Pan American's Ocean Clippers

The
Flying Classics

SERIES

Other Books in the Flying Classics Series

Pan American's Ocean Clippers

BARRY TAYLOR

TAB AERO

Blue Ridge Summit, PA

FIRST EDITION
SECOND PRINTING

© 1991 by Barry Taylor.
Published by Aero, an imprint of TAB Books.
TAB Books is a division of McGraw-Hill, Inc.

Library of Congress Cataloging-in-Publication Data

Taylor, Barry.
   Pan American's ocean clippers / by Barry Taylor.
      p.   cm.
   ISBN 0-8306-8302-X (pbk.)
   1. Pan American World Airways, Inc.—History.   2. Seaplanes—
United States—History.   3. Transpacific flights—History.
I. Title.
HE9803.P36T39   1990
387.7'06'573—dc20   90-74
                                                                CIP

TAB Books offers software for sale. For information and a catalog, please contact TAB Software Department, Blue Ridge Summit, PA 17294-0850.

Acquisitions Editor: Jeff Worsinger
Book Editor: Norval G. Kennedy
Production: Katherine G. Brown
Series Design: Jaclyn J. Boone
Cover Illustration: Larry Selman, Waynesboro, PA

Pan American's Ocean Clippers

BARRY TAYLOR

TAB AERO

Blue Ridge Summit, PA

FIRST EDITION
SECOND PRINTING

© 1991 by Barry Taylor.
Published by Aero, an imprint of TAB Books.
TAB Books is a division of McGraw-Hill, Inc.

Library of Congress Cataloging-in-Publication Data

Taylor, Barry.
    Pan American's ocean clippers / by Barry Taylor.
        p.   cm.
    ISBN 0-8306-8302-X (pbk.)
    1. Pan American World Airways, Inc.—History. 2. Seaplanes—
United States—History. 3. Transpacific flights—History.
    I. Title.
HE9803.P36T39 1990
387.7'06'573—dc20   90-74
                                                              CIP

TAB Books offers software for sale. For information and a catalog, please contact TAB Software Department, Blue Ridge Summit, PA 17294-0850.

Acquisitions Editor: Jeff Worsinger
Book Editor: Norval G. Kennedy
Production: Katherine G. Brown
Series Design: Jaclyn J. Boone
Cover Illustration: Larry Selman, Waynesboro, PA

Contents

Acknowledgments

Writing a specialized book of this type is always a cooperative undertaking, and I would like to acknowledge the help and assistance I received from many people. The cooperation of Pan American World Airways was obviously very necessary in the writing of this book, and I particularly want to thank Liwa Chiu, librarian at Pan American's headquarters in New York City, who unfailingly produced a mass of material from Pan Am's ample files, and Thor O. Johnson, Vice President, Cargo Sales and Services. The courteous research library staff of the National Air and Space Museum, a true wonder in itself, was also much appreciated.

Arthur and Jane Hess and Brian Kelly helped in special ways.

Also thanks to Jeff Worsinger and Norval Kennedy at TAB Books and to my agent, Ray Powers, for being so patient.

Finally, my thanks, as always, to Trisha Taylor, whose aid and comfort are always crucial but seldom sufficiently repaid.

Introduction

There has been almost a mythology associated with Pan American World Airways and its giant flying boats that flew the Pacific and the Atlantic. Probably no aircraft has captured the imagination of the American public as much as the *China Clipper*. These airplanes were true wonders of their age, machines that dramatized the daring and spirit of American enterprise more than any other, perhaps before or since.

Pan American World Airways is still one of the world's outstanding airlines, but at one time it dominated the skies as the "chosen instrument" of America's international presence. The pilots were pioneers, heroes of the popular culture, and the aircraft that bore the winged globe were the subject of front-page news stories and coast-to-coast radio coverage. The Martin M-130, the Boeing 314, the series of Sikorsky amphibians and flying boats, and the beautiful Consolidated Commodore still evoke a magic for the serious aviation historian and the general public alike. Like Robert Louis Stevenson's

> All the old tales retold
> Of buccaneers and buried gold,

I hope *Pan American's Ocean Clippers* will be read by those who still dream of the adventure.

Barry Taylor
Charlottesville, Virginia

About the author

Barry Taylor is an information officer at the University of Virginia at Charlottesville. He has been a journalist for more than 20 years, writing for *Aviation International News, World War II, Military History, Wild West,* and *Dowline* (Dow Jones and Co.). He was an engineering writer for Lockheed Missiles and Space Company. *Pan American's Ocean Clippers* is Taylor's first nonfiction book, which complements two novels.

1

Juan Trippe's airline

Jack Whitbeck, manager of the Pan American Airways base at Key West, Florida, stared dismally out through his office window at the pouring rain. Whitbeck was known as a steady man . . . dependable. But even though his red goatee had earned him endless ragging from the pilots, who called him "Pink Whiskers," he was not noted for his humor. And today he found even less than usual that was amusing.

Under the terms of the Foreign Air Mail (FAM) Route 4 contract with the United States Post Office, Pan Am had to deliver mail to Havana by October 19, 1927. And here it was, only two days to go, and the new Fokker F. VII trimotors the airline had ordered from the Fokker factory at Hasbrouck Heights, New Jersey, had not appeared. What's more, there was no place for them to land at Key West. A reported hurricane was on the way. Rain had been falling heavily, and the island's Meacham Field was no more than a swamp, pitted with deep, rain-filled holes and strewn with rocks.

Juan T. Trippe, president of the embryonic airline, had rushed to Washington to try for an extension. But the post office was adamant. If no mail reached Havana by October 19, the contract was null and void for nonperformance. At stake was not only the mail contract and a $25,000 performance bond, but the very existence of the airline itself.

Time was running out. With fewer than 24 hours to go before the deadline, frantic phone calls were being made up and down the East Coast. An F. VII reached Miami, but there it sat, unable to land at Key West.

Then Trippe had an idea. A seaplane. If they could only get a seaplane from somewhere, the contract could be fulfilled. Desperately, Whitbeck

I

called a friend in Miami. Yes, a single-engined Fairchild FC-2 floatplane belonging to West Indian Aerial Express had landed there, leaking oil, on its way to Haiti. The pilot, Cy Caldwell, was brought to the phone. Would he fly seven bags of mail to Havana? Caldwell hesitated. After all, the plane was not his, and then there was the flight plan . . . Whitbeck made him an offer. Would $145 help him change his mind? It was easy money for a poorly paid pilot.

Caldwell landed his tiny FC-2, sporting the name *La Nina*, at Key West just before dark. The next morning, October 19, seven sacks of mail weighing some 251 pounds were loaded aboard, and at exactly 8:04 a.m. Caldwell was in the air. Sixty-two minutes later, after flying at height of 1,000 feet and pushed along by a brisk tail wind, *La Nina* landed in the harbor at Havana. The flight had beaten a cablegram reporting his departure from Key West.

The Havana postmaster rowed out in a small boat to pick up the mail. In a few minutes the transfer was made, and Caldwell took off for the Bahamas on his way to Haiti. But he had earned his place in aviation history. Caldwell and *La Nina* had saved Pan American Airways from probable extinction.

Nine days later, on October 28, Meacham Field was in better shape, but the usable portion of the runway was no more than 1,600 feet long and 15 feet wide. Nevertheless, a Pan American-owned Fokker F. VIIa piloted by Hugh Wells managed to take off with 772 pounds of mail. One hour and twenty minutes later, the F. VIIa, soon to be named the *General Machado* after Cuba's dictator, circled over Morro Castle and landed in Havana in driving rain.

It was Pan American's first regularly scheduled flight, and everyone connected with the enterprise, the backers and finance men, the managers, the two-man aircrew and the mechanics, must have felt a certain sense of history. But possibly there was one man who had not the slightest doubt that these first flights to Cuba were the initial steps in the creation of a giant airline with a worldwide network of routes, America's chosen international flag carrier. That man was the president of Pan American Airways, Juan Trippe.

Trippe and Pan American Airways

The Trippe family can trace its lineage back to one of the earliest English settlements near Baltimore. A Henry Trippe had settled in Maryland in 1663. Another member of the clan, Lieutenant John Trippe, was wounded off Tripoli in 1805 during America's war with the Barbary pirates. *Paratus et Fidelis*, "Prepared and Faithful," says the family motto, and the Trippes have never thought not to heed its enjoinder.

Juan Terry Trippe was born at Sea Bright, New Jersey, on June 27, 1899, where the family was spending the summer. His mother had expected a girl that she intended to name Juanita after a favorite aunt. When a boy arrived, she decided not to waste the name. It gave him a sort of Latin-American air, and he would always hate it.

The boy grew up in a financially comfortable atmosphere. His father, Charles White Trippe, was a Wall Street investment banker, and his mother's side of the family, the Terrys, were notably wealthy. The Trippe family, in fact, always seemed to be where the money was. Juan climbed trees with William Rockefeller. Another boyhood friend was David Robbins, heir to the Robbins Conveyor Belt Company.

When Juan was 10 his father took him to see an air race over New York Bay. The Statue of Liberty was one of the turning points. From then on, he had a lifelong fascination with flight and was determined to fly an airplane. But the elder Trippe was known for his carefully planned approach to life. First, Juan would learn Morse code and radio, and at 17 he was sent to the Marconi School. Next, he went to the Curtiss Flying School in Miami. By 1917, Juan had 100 minutes of dual flying time; in those days, flight time was counted in minutes.

At Yale, the big, hulking youth played football as a guard and joined various societies, a move that gave him more of the connections that would help him throughout his career. The connections would read like a roster of monied families: Cornelius V. ("Sonny") Whitney of the New York Whitneys, John Hambleton of a Baltimore banking family, and William H. Vanderbilt of the railroad Vanderbilts.

When the United States entered World War I, Trippe joined the Naval Reserve Flying Corps, earning his wings as a bomber pilot instead of flying the more colorful fighters and interceptors — already he was thinking of the future. In 1920, a civilian student once more, he helped organize the Yale Flying Club. Among the charter members were his socially prominent friends.

After graduation, he began a Wall Street career but within a year he had succumbed to the lure of aviation. In the summer of 1923, he talked his friend John Hambleton into becoming a partner with him in purchasing seven surplus Navy seaplanes for $500 each. They formed Long Island Airways, with Trippe serving as president and, initially, as pilot and mechanic. One of Trippe's first steps was to replace each 90-horsepower Curtiss OX-5 engine with the Hispano-Suiza 220-horsepower engine to carry two passengers instead of one, doubling the usual $5 charge for each trip.

Long Island Airways was not to last long. It was really more of an air taxi service than an airline, flying wealthy people out to their estates on the New York island and to fashionable beach resorts. The gypsy pilots Trippe hired believed firmly in loose takeoff times and plenty of wine, women and song, and within two years, the company collapsed under the weight of financial and equipment problems.

The United States passed the Air Mail Act in 1925, also known as the Kelly Act, which stipulated that the government should get out of carrying mail by air and no longer compete with railroads and concurrently "encourage commercial aviation." The post office, in a slightly different way than what the act intended, decided it would ease out of the airmail business by helping to establish private lines that it would pay to carry the mail, which was, in effect, a government subsidy.

The first contract, Civil Air Mail Route 1, New York to Boston, was awarded to Colonial Airways: Managing Director Juan Trippe.

Colonial was carrying passengers between New York and Boston by April, 1927. And then occurred one of the most dramatic events in aviation history: Lindbergh flew the Atlantic. The tall, lanky flyer became a national hero. Aviation was now fashionable, the new gospel of the age. A vision that captured everyone's imagination, young and old alike. Types of aircraft were knowledgeably discussed and evaluated. Pilots' names were known like those of movie stars, their activities front-page news. It was the go-go years of the '20s. Everyone wanted to fly.

But Trippe's grasp of the possibilities of air travel constantly over-reached that of his partners. He was the first in the United States to see the potential of the Fokker F. VII, the workhorse trimotor of the pioneer Dutch KLM airline, which had been operating since 1919. Colonial bought two of the ships, but his partners feared they would bring financial loss. The 26-year-old Trippe was committing them to expensive multiengined aircraft. Why not the tried-and-true, single-engine, open-cockpit craft flown by other airlines?

Abandoning the parochial views of his backers, Trippe joined with John Hambleton and Cornelius Vanderbilt in forming Aviation Corporation of America on June 2, 1927. The company's directors included such wealthy Trippe friends as John Hay Whitney, Seymour Knox, cousin of the five-and-dime millionaire Frank Woolworth, and the ubiquitous W. Averell Harriman. Trippe, who had invested $25,000 of the company's $300,000 capitalization, was named managing director. Quickly, he received his partners consent to invest much of the funds in a newly formed New York Corporation called Pan American Airways, Inc.

Pan American had a curious birth. It is probably the only American airline — perhaps the only major American corporation — that came into existence because of a fear of Germany.

Major Henry H. ("Hap") Arnold, who later would command all U.S. Air Forces during World War II, was stationed in Washington as an intelligence officer. Across his desk had come a number of reports about a new airline in Colombia named Sociedad Colombo-Alemana de Transportes Aereos (SCADTA). Everything about SCADTA was German: pilots, financial backing, and Director Peter von Bauer, who had arrived in Colombia shortly after World War I. Colombia had never forgiven the United States for the loss of Panama, and Arnold's information was that SCADTA was set to beat the United States and establish routes to Panama and as far north as the American border.

Germany was prevented by the Treaty of Versailles, which ended World War I, to engage in international air commerce or to establish an air force. Nonetheless, the Germans were using the many German-owned airlines in South America to provide a proving ground for its aircraft industry and to train a cadre of experienced flyers. Arnold, visualizing Germans sitting on the banks of the Panama Canal, was worried.

Arnold formed an airline named Pan American Airways with three other officers, including Major Carol Spaatz, who would also become a senior air force commander in World War II. Its objective was to establish a route from Key West to Havana, across to Yucatan in Mexico, and down to British Honduras, Nicaragua, and finally Panama.

The airline was set to go into business with some well-connected backers. Pan American won the coveted FAM 4 airmail contract on July 16, then things began to go wrong. The army became embroiled in the General Billy Mitchell affair, and Arnold and Spaatz decided they must stay with the army in an effort to build up the air corps.

A former naval officer and Wall Streeter named Richard D. Bevier became president of Pan American, with a young ex-air corps captain named John Montgomery as vice president and general manager.

Then the money backing the fledgling company suddenly dried up. Worse was to come. Trippe and Hambleton, in a somewhat devious move of questionable ethics, flew to Havana and secured sole landing rights for AVCO. Pan American's mail contract was now worthless.

Another competing group for FAM 4 was led by Reed Chambers, a famous World War I pilot, and included such moneymen as Richard B.

Hoyt, board chairman of Curtiss-Wright, and Percy Rockefeller. Originally, they had been investors in Florida Airlines, which had been set up by Eddie Rickenbacker, probably the most famous American fighter pilot of all time. But the company was dogged by bad luck. Commercial aviation was slower to catch on in the South than elsewhere in the country. Three of the company's new aircraft were involved in a crash at Nashville, and in the spring of 1927, Florida Airlines went into bankruptcy.

With no place else to go, the two competing groups went to Trippe and his Aviation Corporation of America. A deal was cut, and on October 11, Trippe's AVCO became partners with a new holding company named Atlantic, Gulf and Caribbean Airways, Inc., in operating Pan American Airways as a subsidiary. Trippe became president and general manager of Pan American. The three groups would merge on June 23, 1928.

In a subtle name change, Aviation Corporation of the Americas became the holding company for Pan American Airways, Inc., the operating subsidiary. Trippe, with the controlling interest in AVCO, remained as president and general manager of Pan American. Aviation Corporation of the Americas would dissolve and become Pan American Airways on April 29, 1931.

Chambers, Rickenbacker, Arnold, and Spaatz — the real flyers — dropped out; only the entrepreneurs and moneymen remained. Trippe, 28 years old, had won. He would be a millionaire before his 30th birthday. From now on, American aviation in the Caribbean and South America would mean Juan Trippe's airline.

Control of the Caribbean

Mail and passenger service between Key West and Havana was established and Trippe intended to move quickly to consolidate his position in the Caribbean. Even before winning the mail contract with the flight of *La Nina*, he had presented his company's directors with an ambitious plan for the airline. Key West to Havana was only the first step.

Pan American would develop two routes: one going from Miami to Cuba and then across to Mexico and down to South America, and the other route extending down the chain of Caribbean islands to Trinidad. The United States would be linked by air to as far south as Valparaiso, Chile, and the company would secure landing concessions in Cuba, Mexico, Costa Rica, Honduras, Guatemala, El Salvador, Peru, Chile, and Venezuela. The vision held the directors spellbound.

Pan American was awarded FAM 5, Miami-Cristobal via Cuba and Central America on July 13, 1928. The bidding for FAM 6, Miami-San Juan, was in full swing, and here Pan American found that its early savior, West

Indian Aerial Express, was in the way, run by a barnstorming pilot named Basil Rowe. WIAX had originally been formed to carry supplies to isolated sugar plantations in Cuba and by 1927 was carrying mail to Haiti and passengers to San Juan and Santo Domingo.

Bids for FAM 6 were opened on July 14, 1928, and Pan American won the contract at the top rate of $2 per mile. The pragmatic Rowe sold out to Trippe and joined Pan American, where he would have a distinguished career as a pilot. Pan Am took over WIAX's aircraft, including the *Santa Maria*, its flagship, a 10-passenger Keystone Pathfinder trimotor. More valuable to Pan Am were the landing rights that came with the airline. FAM 6 was, in fact, more than it seemed. The route extended down the Caribbean islands to Trinidad, a total of 1,930 miles.

Trippe had won FAM 7, Miami-Nassau, by January 1929 and then cannily bought out the American-run Mexican airline, Compania Mexicana de Transportacion, S.A., as a prelude to entering the bidding for FAM 8, Brownsville-Mexico City. Pan American again won with a bid at the top rate of $2 per mile and was granted the route by a friendly post office over the protests of the other six bidders who had all entered lower bids; they did not have *landing rights*. Trippe had outfoxed them.

The president of Pan American was a visionary and a genius at building an airline. But there is also little doubt that Trippe had an edge in the bidding wars for the mail routes. His influential friends gave him ready access to those who count in Washington. There was also a feeling at that time that Pan American was at the vanguard of America's twentieth century manifest destiny, a view subscribed to by United States Postmaster General Walter Folger Brown. His "impartial favoritism" contributed greatly to Trippe's success in eliminating competitors.

Brown was able to award the Pan Am the routes despite the fact that Pan Am was not the lowest bidder due to the vaguely worded Foreign Air Mail Act, which authorized the postmaster to award the contracts to the "lowest *responsible* bidders that can *satisfactorily* perform the service in the interests of the United States government." Nor was Trippe bashful in exploiting an opening.

President Franklin Delano Roosevelt would later describe Trippe as a "fascinating Yale gangster" and a "scoundrel." "Trippe is an unscrupulous person who cajoles and buys his way," said Secretary of the Interior Harold L. Ickes. An airline official who was a Trippe supporter had to admit that he was the sort of person who "if the front door was open . . . would go in by the side window."

But Pan American reflected contemporary morality. And if it was ruthless in looking for subsidies or lucrative mail contracts, and if it did not make any attempt to reduce rates as equipment improved, it was a pioneering enterprise, always facing new and unknown hazards.

Trippe, with what has been described as his "devilish" smile, plowed on. He bought out a small, crop-dusting air service in Peru and renamed it Peruvian Airlines. He then set up the Chilean Airways Corporation in Santiago and formed a national airline, of sorts, in Colombia called Socie-dad Colombo-Americano de Aviacion, primarily set up to harass the well-entrenched SCADTA. One of the strongest opponents he was to face in South America was the giant W.R. Grace Corporation, which, certain people said, owned "practically everything on the West Coast." Grace was strong enough to weather any assault on its position from the upstart Pan Am; if there was going to be an airline controlling air travel along the west coast of South America, Grace was going to own it.

Grace, however, was also blocked by Pan Am from extending any airline from South America to the United States. Stalemated, both compa-nies formed a joint subsidiary called Pan American-Grace Airways, later named PANAGRA, with each side putting up $1 million in capital. PANA-GRA absorbed Peruvian Airlines on March 25, 1929, and a few days later, FAM 9, the route down the west coast of South America, was predictably in hand.

The year 1929 saw perhaps the most intensive effort by Trippe to dominate the Caribbean. Charles Lindbergh had joined Pan Am as a technical advisor after he made a goodwill tour of the Caribbean in late 1927. Trippe had the best pilot. Now he wanted the best plane.

Igor Sikorsky's amphibians

Count Igor Sikorsky, a refugee from the Russian Revolution, arrived in the United States in 1919. He was already established as a leading figure in aviation; he had designed giant four-engine bombers for Russia during the war. There is a story that it was Sikorsky who had conceived of the idea of a multiengine aircraft when one of his early single-engine designs was forced down with a mosquito-clogged carburetor.

Sikorsky's factory near Long Island Sound built a five-place floatplane in 1925 for an oil company in South America. This was followed by the S-34, a twin-engine amphibian, which was fated to suffer an engine failure on its test flight and flipped over. Sikorsky Aero Engineering Corporation, struggling to survive, built another amphibian, the S-36, and leased one to Pan American Airways for evaluation.

The airline saw that it had broad implications for air transportation in South America, where there was a notable lack of roads, railways, and airport facilities. Andre Priester, Pan Am's Dutch-born chief engineer and operations manager, said, "A seaplane carries its own airport on its bottom."

Sikorsky began work on a new aircraft, the S-38, called the "ugly duckling" and the "flying tadpole." The S-38 actually looked like a shoe-tree to which twin tailbooms had been attached. Its wooden-frame hull was covered in aluminum and divided into six watertight compartments. Two 410-hp, Pratt & Whitney Wasp engines were clamped to an overhead wing, and, even though the S-38 carried a total load of 9,900 pounds, only 300 horsepower was needed for level flight, which meant there was ample power in one engine for takeoffs, climbs, and landings.

Beneath the upper wing was a smaller lower wing that served to strengthen the structure and carry the floats. Both wings were made of wood and metal and covered with a doped fabric. Their sesqui-arrangement gave the aircraft the aerodynamic advantages of the monoplane with

Pan American World Airways

Crew of the Sikorsky amphibian NC-142M at Miami in April 1930: (from left) Bert Denicke, radio operator; Charles A. Lindbergh, pilot; Basil L. Rowe, copilot.

the structural advantages of the biplane, at the same time keeping the major lifting surfaces well above the surface of the water. The idea of the twin boom support was to keep the tail surfaces high and out of the water but well within the slipstream for better control.

The amphibian's wheels did not fully retract but tucked in alongside the fuselage for water operations. A wheel on the same side as a turn was lowered into the water for single engine steering. The passengers sat in eight wicker chairs, advertised as "comfortable," while the pilot's compartment had sliding glass windows for ventilation.

The S-38 was an excellent ship, and pilots usually praised its abilities. A somewhat flat bottom, however, often made landings and takeoffs in rough water an adventure. Pilot Basil Rowe would later say, according to an article published in the *Journal* of the American Aviation Historical Society, "(the flat hull) made *stall* landings somewhat rough at times, which is the reason that we always made *step* landings — the equivalent to a *wheel* landing in a landplane.

However, if the water was rough or rolling such that a landing was not practical and it was necessary to use the standard stall landing." Another pilot: "The S-38 was a good aircraft as far as landing or taxiing was concerned (but) in rough water or swells it would porpoise before settling in. . . ." All pilots were unanimous, in declaring that takeoffs were almost always a problem. The flat hull meant the S-38 sat low in the water, and spray thrown by the props obscured the pilot's vision until they got onto the "step."

Then, said Basil Rowe, who became chief pilot of Pan American after leaving West Indian Aerial Express, "you were into the air like a scared jackrabbit." Water would also get into the carburetor scoops, causing engine revs to drop off. The crew would have to change spark plugs and start all over again.

Biplane construction made visibility for the pilot somewhat restricted, especially on the right side. The placement of the wheels far back from the nose also gave the aircraft a tendency to sink into soft dirt, tipping the plane forward. When this happened, the pilot simply let the amphibian settle back; little, if any, damage was ever done. Nevertheless, the aircraft was easy to handle, with good cross wind characteristics due to its low profile and easy taxiing habits.

Sikorsky built 38 S-38s for Pan American at a cost between $50,000 and $54,000 each. The initial aircraft, the S-38A, and the first five of the succeeding S-38Bs, were distinguished by their vertical windshields, while the remainder had a graceful slope. The S-38B also used the more powerful 525-hp Hornet engine.

Trippe saw the S-38 as the means to expand his domain throughout South and Central America: "America has the first chance to dominate the future highways of world trade since the days of the clipper ships a hundred years ago." The analogy was to be prophetic.

Lindbergh's flight

Trippe decided that Lindbergh, his technical advisor, would pilot the airline's trailblazing flight for FAM 5, connecting Miami with Cristobal, via Havana, Belize, Managua, and Punta Arenas in Costa Rica. Trippe would accompany the flight on its first leg and an old friend, John Hambleton,

Pan American World Airways

Charles A. Lindbergh and Juan Trippe at Panama in September 1929.

would be copilot. The S-38 (NC-8000), the second model built by Sikorsky, was wheeled out of its hangar at Pan Am's Miami base and rose into an overcast sky at 6 a.m. February 4, 1929, Lindbergh's 27th birthday.

Large crowds were at every stop and the trip encountered only a few misfortunes. A ramp had been constructed at Belize jutting out nearly 200 feet into the water. Lindbergh eased the aircraft forward, but its wheels sank into the soft sand on the beach. No damage was done and a tractor pulled the S-38 onto more solid ground.

They were two hours ahead of schedule and circled Managua until the announced landing time, while enthusiastic crowds cheered from the rooftops.

The final leg brought them into France Field at Cristobal near the Panama Canal at 4 p.m. on February 6. Flying time for the 700-mile trip was almost seven hours.

They started back on February 11, and again the trip was largely without incident. Ambassador and Mrs. Dwight W. Morrow chose Mexico City to announce the engagement of their daughter Anne to Charles Lindbergh, producing even more publicity for Pan American.

The flight was late getting into Miami because Lindbergh decided to scout along the Yucatan coast for possible landing sites. They refueled at Cozumel and arrived at Miami after dark. Cheers, especially for the young, daring Charles Lindbergh, roared out from a crowd of 3,000.

The inauguration flight of FAM 6, from Puerto Rico to as far south as Paramaribo in Dutch Guiana, was scheduled for September, and Trippe decided to make this trip a diplomatic journey of goodwill. Not only would Trippe and his wife Betty accompany the flight on a 7,000-mile tour of the Caribbean, but Lindbergh's bride Anne, whom he had married in May, would also be along. The fathers of both Anne Morrow Lindbergh and Elizabeth Stettinius Trippe were connected to the banking house of J.P. Morgan & Company.

The two couples departed on September 23 in the Sikorsky S-38 NC-75K. Basil Rowe was copilot. Trippe was determined it was going to be a public relations coup. Every routine situation report on the flight was rewritten into more flowery paragraphs at the Miami base and then mimeographed and distributed to reporters, who would immediately send the information on to their newspapers.

The flight had a beauty of its own. The islands would appear ahead, rising from a brilliant blue sea. Below them, suddenly, a white beach, and then they would skirt along green jungle stretching up the sides of rugged mountains, each with puffs of cloud drifting away from its summit. Flocks

Charles and Anne Lindbergh with Juan and Elizabeth Trippe at Miami in 1929. Behind them is a Sikorsky S-38.

of red birds, startled, soared up to almost keep pace with them before falling away.

As they swung down through the island chains of the Caribbean towards South America, Trippe, wearing what Anne Morrow Lindbergh would remember as a "glaring white suit" and brown-and-white saddle shoes, called on the officials of 16 governments in 20 days. There was a constant round of dinners, speeches, balls, and receptions. Everywhere they stopped, adoring crowds pressed in on them. Bands would strike up the "Lucky Lindy."

When they landed, the cabin of the aircraft was soon awash in flowers. Rhapsodic newspaper columns described their journey in detail. The air mail mission was completed at Paramaribo, and after a day and a half of rest, they departed once more for home, carrying the first northward mail from Dutch Guiana to Trinidad.

Lindbergh decided that he needed just the right angle for a photograph and climbed out over the bow of the S-38 without a parachute and proceeded to calmly take pictures 1,500 feet in the air.

Newly married Anne Lindbergh watched her husband risk his life and said nothing. A tiny, slim woman with an elfin sense of humor, she had spent hours of the trip writing in her journal. Later, she would say she had found the Trippes "remarkable" and often fun, although she noticed that Juan had a tendency to be "prissy." Throughout the whole trip, for example, even though weight was so critical that they had to leave behind the flowers, Trippe carried clean sheets in the aircraft for his own and his wife's beds.

The Lindberghs withdrew from the flight at Trinidad so they could visit Central America before returning to Miami, and the S-38 went on piloted by Basil Rowe.

Despite the festive tone of these inaugural trips, they had the very serious purpose of blazing new routes around the Caribbean and down to South America. Beneath the outward appearance of glamour and the trappings of stardom surrounding the Lindberghs, Juan Trippe never forgot for a moment that he was forging an airline that he intended to dominate the skies around the world.

Out of Pan American's Caribbean routes would emerge many of the overwater flying techniques that would subsequently have immense value: celestial navigation, long-range radio direction finders, and multiple crews.

Thank God at 11 a.m.

Lindbergh was pilot again on April 26, 1930, with Basil Rowe as copilot and Bert Denicke as radio operator, when they forged another air mail route across the Caribbean, crossing the sea from Havana to Puerto Cabezas, Nicaragua — the world's longest scheduled overwater crossing at that time.

Every possible ounce of excess weight was removed from NC-142M, including the floor. Two cabin tanks, each containing 100 gallons of fuel, were installed, which together with the aircraft's main tanks amounted to 520 gallons of fuel.

They left Miami at 3:29 p.m. on the first leg to Havana and passed a Pan American Fokker F-10 inbound from Cuba with about 500 feet separating the planes. The usual crowd greeted them at Havana, but Lindbergh asked that festivities be cancelled so the crew could get some rest for the flight the following day.

April 27 dawned fair and clear and they took off carrying 444 gallons of fuel. They passed Cape Gracias a Dios on the farthermost northeast coast of Nicaragua at 11 a.m. Rowe saved time, with a touch of whimsy, and noted passage on the routine position message as "Thank God at 11:00 a.m." and passed it to Lindbergh, who was flying, for his signature.

The meticulous Lindbergh, who often had little sense of humor when it came to flight, gave Rowe a questioning look, and the copilot had to explain that it was the Spanish name translated into English. Lindbergh said he thought the position in Spanish would sound better and, with a sigh, Rowe destroyed his play on words and the message was sent with the Spanish name. They ran into heavy cloud and rain as the aircraft and a tropical storm arrived simultaneously at Cristobal. "It was raining so hard," said Rowe, that "(Lindbergh) could only see to land by opening the top of the cockpit and half standing on the rudder pedals."

The crew transferred to another Sikorsky S-38, NC-9776, for the trip back. As they approached Bluefields on the coast of Nicaragua, a wild vibration shook the aircraft and its airspeed fell off. Lindbergh crawled back into the rear cabin, stuck his head out through the rear hatch, and saw that the horizontal member between the V struts that supported the tail structure had broken, and the two ends of the strut were flailing wildly. He then slid along the afterdeck until just his toes were hooked over the edge of the hatch. Using his hands, he bent the two broken ends down

The paint scheme of this Sikorsky S-38 is a hint that the aircraft was probably an early prototype.

against the V struts, which seemed to stop the tail section wavering. They landed at Puerto Cabezas and said nothing about it to the press. The rest of the flight was almost an anticlimax.

The workhorse amphibian

Pan Am was linking all the capitals of Central America by air by early 1931. It had carried 20,728 passengers in 1929, which, by the following year, jumped an incredible 60 percent. The 1930 fleet stood at 111 units. The airline's international routes had grown in four years from the 110 miles between Key West and Havana to a network 200 times longer.

Pan American's workhorse airplane continued to be the Sikorsky S-38 amphibian, and the flying shoetree became a familiar sight around the Caribbean as Pan Am pioneered new routes and established bases up remote rivers and on desolate coastlines. Pilot Basil Rowe would look back at those times and remember the keen edge of excitement, the feeling that they were all doing new and glorious things. Another pilot said, "Pan Am was like a religion."

The aircraft were unpressurized and it was impossible to attain altitude. The trade winds blew constantly at 35 mph, forcing the aircraft to fly eight to 10 feet off the water, otherwise the wind would cut their speed by one-third. Tailwinds helped at 8,000 feet.

Always there was the new and unexpected, the days often passing like magic. The solitary S-38 would approach a coast where muddy, silt-laden rivers roiled the water far out to sea. Officials from a tiny village or a town would put out in boats to greet the aircraft, and Rowe would put on a show, coming in with a flourish, "starting up the flamingos from the jungle shore." Then, nattily attired like all Pan American aircrews in navy blue uniform coat and white pants, he would take the town officials up for a hop, and there would be a big fiesta and local holiday.

Basil Rowe would be listed in Robert Ripley's "Believe It or Not" in 1955 for having flown 5,594,000 miles and logging 35,000 hours [the equivalent of nearly four years] in the air. He was a small, dapper man, who would fly for the Air Transport Service during World War II and end his long aviation career flying DC-6Bs, transporting American troops back from Korea. He retired to Florida to play tennis, not even bothering "to look up from balancing my tennis racket" when an aircraft passed overhead.

One constant hazard to navigation during those early flying years, he would write in his autobiography *Under My Wings*, was the lack of reliable maps. There was simply nothing available that could reliably tell them the most important thing a pilot wanted to know: mountain elevations.

Rowe and other Pan Am pilots tried to resolve the problem by tearing maps out of children's school geography books, but the elevations were incorrect. The mountains in South America and much of the Caribbean had been surveyed by the Spanish who noted mountain heights, often inaccurately, in meters. When the schoolbook maps were printed, the printers simply copied the figures as feet. A mountain charted as 3,000 feet, said Rowe, could actually be 9,810 feet—rather disconcerting to a pilot coming upon one after being in a cloud.

Rowe and the other Pan Am pilots began to make their own maps. They would fly alongside a mountain peak and, with the copilot flying, spread the map out on their knees and write the elevation. Gradually, pilots corrected the shape of rivers, changed coastlines, and added lakes, even naming the geographic features: Hogsback Mountain, Banjo Lake.

Pilots being pilots, some of these names had interesting stories behind them. One bay was named Fuller's Folly after a pilot named Bill Fuller. Fuller was piloting an S-38 from Nassau across the water when he noticed his copilot had fallen asleep. Flying along the coast of the island, he decided to drop down to water level, just enough to get the keel in the water and the tremendous noise would startle the copilot awake. Trouble was that as the aircraft touched the water, Fuller seemed to have misjudged things slightly because the impact peeled off the bottom of the aircraft like an orange skin. A wideawake Fuller fought the S-38 back into Nassau "looking down between his legs at the open water."

Then there was Spook-Gear Landing, a stopover point in the Caribbean. Apparently a certain Pan Am pilot named Harrison, who did not fly amphibians, loudly and repeatedly let it be known that a only a pilot who was absolutely stupid would land an amphibian without remembering to put the wheels down. Actually, it happened frequently. There were no warning buzzers in those days to notify the pilot, and it was easy to forget while managing a busy cockpit.

Harrison made his first flight in an amphibian and approached the stopover point for his first landing. Rowe was on the ground and watched the approach. There was not a wheel in sight. Harrison's aircraft hit the ground, skittered along for about a hundred feet, then flipped over on its back. Rowe was then amazed to see the wheels slowing extend up, into the air. Harrison claimed he had the wheels down all the time. . . .

Pilot Frank Chapman also joined Pan Am to fly passenger airplanes. But after two weeks' indoctrination and trips out on the 26-foot motor launch "Panair II" to learn seamanship, he was then taught Pan Am's radio letdown procedures, which was standard operating procedure when Pan Am airplanes flew on instruments. His first aircrew duty with the airline was radio officer on the Havana-Nassau run; he also handed out blue box lunches to the passengers. When an aircraft landed and taxied to a stop, Chapman would scoot under the instrument panel to open the hatch and grab the buoy line.

Pan American's radio communications network was centered around radio station WKDL at Dinner Key, Miami. The station was staffed by 10 operators in two shifts. WKDL used the international Morse code to reach

The prototype Sikorsky S-38 amphibian, NC-5933, went into service with NYRBA in July 1928, sold to Pan Am in 1930, and scrapped in 1931.

out to 20 countries and all Pan Am airplanes in flight. Basil Rowe surveyed a new route, Canal Zone – Kingston – Cienfuegos – Miami on December 3, 1930. Because of the long water jump from the Canal Zone to Kingston, Jamaica, the aircraft was lightened by every possible ounce. Navigation was "all dead reckoning," said Rowe, which, according to Will Rogers, meant "unless the pilot reckons correctly, I'm dead."

The following March, 1931, a violent earthquake struck Managua and Basil Rowe immediately flew in an S-38B, NC-9151. The aircraft landed on Managua Bay near dark and the crew stared in awe at the burning city silhouetted against the twilight sky. The S-38's radio gave the Nicaraguan capital its only radio link with the outside world and Pan American coordinated extensive relief efforts.

Over the coming days, Rowe flew dozens of relief missions, and spent so much time delivering bread that he became known as the "Flying Baker." The Pan Am office was totally destroyed; passengers and staff slept on cots set up on the airfield. Pan American planes had flown out 98 passengers by noon April 1.

Mercy flights became almost a Pan Am specialty. Another disaster struck Central America on September 10, this time a violent hurricane sweeping across Belize, British Honduras; Pan Am aircraft were again on the spot. The first on the scene, E.S. Rodenbaugh, a pilot, was unable to find a place to land. Circling the city, he dropped medicines and mail and radioed, "City entirely washed out. No buildings undamaged. Houses tossed in a pile like toys. . . . Our hangar is a place of refuge for forty or fifty people and no other large buildings are left."

Basil Rowe later flew in NC-8044 to deliver supplies, medicines, and Red Cross personnel to the stricken city. Once again, Pan Am's office radio became the only link to the outside world.

A few years later, Rowe piloted S-38 mercy flights into Santiago de Cuba to assist survivors of an earthquake, and on September 5, 1935, he flew relief supplies to the Florida Keys following a devastating hurricane that swept across the islands leaving nearly 700 dead or missing. The entire town of Islamorada was swept away by the storm.

Pan American's S-38s were often caught up in several revolutions and outbreaks of civil violence that occurred in Central and South America during those years, and more than one Pan Am airplane took off under fire. One such event, for example, was the Cuban revolution that occurred on August 12, 1933. Cuban dictator General Gerardo Machado finally saw the writing on the wall and decided to leave the country after several years of internal strife.

Pan American World Airways

Sikorsky S-38 taking on cargo in Central or South America. The pilot's rank insignia and cap badge indicate that this aircraft was being flown by a Pan Am subsidiary.

Machado and his party, which included the secretary of the treasury and other politicians and military officers, arrived at the Havana airport at 2 p.m. where a chartered S-38B, piloted by Al McCullough and belonging to Compania Nacional Cubana de Aviacion, a Pan American subsidiary, was waiting. Passengers milled around nervously while the Cuban Aviation Corps, which was in charge of the field, debated for nearly an hour and a half about whether to allow Machado to depart.

Word of the fleeing dictator was not long in getting around and suddenly a shouting, angry mob charged onto the field. Permission or not, McCullough decided it was time to go. Everyone scrambled on board, and the S-38 lifted off just ahead of the angry Cubans.

Meanwhile, Leo Terletzky, Pan Am pilot, was also having a narrow escape. Secret police Chief Dr. Orestes Ferrara, whose tenure in the post had not earned him many friends, had hidden himself aboard Terletzky's S-38, which was being readied in Havana Harbor. The Cuban was discovered by the Pan Am station manager, 26-year-old S.B. Kauffman, who ordered Ferrara off the aircraft, but the police boss pulled a gun. The airplane was then towed out to the overnight buoy to wait for the other passengers and their luggage to be brought out by launch. Terletzky and Kauffman arranged a signal; if the pilot saw Kauffman waving a red flag from the shore he was to take off at once.

It was not long before a howling mob appeared brandishing weapons. Kauffman frantically waved a red flag from the window of the Pan Am office. Terletzky scrambled to start the engines, a job that had to be done by hand, but they were balky. Finally, he got one engine going, and the amphibian began working its way farther out into the harbor for a takeoff run. The S-38 took off in the proverbial hail of fire, and later, nine bullet holes were counted in the fuselage. Fourteen angry Pan Am passengers and their luggage were left behind on the dock at Havana.

Trippe completes the circle

The S-38 was an excellent aircraft for water operations, but there was another airplane, a true floatplane, flown by Pan American during those years that was an even better aircraft, the graceful Consolidated Commodore. Pan Am's acquisition of this fine aircraft starts with a business rival, the New York, Rio, and Buenos Aires Line (NYRBA) and the flamboyant personality of Ralph O'Neill, founder and president.

Time has not dimmed the legend of Ralph O'Neill nor his reputation for vision, drive and eccentricity. He had been a pilot and won three Distinguished Service Crosses for shooting down Germans in World War I. Later, he was Boeing's marketing representative in South America because he could speak Spanish fluently. His job vanished when he flew the demonstrator into a mountain in Uruguay, utterly destroying the aircraft and almost himself.

But O'Neill also had a dream: an 8,000 mile-airline that would link the entire east coast of the Americas from New York to Buenos Aires. So, like any good entrepreneur, he went to New York and found backers, primarily Remington Rand's James Rand, plus Reuben Fleet of Consolidated Aircraft.

Perhaps NYRBA constituted the greatest threat to Pan American and to Trippe personally. What's more, there was something of a grudge match here. Two of O'Neill's backers, Richard Bevier and John Montgomery, had been forced out of Pan American by Juan Trippe.

NYRBA, called "Near Beer" by both friends and enemies, was founded on March 17, 1929, with a public offering of $5 million in stock. O'Neill promptly ordered six Commodores, several Ford Trimotors that would connect Buenos Aires with Santiago, Chile, and S-38s for flights

Interior of the Sikorsky S-38.

along the Brazilian coast. NYRBA's Ford Trimotors began flying between Buenos Aires and Montevideo on August 29, 1929, and were soon crossing the 20,000-foot Andes twice a week to connect with Santiago. The passage across the Andes was an adventure in itself, with some of the roughest air encountered by pilots anywhere. Passengers took a whiff of oxygen from handy cylinders whenever they felt they were going to pass out.

One day in the fall, 1929, a Pan American pilot, Ed Musick, watched the first NYRBA Sikorsky S-38 land at Miami: destination Argentina. Musick, an ex-Marine Corps pilot, wandered over to talk to the NYRBA pilots and found them to be navy-trained veterans; they were also full of enthusiasm about their fledgling airline. What's more, they were expecting delivery of another airplane, one even better than the S-38, now being built at the Consolidated factory at Buffalo, New York.

Consolidated Commodore NC-669M was scrapped in 1946.

That evening Musick confided to his wife that Pan Am was going to have a fight on its hands. NYRBA, he said worriedly, could block them out of South America unless Pan American moved fast. Later, when he had seen his first Commodore, Musick would say that the flying boat made Pan Am's S-38s look like "student trainers."

The Commodore was an airplane that even today looks elegant. Its twin Pratt & Whitney 575-hp Hornets and 100-foot wingspan gave it a range of 1,000 statute miles. It could carry 22 passengers at over 100 miles per hour and no expense had been spared on the creature comforts; gone, for example, were the uncomfortable wicker chairs of other aircraft. Three passenger compartments, accessed by walking down a thickly carpeted center aisle, had seats upholstered in fabric for the first time on any airplane. NYRBA's O'Neill was ecstatic. The Commodore would set the standard for aircraft travel throughout the Americas, perhaps even the world.

O'Neill pushed William Grooch, operations manager and pilot, to rush through the testing on the Niagara River, where the first Commodore was launched. NYRBA's president wanted the airplane in Washington, where he had arranged an elaborate dedication ceremony crowned by a christening of the aircraft by President Hoover's wife. Grooch hustled the aircraft out of the factory and on toward Washington, but landing for the night off Staten Island in heavy seas became a disaster when the airplane's hull was ripped open on a concrete ramp. Nothing could delay the ceremony. A hurriedly patched together Commodore arrived at the Anacostia

Takeoff preparations for Consolidated Commodore NC-669M *Brazil*.

Naval Air Station where O'Neill was chagrined to see the first lady arriving on the arm of none other than Juan Trippe.

The plane's damaged hull was more or less repaired and, named the *Buenos Aires*, crammed with passengers and gear for the inaugural trip to South America. All went fairly well until Havana. O'Neill had invited a dozen government officials for a courtesy flight, but more than two dozen showed up. Not wanting to be impolite, O'Neill loaded them all in, and with William Grooch at the controls, the Commodore took off. Heavy rain squalls suddenly appeared and visibility was almost nil. A sweating Grooch set the overloaded aircraft down, but it smashed into the high swells, the bottom seams opened, and water poured in. Grooch desperately beached the aircraft. The passengers, up to their knees in water, were in hysterics.

Nevertheless, despite a somewhat haphazard working style, O'Neill had four Sikorsky S-38s, four Commodores with 10 more on order, and three Ford Trimotors in full operation by early 1930. NYRBA had mail contracts with the Brazilian and Argentine governments, but the United States Post Office had not yet let bids for FAM 10, the mail contract for the same route. Matters were not helped for the airline when O'Neill, in a widely circulated statement in the press, accused Postmaster Walter Brown of selling out to Pan American.

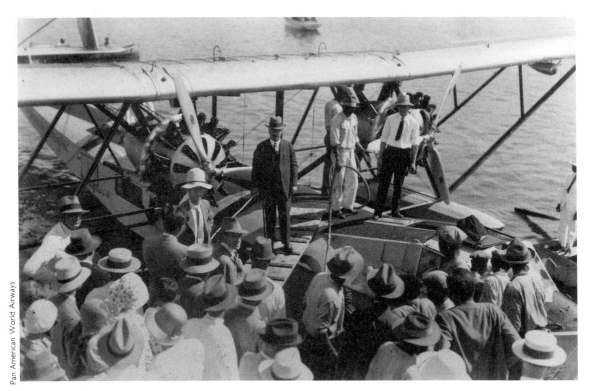

Passengers boarding a Consolidated Commodore.

O'Neill also proved to be less of a businessman than Trippe, committing himself to mail contracts with South American governments at absurdly low rates, which Trippe would never do. What's more, the low mail rate charged by NYRBA was half the rate of the Pan American system, the officially recognized rate between the United States and foreign governments. Thus, "Near Beer" was disturbing American plans for foreign airmail routes and a standardized system of return payments from foreign countries. Pan Am's Trippe, of course, did his utmost to exploit the ill will this earned NYRBA.

FAM 10 was crucial if the airline was to survive because most mail was generated in the United States. NYRBA was losing money at the rate of $400,000 a month by early 1930 and was virtually bankrupt. Relations between Pan American and NYRBA people in South America, meanwhile, deteriorated to the point of hostility, with NYRBA ground crews, at one point, refusing to help the crew of a Pan American survey craft at Lake Montenegro, in northern Brazil.

With almost certain knowledge that the airmail contract was marked for him, Trippe launched a bid to acquire NYRBA. He even had the gall to

Consolidated Commodore *Brazil* was delivered directly to Pan Am with company colors of NYBRA. NC-699M was the 13th Commodore built.

The Consolidated Commodore was the first passenger aircraft to have upholstered seats.

list FAM 10 as an asset when negotiating the terms of the merger; O'Neill never had a chance. Aviation Corporation of the Americas took over NYRBA on September 15, 1930. Nine days later the postmaster general awarded Pan American Airways the South American contract. Pan Am's bid was the usual maximum rate of $2 per mile.

Although it is said that O'Neill was offered a position in Trippe's company, he departed for a mining venture in Bolivia, a disillusioned and bitter man. He had built a magnificent airline and lost it all. Most of his pilots, however, did better. They were taken on by Pan Am at lower salaries.

Trippe had already made a quiet agreement with Peter von Bauer in February 1930 to acquire 84 percent of SCADTA's stock for $1 million. SCADTA terminated its service to the Canal Zone and Ecuador and became little more than a feeder line to the Pan American/PANAGRA network. Bauer remained as president of the airline because of Colombian citizenship laws.*

Landing privileges at Barranquilla helped Trippe fit the last piece into his circle of routes around South and Central America. There was nothing else in his way. But now he was looking for an aircraft that would be even more advanced than the Commodore. A commercial airliner that would boast four engines, signifying a change that was not only a technical advance but one that had profound emotional and psychological implications for the air age. That plane would be the Sikorsky S-40.

As for the Commodore, NYRBA's aircraft were all transferred to Pan American Airways, and eventually the airline would have 14. They went on to give exemplary service in the Caribbean, and one or two even found their way to China. Pan American did not retire the last two of these beautiful machines until September 1946 after 16 years of service.

---

*SCADTA would cause more problems for Trippe, however. At the beginning of World War II, he was accused by the Justice Department of being rather slow in purging the airline of its German pilots and staff. The company was eventually nationalized by the Colombians, merged with another airline called SACO, and survives today as the national airline, AVIANCA — the oldest in the Western Hemisphere.

Performance Data
Sikorsky S-38

	S-38A	S-38B
Type	Amphibian	———
Length	40 feet	———
Span	72 feet	———
Height	14 feet	———
Gross weight	9,200 pounds	9,900 pounds
Engines	P&W Wasp×2	P&W Hornet×2
Horsepower	410	450
Range	595 statute miles	———
Fuel capacity	330 gallons	———
Useful load	9,900 pounds	———
Cruising speed	112 mph	110 mph
Service ceiling	20,000 feet	19,000 feet
Climb rate	940 feet/minute	880 feet/minute
Passengers	8	———
Crew	3	———

Performance Data
Consolidated Commodore

Type	Boat
Length	68 feet
Span	100 feet
Height	16 feet
Gross weight	17,650 pounds
Engines	Pratt & Whitney Hornet×2
Horsepower	575
Range	1,000 statute miles
Fuel capacity	650 gallons
Cruising speed	102 mph
Service ceiling	10,000 feet
Passengers	22
Crew	4

Pan American's Sikorsky S-38s
(in order of construction)

Model	Reg. No.	User	Original Area of Use	Remarks
S-38	NC-5933	NYRBA	Carib.	Scrapped 10/7/31
S-38A	NC-8000	Pan Am	Carib.	Inaugurated Pan Am's service 10/31/28
S-38A	NC-8020	Pan Am	Carib.	Damaged 12/30/29; scrapped 1933
S-38A	NC-8044	Pan Am	Carib.	Relief flight to Belize 9/13/31; scrapped 5/26/33
S-38B	NC-9775	Pan Am	Carib.	
S-38B	NC-9776	Pan Am	Carib.	Lindbergh-Rowe's survey flight 5/1/30
S-38B	NC-9107	Pan Am	Carib.	Transferred to SCADTA; crashed 3/10/34
S-38B	NC-9137	Pan Am	Carib.	Rowe's survey flight to Paramaribo 7/17/29
S-38B	NC-9151	Pan Am	Carib.	Relief flight to Managua 4/1/31
S-38B	NC-197H	Pan Am	Carib.	Crashed 9/19/29
S-38B	NC-73K	NYRBA	Carib.	Transferred to Panair do Brasil (Pan Am sub.)
S-38B	NC-74K	Pan Am	Carib.	Allocated to Cia National Cubana de Aviacion (Pan Am sub.)
S-38B	NC-75K	Pan Am	Carib.	First air mail flight to Paramaribo; crashed 1938
S-38B	NC-113M	NYRBA	Carib.	Crashed 9/25/32
S-38B	NC-142M	Pan Am	Carib.	First air mail Miami-Canal Zone 4/26/30
S-38B	NC-143M	Pan Am	Carib.	
S-38B	NC-144M	PANAGRA	So. Am.	First air mail to Managua 5/21/30
S-38B	NC-145M	Pan Am	Carib.	Transferred to Panair do Brasil; crashed 1933
S-38B	NC-146M	Pan Am	Carib.	
S-38B	NC-300N	PANAGRA	So. Am.	Transferred to SCADTA
S-38B	NC-301N	NYRBA	So. Am.	Transferred to SCADTA
S-38B	NC-302N	NYRBA	So. Am.	Dismantled 1930

Pan American's Sikorsky S-38s
(in order of construction)

Model	Reg. No.	User	Original Area of Use	Remarks
S-38B	NC-943M	NYRBA	So. Am.	Transferred to Uraba, Medellin and Central Airways (Pan Am sub.)
S-38B	NC-944M	NYRBA	So. Am.	Crashed 6/14/32
S-38B	NC-945M	PANAGRA	So. Am.	Named the *San Juan*
S-38B	NC-946M	NYRBA	So. Am.	Scrapped 1933
S-38B	NC-3V	SCADTA	So. Am.	
S-38BH	NC-16V	CNAC	China	Crashed 11/24/33
S-38B	NC-304N	Pan Am	Carib.	First air mail Miami-Merida 11/12/29; transferred to Panair do Brasil
S-38B	NC-306N	PANAGRA	So. Am.	Crashed Ecuador 2/7/31
S-38B	NC-308N	NYRBA	So. Am.	Transferred to Panair do Brasil
S-38B	NC-309N	Pan Am	Panama	Transferred to SCADTA; crashed 1931
S-38B	NC-17V	CNAC	China	Crashed 4/10/34
S-38B	NC-18V	PANAGRA	So. Am.	
S-38B	NC-19V	PANAGRA	So. Am.	
S-38B	NC-21V	Pan Am		Destroyed Biscayne Bay, Florida 12/11/41
S-38BT	NC-22V	PANAGRA	So. Am.	Named *San Blas*
S-38BH	NC-40V	CNAC	China	Destroyed 8/13/35

Pan American's Consolidated Commodores
(in order of construction -
the last three were delivered directly
to Pan American Airways)

Reg. No.	Name	Area of Use	Remarks
NC-855M	*Buenos Aires*	So. America	Retired 1938
NC-658M	*Rio de Janeiro*	So. America	Retired 1932
NC-659M	*Havana*	Caribbean	Retired 1935
NC-660M	*Cuba*	Caribbean	Destroyed Dinner Key, Miami 1935
NC-661M	*New York/Santos*	So. America	Retired 1940
NC-662M	*Uruguay/Sao Paulo*	So. America	Transferred to Brazilian military as *Manaus* 1944
NC-663M	*Trinidad*	Caribbean	Transferred to China 1937
NC-664M	*Puerto Rico*	Caribbean	Sold 1937
NC-665M	*Argentina*	So. America	Transferred to China 1937
NC-666M	*Miami*	So. America	Transferred to Brazilian military as *Belem* 1941
NC-667M	———	Caribbean	Transferred to Bahamas Airways as VP-BAA, 1949
NC-668M	———	———	Crashed Dinner Key, Miami 9/24/43
NC-669M	*Brazil*	———	Scrapped 1946
NC-670M	———	———	Scrapped 1946

Sikorsky S-40:
The first Clipper

Excitement crackled in the atmosphere at the Berlin Air Show of 1928. Aviation was the wave of the future. Now it was a global race to produce the next, more grandiose design. Each rumor seemed to top the last.

"My friend, Dornier is building a flying ship that can carry 100 passengers!"

"Incredible, but have you heard about Aeropostale. . . ?"

Juan Trippe examined the displayed aircraft and listened to the talk, but he was thinking of his trip over to Europe as a first-class passenger on a luxury steamship. He was visualizing something special for Pan American: A giant flying machine, with all the mystique and glamour of the great ocean liners. A *Normandie* of the air.

Long-distance flying over water would require the power and range of four engines. It would have to carry more passengers than any aircraft now in service to be economical. The tough question was what kind of aircraft should it be: landplane, lighter-than-air, or flying boat?

Airports with the long concrete runways that could support heavy machines were few and far between in the '20s, perhaps no more than a couple in the United States: Detroit's Dearborn and New York City's Floyd Bennett Field. Europe had a few more, mainly to offset the wet, cold springs that turned unimproved airfields into muddy quagmires. Large commercial aircraft also paced the development of bombers, particularly in America, and not until the late 1930s did Boeing's bomber production open the technical path for the large airliner.

Lighter-than-air aircraft were ponderous and slow and required extensive and costly aircrews and enormous ground installations. Certainly the Germans had pioneered the use of long-range, transoceanic airships with their *Graf Zeppelin* and *Hindenburg*. It would not be until 1937, when the latter's disaster occurred, that faith in the airship was extinguished. But, for a while, the lighter-than-air mode of travel had its adherents, as long as the commercial viability of operating a service across the Atlantic Ocean more than compensated for the airship's drawbacks.

Trippe, however, was building an international airline with long routes over water. He was drawn to the flying boat. But this type of transportation had its drawbacks, too. Transporting passengers by launch across a choppy stretch of water to board an anchored airplane rising and falling in the swell could be an ordeal. A marine base, perhaps with facilities constructed on pontoons, was also an expensive proposition. Nevertheless, the flying boat possessed the unquestionable advantage of providing its own landing field. And the ocean was free. Presumably, there was also the enhanced safety factor because a flying boat could always land on the water and perhaps float. A landplane would have no place to set down until it reached land.

The choice for Trippe was the amphibian or the flying boat and he turned again to Sikorsky. They hammered out an agreement in 1929: two four-engined aircraft would be built, designated the S-40, with an option for a third. Cost per copy was $125,000. European airlines, with the possible exception of Britain, had substantial government subsidies and were about five years ahead of the United States in aircraft design, particularly giant marine aircraft that could cross oceans. Europeans felt that aircraft routes were strategic arteries, instruments of national policy. Airlines were creatures of their governments, merely another device to bind the colonies to the motherland and preserve its hegemony in international markets.

Trippe already had his eyes on the Atlantic and the Pacific and knew that in this arena he would be facing a vastly different competitive atmosphere than in the easily dominated, economically backward countries of South and Central America. Britain's Imperial Airways was already linking London to New Delhi in India. KLM, a great pioneering airline, had a route extending all the way from Europe to Java in the Dutch East Indies and was also serving the north coast of South America. The French were flying across Africa and reaching as far afield as Saigon in the Orient, while the Germans, who had already established a presence in China and South

America, were rumored to be building immense aircraft that would fly the Atlantic.

If America was going to be in the game, time was of the essence.

Development of the S-40

Sikorsky began testing various hull shapes on the Housatonic River, near his Connecticut factory, by towing them from a boom attached to a speedboat. Each wooden model was around six feet long and each made approximately 2,000 runs. Nine different hull models received initial testing, three of them in the Washington Navy Yard Basin, before the first water test of the final design was made in April 1929.

Lindbergh was closely consulted for his expertise. He was disappointed that in appearance the S-40 looked like an enlarged S-38: wings externally braced, tail mounted on outriggers, more struts. He began to refer to it, somewhat disparagingly, as the "flying forest." Better aircraft were coming off the drawing boards, but Sikorsky could not develop a radical new design before the scheduled completion date.

The S-40 was Sikorsky's aircraft all the way, a boyhood dream of a mighty aircraft come true. But the designer knew he had to satisfy three people: Trippe, Lindbergh, and Andre Priester, Pan American's operations chief. Trippe wanted to design an aircraft with a high useful load and range and make the passengers' cabin look like the first-class quarters aboard an ocean liner.

Lindbergh had to think about the pilot; Sikorsky knew Lindbergh was already upset about the S-40's lack of an advanced design, so he listened carefully to the Lone Eagle's suggestions, particularly concerns about how well the pilot could see. Curtailed visibility was a notorious problem with floatplanes and amphibians due to spray striking the propellers and gushing over the windshield during takeoffs and landings. The S-38 pilot was blinded for several crucial seconds during takeoff before the aircraft got up on the step, when the floats are merely skimming across the surface of the water. Placement of the cockpit was crucial to Lindbergh, and Sikorsky placed it right where the pilot wanted it: forward of the engines and about one-third of the way between the wing and the nose.

Andre Priester's concerns were the thousand-and-one details that went into building and crewing an aircraft, from the selection of batteries to, literally, the details on the buttons of the crews' coats.

The thin, bald Dutchman was already something of a legend at Pan American, and, indeed, in the airline industry. He was born in 1891 in Java,

Dutch East Indies, the son of a minor colonial official. There are stories that he tended to exaggerate the importance of his background, one being that he supervised KLM's operations in Amsterdam. Nevertheless, one day he showed up in the United States and landed a job as the operations manager for the Philadelphia Rapid Transit Airline, which was connected to the Philadelphia Exposition of 1926.

Priester gained a reputation as a somewhat dour, exacting manager — the exact antithesis of the free-spirit pilots who worked for him — and there are many stories about his stern admonitions delivered in a thick accent that he kept all his life. Perhaps this is the reason why Trippe hired him as Pan American's operations manager in 1927. Trippe had his own ideas about how he wanted the pilots of Pan American to behave: reliable, professional, competent, and smartly dressed at all times, like a very good chauffeur.

As development of the S-40 proceeded, it was soon apparent that the very size of the aircraft created manufacturing problems. Weight for one thing. You were talking about an aircraft weighing more than *17 tons*. Hull construction was all-metal duralumin, with riveted Alclad metal sheets. The fabric-covered wing area measured 1,740 square feet. The weight of each aileron, stress tested to 945 pounds, was 53 pounds. The area of the twin-boom tail assembly was 461 square feet.

Fuel capacity was originally 1,040 gallons, each pontoon — supported by rods extending more than 12 feet from the fuselage — carrying approximately 250 gallons and four more fuel tanks in the wings. Any fuel tank could feed any engine, and all fuel lines and valves were placed outside of the cabin area to allow passenger smoking and to lessen the likelihood of fumes accumulating.

Maximum theoretical load for passengers and cargo was 58,000 pounds, all to come down on the landing gear. The amphibious S-40's retractable gear weighed a total of 1,700 pounds and incorporated the largest aircraft landing wheels (14-inch diameter) ever built. The gear and tire as a single assembly was built to support 153,000 pounds. A smaller retractable wheel was also positioned at the rear of the hull; the wheel could serve double duty as a rudder when levered down by the pilot.

The S-40 was also well prepared for marine operations and carried more than 3,000 pounds of anchors, mooring gear, emergency radios, life vests, inflatable rafts, and other survival gear. All of this weight had to be deducted from the revenue generating load the aircraft could carry.

A hitch developed when it was discovered that spring manufacturing was a very specialized procedure. No aircraft springs were available for an airplane of this size and weight. Sikorsky came up with a solution. He turned to the railroads, and the springs used on medium-sized railway cars proved to be just right.

Four nacelle-housed, 575-hp Hornet engines were hung below the S-40's upper wing. Each engine drove two-bladed propellers that cut an arc $10\frac{1}{2}$ feet in diameter. The S-40 was designed to fly and climb with the load on any three engines and maintain altitude on any two.

Ease of maintenance, particularly in remote areas where skilled mechanics would be at a premium, had a high priority. The control cables, for example, were housed in a rectangular conduit attached to the outside of the hull. And, ever mindful of exactly where the S-40 would be going, and what type of facilities could be expected there, Trippe ordered each aircraft to have a special engine mounting ring installed on the cabin roof forward of the rear hatch. This allowed a spare engine to be bolted to the roof and delivered to remote Pan Am stations without taking up cabin room.

The aircraft was ready for flight tests in April 1931. Boris Sergievsky, Sikorsky's test pilot, guided the aircraft out onto Long Island Sound for an initial series of test runs. Then the moment arrived that everyone had been waiting for. Sergievsky revved the engines to a takeoff speed of 1,950 rpm during a one-mile run. Roaring through the water, he eased back the stick, and the huge plane soared up into the air in a shower of spray. Despite all the misgivings and the muttering that the aircraft would never fly, the S-40 worked. The most difficult test occurred in August when the S-40 taxied out in a very rough sea on one of the windiest days of the summer. The S-40 took off and landed repeatedly with no ill effects, despite tons of water crashing down on its hull.

Testing determined that the aircraft would have a cruise of speed of 115 mph and a range of 700 miles, which could be doubled with a reduced payload coupled with extra fuel tanks. Rate of climb was 712 feet per minute, and the aircraft could level off at a service ceiling of 13,500 feet. Ground and water landing speed was established at 65 mph.

Sikorsky was sure his design was sound. The aircraft was unusually dry, with relatively little water splashing on the windows and exterior cabin walls. What's more, flight characteristics were encouraging; with a gross weight of approximately 25,500 pounds, the aircraft had risen into the air in approximately 16 seconds.

Pan American had to address passenger comfort and Trippe and Priester were exacting. The S-40 would rarely carry more than 30 passengers, but was rated to carry 45, and Trippe wanted them to feel they were in a luxury liner.

Immediately aft of the cockpit were two suites for the traveler who wanted true opulence in the air. Each suite was separated by the main aisle, softly carpeted in blue, and privacy was ensured by pull drapes and doors in the bulkhead.

Next in line were three standard compartments, each with eight passenger chairs, upholstered in blue and orange, and designed in the Queen Anne style. Seating was four abreast. Each seat had an electric light, a steward call button and — before the age of warnings from the surgeon general — an individual ash tray and cigarette lighter. Metal-mesh overhead racks provided storage for the passengers' luggage during short hops.

The finish was truly awesome: polished walnut paneling on walls and bulkheads, blue carpeting stretched throughout the passenger areas, and soft lighting glowing from above. Each compartment was wider than a Pullman car, with eight-foot ceilings and large square windows, which could be opened during flight. Rope blinds shaded the windows, textured in gray silk and complemented by a Sikorsky *Winged-S* chrome latch. Each compartment, naturally called a *cabin*, had crafted wood pictures depicting a history of man's travel, from hunting game to the world's first four-engined aircraft designed by Sikorsky.

A smoking lounge aft of the passenger compartments was adorned with life rings hung on the walls to continue the nautical theme. Directly behind the lounge were two lavatories and a compartment for mail and baggage. Hot meals could also be prepared on board, another first for Pan American aircraft.

All this luxurious space for the passengers did come at a price. One of the first things to go was the crews' sleeping quarters. Pan American felt the space could be more profitably used for passengers and luggage, besides, the crew would not need to rest on short hops around the Caribbean.

Passengers were supposed to have a feeling of greater security when over water with compartments that were fitted with five watertight bulkhead doors, each with large latches and a porthole just like an ocean liner. The doors were heavy and awkward to open, and whether they actually gave passengers a more comfortable feeling or not is hard to say.

Basil Rowe arrived on September 25 to test the aircraft and pronounced it "perhaps one of the best and most serviceable of any that Sikorsky has built." The aircraft seemed to have no bad habits, except a heavy lateral control forced pilots to exert control wheel pressure to keep the wings level. Sikorsky incorporated a greater gear ratio to help lateral control. The aircraft controls should have been completely redesigned, but the gearing change was sufficient to overcome the problem.

Testing was completed by early October and Rowe flew the S-40, now registered NC-80V, down to Washington where Mrs. Herbert Hoover would christen the aircraft. Trippe had already settled on a name. Henceforth, his aircraft would bear the name of the ships that bore American commerce across the oceans: the fastest vessels of their day. Before an excited crowd of 12,000 people, including the representatives of more than a dozen countries, the first lady christened the plane *American Clipper*, breaking a bottle of Caribbean water across its bow because Prohibition prohibited the traditional champagne. Trippe gave a speech that was broadcast over a nationwide radio hookup, and then, with military bands playing the national anthem, the blue-hulled S-40 taxied out onto the Potomac River for a demonstration flight. The *New York Times* called it, "America's mightiest airplane."

The S-40 would be the first Pan American aircraft to bear the name of *Clipper*, which became a registered trademark of Pan American. It was the flagship of the Pan Am fleet, the first example, Trippe said, of "the great airliner of tomorrow that will speed trade and goodwill among the nations." He had actually paid $138,772 as the final cost for the *American Clipper*. It was a more dignified, more confident Trippe, perhaps helped by the fact that, after four years, his airline had shown its first profit, $105,452 on revenues of $7,913,587.

The *Clipper* brought a new aura to the airline. Pan American would operate planes like ocean liners; time aboard "ship" was measured in bells, speed in knots; the nautical terms *port*, *starboard* and *beam* were introduced. And now there were naval terms for the flight crew: the pilot became the captain; copilot, first officer; mechanic elevated to flight engineer; and the Marconi operator became the radio officer. And, of course, a steward assisted the passengers and was in charge of a galley.

The nautical theme was carried over to the dress of the crew. Pan American pilots, navigators and radio officers already wore uniforms of navy-blue serge, with gold wings over the breast pocket. Ranks were designated by stars on the wings: captain, two; first officer, one. Later, those with a super rank of master ocean pilot wore three stars. Gold rings on the cuff and braid on the peak of the cap were not added until World War II.

Stewards' uniform was dark trousers and a sparkling white, waist-length jacket, with a white shirt and a black necktie. They had much to do besides serving refreshments and meals, including pointing out scenic attractions from the windows, helping passengers with customs forms and other official procedures, and the all-important distributing remedies for airsickness.

One of the early Pan Am stewards in the Caribbean was a young Cuban-American named Charles B. Rebozo. Years later, after he had become a self-made millionaire, he would be known as the friend and confidant of Richard M. Nixon.

First flight

The amphibian's inaugural flight was scheduled for November 19, 1931, with Lindbergh, now twenty-nine years old, as captain and Basil Rowe as first officer. The aircraft stopped at Norfolk, Savannah, Charleston, and Jacksonville, where large crowds turned out to see the Sikorsky wonder plus the thrill of seeing Lindbergh.

Thirty-two passengers were taken on board at Miami's Dinner Key, including Sikorsky. The run was Miami to Kingston, Barranquilla, and then on to Cristobal in the Canal Zone. Before departing, however, Lindbergh had to make 10 practice takeoffs and landings to meet Pan Am's regulations. He had never flown the S-40 before.

Lindbergh lifted the *Clipper* off the blue water surrounding the Pan Am base at Dinner Key on Biscayne Bay and headed for the first overnight stop, Kingston, Jamaica; Basil Rowe was first officer. Lindbergh and Sikorsky attended a dinner that evening with approximately 300 guests assembled by Kingston's Chamber of Commerce. Lindbergh was slated to be the principal speaker and was waiting to get up to begin his address when a nervous waiter spilled a pitcher of cream all over him. The Lone Eagle would later complain somewhat testily that he realized a basic difference between the Americans and the British from that incident: the Brits in the audience ignored the accident, while the Americans laughed.

The next day they departed for Barranquilla: six hundred miles of open water, the longest nonstop commercial flight ever attempted to that point. The aircraft was being refueled at Barranquilla when gasoline sloshed across the wings and into the water due to the choppy waves. Lindbergh noticed people on the dock nearby were smoking and hollered to them to put out their cigarettes. The startled smokers complied immediately by ditching them into the water. Luckily for Pan Am and the crew, there was no fire. The S-40 reached Cristobal on November 22, where General Bliss, the postmaster of the Canal Zone, greeted Basil Rowe and the passengers and ceremoniously accepted the mail. Lindbergh, meanwhile, had remained in Barranquilla for a few days and would rejoin the flight on the return trip.

The only untoward incident on the return trip with Lindbergh again acting as captain occurred right at the end of the flight. NC-80V arrived at Miami after dusk with no idea of wind direction. The S-40 had no night flying instruments and Lindbergh put the plane down more or less blind.

There was a little porpoising, and then the aircraft swerved abruptly to the left, tossing some passengers from their seats.

In a sort of "after-you-Alphonse" routine, both Lindbergh and Sikorsky claimed it was their fault. Even Sikorsky would later insist that there was a design error in the hull. Lindbergh laughed when he heard that Sikorsky continued to claim that the difficult landing was his fault: "That's quite typical of Igor to take the blame himself and never blame the other fellow."

Perhaps, however, Sikorsky's mistake was excusable. Trailing models in the water simply did not have the accuracy attained with the elaborate instrumentation and test basins of later years.

'Flying Down to Rio'

Sikorsky delivered the second S-40 (NC-81V) to Pan American on November 16, 1931. The aircraft's cost was $136,597. The *Caribbean Clipper* was soon flying across its namesake sea carrying passengers and mail. The *Southern Clipper*, NC-752V, the last of the S-40s, joined its sister aircraft on August 30, 1932. Pan American paid $137,281 for NC-752V.

Pan American World Airways

Sikorsky S-40 *Caribbean Clipper* (NC-81V) that, like all S-40s, carried a crew of six and up to 38 passengers.

Sikorsky S-40 *Southern Clipper* (NC-752V).

Pan Am's three S-40s went on to accumulate a thousand flights in the Caribbean from November 1931 through January 1934. They seldom carried more than 30, but all three aircraft were a commercial success. On-time arrival averaged 99 percent. Travel on the S-40, advertised as the "Pullman of the Skies," became extremely popular, the flights booked weeks in advance. The service to the Caribbean and South America was so well publicized, in fact, that Hollywood saluted it with the 1933 musical classic, *Flying Down to Rio*, which starred Fred Astaire, Ginger Rogers, and Dolores del Rio.

America had fallen in love with the S-40, and nowhere was the airplane more popular than on the short hop between Miami and Havana. Cuba's capital was the gambling mecca of the Western Hemisphere in the '20s and '30s, a city that was truly wide open and a magnet to high rollers from all over North America; more than once, patient Pan Am crews had to contend with drunk and angry passengers, returning home with empty pockets and crushed dreams of making the big one.

On one flight, with Ed Musick at the controls, a drunk and wild passenger went berserk, brandishing a knife and screaming that he was going to kill everyone. There was pandemonium on the aircraft as the other passengers scrambled to get out of the way. Musick turned the controls over to his copilot, grabbed a pistol and ran aft. The two confronted each other for a moment, the passenger with his knife raised and Musick leveling his gun. Suddenly, the plane hit an air pocket and wavered. The unsteady passenger groped for a handhold and Musick decked him

Pan American World Airways

Interior of the Sikorsky S-40.

with one punch. Crewmembers locked the drunk in the lavatory and the rest of the flight proceeded on schedule. Musick later had to explain his swollen and cut knuckles to his wife.

Many captains allowed passengers to come up to the cockpit and look around after cruising altitude had been reached. On one Havana-Miami flight, with Captain Art Peters at the controls, an obviously inebriated passenger — "packing a full load of Cuba Libras" — staggered up to the flight deck, took one look around, and then fell back; he reached up and grabbed the overhead engine throttles, cutting power on all four engines. There was momentary panic in the cockpit before the engines were restarted. The passenger was firmly told to go back to his seat. Fifteen minutes later, here he comes again. And again he tripped and cut the power to all four engines. This time, he was led back to his seat, and Peters told the steward to strap him in and keep him there.

Another unusual flight took place when Basil Rowe, at the controls of the *American Clipper*, raced an ox-drawn cart. The idea was to publicize the difference between modern transportation and ancient transportation, in this case, a Cuban cane cart. Both vehicles were supposed to start at the same time from Havana. The rules required Rowe to estimate the distance the cart would cover in the time it took the S-40 to fly to its base at Miami. Rowe's guess was that the cart would travel at four miles per hour. Full corporate publicity drums were rolling and competition day arrived with a great deal of excitement. Away went the cart, oxen straining, and off flew a determined Rowe at the controls of the S-40. Rowe's estimate proved to be way off.

He later explained that he had failed to take three things into account: the Cuban sneakily goaded his oxen with a secret weapon: a nail at the end of a pole. Next, the S-40 had to buck a strong headwind. And, finally, the Cubans could not resist gambling. Everyone placed money on the nose of the oxen, and the beasts, beautifully handled, cranked up their speed to 10 miles per hours. Rowe, meanwhile, was battling a fierce northeaster, but ingenuity was the hallmark of the Pan Am pilot. Cannily, Rowe set the S-40 down on a stretch of calm water, radioed just landed, and taxied in the rest of the way. Rowe excused the deception by saying no one was sticking a nail into his *Clipper*.

Art Peters began flying S-40s between Port of Spain and Caracas, with stopovers at various small coastal towns in between. For the citizens of many of these towns, the Pan Am flying boat was their only contact with the outside world apart from the occasional tramp steamer or mail boat. The whole population from miles around would show up to watch the S-40 arrive. Whenever a crew member climbed up on a wing and measured the fuel in the tanks with a stick, there would be a round of applause.

Sikorsky S-40 *American Clipper* takeoff.

Cockpit crew of the S-40.

Refueling in most of the smaller places was by 55-gallon drum and a hand pump.

Overhauling or changing an engine in the field was also an ordeal. Whenever it looked as though an engine had to be changed, the crew would notify Miami and begin getting things ready. First, all accessories, magnetos, starter, generator, and so on, were removed and set aside. The cylinders were pulled from the power case, and the carburetor, exhaust, and intake stacks removed. When all that was left was the bare engine case and the propeller, which could not be removed because of the special equipment needed, the crew waited for the new engine to arrive, usually in a Consolidated Commodore accompanied by two mechanics. The propeller and power case were removed, the new case installed, and the engine rebuilt. All of this usually had to be done with the airplane in the water.

As the months of operating experience went by, it was apparent that, while successful in attracting customers, the three Clippers were barely on the threshold of being profitable to operate. The problem was the heavy landing gear. Originally considered a necessity as a safety factor, the weight became harder and harder to justify. The airline finally stripped the S-40 wheels in 1933, and they became true flying boats.

The profit picture improved until 1936 when the three S-40s were feeling the competition of newer and more powerful aircraft. A major overhaul to increase power and range saw the installation of four 660-hp Hornet T2D1 engines on each aircraft, boosting range to 800 miles. Gross weight went from 34,000 to 34,600 pounds, and useful load rose to 11,400 pounds. The revamped aircraft kept going for several more years, but, gradually, the shortage of parts became acute, and they also became too expensive to operate. The glamour had also moved to bigger and faster craft. The S-40s had their beautiful walnut paneling removed and replaced with a more utilitarian material that was easier to clean. The elegant smoking lounges were converted to a standard, eight-passenger compartment.

All three *Clippers* were retired from regularly scheduled service in June 1940 and farmed out to charter operators. *Southern Clipper*, after an extensive overhaul, became the world's first scheduled air freight carrier. Service began on January 2, 1941, when the S-40A flew from Biscayne Bay to Port au Prince with 3,366 pounds of cargo.

Pearl Harbor prompted the Naval Air Transport System (NATS) to take over the *American* and the *Caribbean* and use them as flying classrooms for navigators and seaplane pilots. The two aircraft operated out of Dinner Key sporting large blister domes cut into their fuselages and in hundreds of flights helped to train young navy aviators. Finally, too old and too worn out for even use as a trainer, the navy junked the *American Clipper* in June 1943 and it was stored in a Miami junkyard, its parts cannibalized. The *Caribbean Clipper* was retired on April 15, 1943, and finally written off in August 1944 and condemned to the scrap heap. The *Southern Clipper*, meanwhile, continued to fly until its license was submitted for cancellation in November 1944 and it, too, was sold for scrap.

Altogether, the Sikorsky S-40s logged slightly more than 10 million air miles during their career. But the S-40s did more for Pan American than haul passengers in comfort. The Caribbean was the proving ground: the aircraft, the laboratory. Technical innovations, such as a dual control panel and two steering columns and an improved gas pumping system, meant that the S-40 was only the prologue to a new era.

The commercial world is not known for its sentimental approach to used-up equipment. The *American Clipper*, the first of its line, the aircraft that without a doubt did more to establish the United States in international aviation than any other, the aircraft that Lindbergh flew to Barranquilla, lay for years in its final resting place, a Miami junkyard, no more than a rusting hulk. Finally, in 1946, it was torn apart and sold for scrap.

Performance Data
Sikorsky S-40

Type	S-40	S-40A
Type	Amphibian	Boat
Length	77 feet	——
Span	114 feet	——
Height	24 feet	——
Gross weight	34,010 pounds	34,600 pounds
Engines	P&W Hornet B×4	P&W Hornet T2D1×4
Horsepower	575	660
Range	800 miles	——
Fuel capacity	1,040 gallons	1,060 gallons
Useful load	10,870 pounds	11,400 pounds
Cruising speed	115 mph	120 mph
Service ceiling	13,000 feet	12,500 feet
Climb rate	712 feet/minute	——
Passengers	34	40
Crew	5	6

Pan American's Sikorsky S-40s
(in order of construction)

Reg. No.	Name	Remarks
NC-80V	*American Clipper*	Flown by Lindbergh on inaugural flight; scrapped 6/24/43.
NC-81V	*Caribbean Clipper*	Scrapped Aug. 1944.
NC-752V	*Southern Clipper*	Converted to freight carrier Dec. 1940; scrapped 11/17/44.

Lindbergh
flies the Pacific

Juan Trippe had briefly met Charles Lindbergh at Teterboro Airfield in New Jersey sometime in 1926. According to Trippe, they discussed a ground radio navigation system, but Lindbergh would later say that he had no recollection of meeting the future head of Pan American that early.

Trippe, however, was amongst the crowd of five hundred that watched Lindbergh take off for his transatlantic flight from muddy Roosevelt Field, Long Island, on May 20, 1927. A few months later, he met Lindbergh at the Commodore Hotel in New York, with the Lone Eagle's lawyer present. Trippe would later say that he told Lindbergh he could not speak to Lindbergh except through a lawyer. That, said Trippe, created a very good impression with Lindbergh.

Whatever it was, it must have considerably impressed the Lone Eagle. He was the man of the hour and had received hundreds of job offers since his great solo flight. Trippe had just departed Colonial Air Transport and was out of work. Yet, they worked out an agreement that Lindbergh would become the technical advisor to an airline that did not yet exist. Nobody ever said Juan Trippe was not persuasive.

The pair became a highly visible partnership. Trippe needed Lindbergh for the millions of dollars worth of publicity the glamorous young flyer brought to Pan Am. But the *quid pro quo* was that Lindbergh was one of the few pilots alive who had the flying skill and daring to pioneer the new routes for the airline. Lindbergh's reward was reinforcement of his love of flying and a devotion to the future of international aviation, and for an American that meant Pan Am.

(This was almost literally true. While Lindbergh made some money from Pan American through attractive stock options here and there, he was never a greedy man. Once he reached a comfortable but rather simple level of living that suited him and his wife with funds obtained mainly from the royalties from their books, he was content. Indeed, in later years, Trippe, not usually known for any freespending habits, had to press compensation on Lindbergh for the valuable work that the flyer was prepared to do for the airline for nothing. Lindbergh eventually became a director of Pan American, but not until 1964.)

Latin America was a Pan American domain and Trippe now looked for a way to expand his airline across the Atlantic. But the thousands of miles of ocean to be crossed were a barrier for any passenger aircraft. A scheduled airline service required intermediate points where aircraft could be refueled and serviced. Every useful landing spot, the Azores, Greenland, Labrador, Newfoundland, Iceland, and Ireland, was under the territorial sovereignty of various European nations, and they were not anxious to let the Americans gain a foothold before their own services were well established.

Competition to be the first to establish a route across the Atlantic was also heating up. The British were now flying the first of the Short Brothers' flying boats, and the Germans were showing their inventiveness by cata-pulting aircraft from the ocean liners *Bremen* and *Europa*.

By some maneuvering, a Trippe specialty, Pan American Airways was able to sign a Tripartite Agreement in 1930 with Britain and France to share the transatlantic mail traffic business. Pan Am's share was a respect-able 50 percent. Even so, Trippe still did not have his landing rights. But there is more than one way to build an airline. Trippe, his goals for the Atlantic momentarily frustrated, suddenly found the Pacific more interest-ing. Lindbergh put forward a plan for a long-range survey flight, an incredible aerial journey along the great circle route of the northern Pacific, from Alaska to China. It was probably the first Arctic flight directed specifically at establishing an airline route.

If Trippe could not, for the moment, reach Europe and Asia across the Atlantic, he would reach it across the Pacific.

The lady learns Morse code

The Lindberghs' living room was a morass of equipment for days. Clothing, radio and navigation gear, and emergency food — the thousand and one items needed for a long-distance flight — were stacked in great piles, each piece carefully weighed on a white baby scale. Whatever they would eventually take was a carefully thought out compromise on weight. Would it be better, for example, to take a shotgun and shells, which can kill birds if needed for food, or simply take an equal amount of weight in food? The shotgun was left behind.

Anne Lindbergh, the daughter of an ambassador, the product of Smith College, gleefully mastered Morse code, navigation and the operation of an airplane's radio. When people would ask Lindbergh whether he had considered the dangers of the coming trip and whether it was really necessary for Anne to go along because there were plenty of navigators and radio operators available, he would just grin: "She's crew."

The aircraft was going to be a specially built Lockheed Sirius, a twin-float seaplane. The Sirius had been designed and built for Lindbergh by Lockheed Aircraft Company, with the company bearing the development costs in expectation that the sale of the aircraft to the famous Lone Eagle would encourage other customers. They were not far wrong, and even before flight testing was completed, the company sold six more of the model. Lockheed charged Lindbergh $17,825 for the aircraft, about the same cost as the Lockheed Vega, which provided much of the aircraft's ancestry.

The Sirius was built as a low-wing monoplane, not a very popular design at that time, but Lindbergh insisted on the type for various reasons, including "safety in a forced landing and wider wheel spread." It had a wood fuselage, two cockpits with sliding glass canopies and massive, all-metal floats built by the Edo Aircraft Corporation. The 600-hp Wright Cyclone engine was coupled to a two-bladed, Hamilton Standard propeller. Wing loading was 29 pounds per square foot. Enough fuel was carried on board to give it a range of 2,000 miles.*

Flight testing of the Sirius proceeded while Lindbergh carefully plotted a spectacular course across the Arctic. First, the easy part: New York, North Haven, and Ottawa. Then they would fly north towards Moose Factory on James Bay, entering the vast Canadian wilderness. Beyond Moose Factory, a small village on Hudson Bay, nothing would be below them but empty tundra. They would cross the 60th parallel and land at the tiny hamlet of Baker Lake, only a few degrees south of the Arctic Circle. Then they would begin the great swing to the east across the Arctic to the next stop, Aklavik on the frigid Beaufort Sea. Then Barrow, Alaska, and, flying south, Shishmaref and Nome on the Seward Peninsula, jutting out into the Bering Strait.

---

*Although the Sirius had some initial popularity, the timing of its introduction was bad. The 1929 stock market crash and the beginning of the Great Depression severely cramped aircraft sales. Lockheed built only 14 of the planes, and production was halted in 1930.

Bearing to the east, they would fly on to Karaginski in the Russian Far East, with a government still not recognized by the United States; south to Petropavlovsk at the tip of the Kamchatka Peninsula, then down through the Kuril Islands, still Russian territory.

The Sirius would then enter the Japanese Empire, home of a vigorous people but lately increasingly at odds with the United States. The Lindberghs would fly from Tokyo south to touch at Osaka and Fukuoka and then cross the East China Sea to China, landing at the mighty port of Shanghai, in 1931 probably at the peak of its importance. They would fly on to Nanking on the northward curve of the Yangtze River, and then reach the end of their journey farther up the river at the city of Hankow.

A great crowd assembled on July 27, 1931, to watch the Lindberghs take off from College Point, Long Island. Radio reporters described every move to home audiences. Spray whipping back, the black seaplane with orange wings bounded across the Sound and then roared into the sky. It banked against the clouds and headed north.

After a quick stop in Maine, the Lindberghs flew on to Ottawa, then beyond the Canadian capital. They soon found themselves flying over a desolate land. Miles and miles of wilderness passed beneath their wings. Anne was busy operating the radio, which was often an ordeal in itself. Operating radio gear in 1931 meant you had to insert a different transmitting coil every time you changed frequencies; the Sirius carried six coils. Another set of coils had to be adjusted correctly to receive. Stick your fingers in the wrong place, easy to do in a bouncing aircraft, and you received a nasty jolt of 400 volts. Anne Lindbergh learned to pick out the correct coils by feel—500 cycles had the most turns of wire. The trailing antenna, which had a heavy ball on the loose end, also had to be reeled out by hand—so far for one frequency, so far for another. And the hand cranking turns had to be precise.

In the far north, they landed at tiny settlements, met by a few Indians or Eskimo trappers and once by a Mountie in a red coat. Herds of caribou, looking like vast shadows, crossed the earth below them. The aircraft roared on, rising and falling on the unseen currents of air. Each person took spells at flying the airplane while the other slept. Anne would later describe the flight in *North to the Orient*. "It never grew dark," she wrote. "For hours I watched a motionless sun set in a motionless cloud-bank. For hours we skirted that gray, treeless coast, stretches and stretches of bleak land scattered with icy lakes. Always the same. Until I wondered, in spite of the vibration of the engine which hummed up through the soles of my feet, whether we were not motionless too."

Darkness at Nome

The Lindberghs found that they could not get fuel for the aircraft at Point Barrow. The supply ship, the *Northland*, had been locked out of the harbor by ice. There was nothing else to do but fly on to Nome with what fuel they had. Soon, they were out of the zone of permanent twilight, and it was getting dark. They had no night flying instruments, and Anne could not contact Nome on the radio. She tried to raise Point Barrow to see if they could relay a message. There was a faint signal. Then it was gone.

"CAN'T..COPY..UR..SIG," Anne sent, "WILL..CONTACT..NRUL (the supply ship *Northland*)."

"NRUL..NRUL..WHAT..TIME..DOES..IT..GET..DARK..AT..NOME?"

The signal to the supply ship also went unanswered; it was growing darker. Anne Lindbergh watched the sparks from the exhaust as they "flashed behind us in the dusk."

By now Nome was worried. A signal was sent out that the famous couple was overdue and presumed lost.

Time went by. The Lindberghs stared anxiously ahead at a dark range of mountains. Then, almost like magic, a signal got through to a relay station on the coast. At Nome there was rejoicing. The Lindberghs were alive. They sent a message that they were putting out flares on the Nome River. But it was too late. There was no way the Sirius could fly on in the darkness. Lindbergh decided to land. Below them, a lagoon, or was it a lake? Lindbergh throttled back and dropped down. They landed safely, and he cut the switches. But when he climbed out of the cockpit to anchor the craft, he discovered the water was only three feet deep.

They arrived at Nome the next day, August 11, 1931, and walked beside muddy streets on sidewalks from the 19th century made of planks like the frontier town.

In Russia, they were met cordially enough and were given gifts and a comfortable place to sleep in a government building. Flying on to Japan, they were caught in a fog so dense while trying to find Buroton Bay in Hokkaido that for a while Anne Lindbergh went through a philosophical bout of fatalism, ready to accept her fate and "not struggle through all the intervening stages of fear." But her husband's skill as a pilot saved them again, and once more the Sirius came down safely.

On the Inland Sea at Osaka, Lindbergh noticed that their luggage on the aircraft had been disturbed, and a youth was found to have stowed away on board. Head drooping sadly, he was led away by the police. They found out later he had hoped they would take him to America, not knowing that the Lindberghs were on their way to China.

China. They flew over a devastated land. The Yangtze River was going through one of its periodic floods, and as they peered down at the countryside, they could see thousands fleeing the water's ravages. At Nanking, the city walls, Anne said, were like "a gray rope around hills and fields, railroads and canals, mud huts and tiled roofs . . . ."

They landed on Lotus Lake just outside the city, the flooded river reaching to the foot of the city wall "like a medieval moat." It was September 19.

Lindbergh volunteered to join the relief effort and map the damaged area for the National Flood Relief Commission. He then flew off to the town of Hinghwa with two doctors and medical supplies on board. At Nanking, meanwhile, the river was a turbulent moving mass of muddy water carrying everything, boats, homes, and corpses, downstream. Thousands of desperate Chinese, literally starving, were trying to find food and shelter. Lindbergh was concerned that the Sirius would be rammed by one of the numerous junks coming down the river, and he asked the British aircraft carrier *Hermes* to lift the Sirius on board with a derrick. The British agreed.

The next morning, however, when they tried to lower it back into the river again, with Charles and Anne already aboard the aircraft, it was caught by the current and swept downstream. Brought up at the end of a cable, one of the aircraft's wings dug down into the water, and it flipped over. The Lindberghs dove out into the water, swam to a launch, and were helped on board. The *Hermes'* derrick then lifted the battered Sirius out of the water and swung it onto the ship's deck. But the aircraft, damaged by the cable during retrieval, was now unflyable and was sent home by ship. The Lindberghs followed on a steamship from Yokohama.

Lindbergh reported back to Trippe that the great circle route to the Orient could be flown, but there were many problems that had to be solved if Pan Am wanted to establish a regular airline service. Unpredictable weather, the total lack of adequate facilities, and the perpetual winter nights of the tundra all meant an enormous commitment of resources. Was it worth it?

Meanwhile, Trippe was thinking ahead, buying two small aviation companies in Alaska for a total of $90,000 as a prelude to establishing a great circle service. The merged subsidiary was named Pacific-Alaska Airways and gave Trippe another two thousand miles of route, but international politics prevented him from getting to the Orient across the Arctic and northern Pacific. The United States would not recognize the government of the Soviet Union, which, in turn, refused to give Pan American landing rights in Siberia, an essential part of the route.

But Trippe was not ready to give up yet. There was another way across the Pacific: the central route — across the vast stretches of ocean from San Francisco to Hawaii and on to Manila. But before he reached the Orient, he had to have an anchor, a base in China.

China
'cross the bay

China National Aviation Corporation (CNAC) — spelled literally as the Middle Kingdom Space Machine Family, in Chinese characters — was established in 1929 by the Curtiss-Wright Corporation. Shanghai was the hub and CNAC began operating west to the city of Chungking, far up the Yangtze, and north to Peking. CNAC's fleet was a strange mixture of the familiar and the unusual; the Yangtze route was flown with Loening amphibians, a clumsy-looking, single-engined biplane with a squared-off rudder; the more streamlined Stinson SM6B was used for the Peking service.

China in the 1930s was a difficult place to run an airline. Civil war disrupted operations, planes crashed, pilots were arrested and killed by warlords. Soon the operation was losing money at the rate of $250,000 a year. Curtiss-Wright wanted to pull out and looked for someone to take over the airline's operation.

Trippe saw CNAC as an opportunity to gain an official foothold on the Chinese mainland. He bought a 45 percent interest in CNAC on March 31, 1933, financing the deal largely with a highly inflated value placed on Pan American stock. The Chinese government, following the current practice, maintained legal ownership of the company.

Two S-38s, which were transported to Shanghai by ship and then assembled, and two Douglas Dolphins helped Pan American quickly expand CNAC's service south along the Chinese coast, linking Shanghai to Canton. Routes would also eventually extend as far west as Chengtu before the aggressive advance of the Japanese disrupted operations in the mid 1930s.

Pan American took delivery of two Douglas Dolphin amphibians in August 1934, which were allocated to CNAC; NC-14239 and NC-14240 were the first commercial aircraft designed and built by Douglas. The Dolphin had two Pratt & Whitney Wasp engines, each rated at 450 horsepower, mounted above each wing, driving Hamilton Standard nine-foot diameter propellers. The Dolphin could carry seven or eight passengers at a cruising speed of 108 mph for up to 650 statute miles.

The aircraft's wingspan was 60 feet, length 43 feet, and height 15 feet. Six compartments separated by five watertight bulkheads divided the hull. The Aerol strut-type landing gear was fitted with a hydraulic retracting mechanism. The pilot could manually crank the landing gear out of the way when the aircraft was in the water. With a single rudder, an all-metal hull and a spruce veneer-covered cantilever high wing, the Dolphin had a modern design. Fifty-eight of them were eventually built, most for the army and navy. Interestingly, the only other two Dolphins in commercial operation were used on the ferry service between Los Angeles and Avalon on Catalina Island.

Trippe's problems in China were just beginning. Buying 45 percent of CNAC did not mean that Pan Am could land any plane in China that was not there to begin with; in other words, while CNAC could buy aircraft and operate wherever it wanted on the China mainland, a foreign airline, Pan American Airways, still did not have any landing rights.

Trippe sent out 42-year-old Harold M. Bixby, a former St. Louis banker and one of Lindbergh's backers on his 1927 transatlantic flight, to act as troubleshooter. Bixby probably did not realize what he was getting himself into. A neat, tall man of impeccable honesty, he waded his way for months through the intricate corridors of the Chinese government with little result. Regardless, a major hurdle was the international treaties themselves, forced on China by the European powers, Japan, and the United States. China was obliged under the terms of these treaties to extend to all other powers any rights granted to one of them. China, moreover, had been embroiled in a war with Japan since the Mukden Incident in September 1931. Extending rights to the Americans would mean they would also have to let in the feared Japanese. Bixby, firmly backed by Trippe, also refused to resort to bribes, the ubiquitous cumshaw, which did not expedite matters with the Chinese officials.

Little apparent chance of gaining direct landing rights on the Chinese mainland from an intransigent government, encouraged Trippe to set his sights on the British Crown Colony of Hong Kong. The colony was also next door to Canton, the southern terminus of CNAC. But the British were not about to help out the Americans, particularly Pan American

Airways, which it rightly saw as a rival to its own, rather backward, Imperial Airways.

Trippe pulled his usual end run. If he could not land at Hong Kong, he would land at the sleepy Portuguese colony of Macao across the bay, or so he made it appear. Portugal, which had nothing to lose and everything to gain, promptly granted him landing rights. A five-year contract gave Pan American the exclusive right to carry mail between Macao and Manila, there, connecting with service to the Americas.

The British, visualizing themselves cut out from a modern transportation system, were now very nervous. Swallowing the bait, the governor of Hong Kong invited Pan Am to send a *Clipper* flight to Hong Kong as a courtesy call. Trippe dealt the next card carefully. A message came back from Pan Am saying, "While we understand that Kai-tak Airdrome is excellent for the purpose which it is designed to serve, we fear that it would not have the proper facilities for handling a ship such as the trans-Pacific Clipper." The British folded. Trippe had his Hong Kong terminus on the China mainland in October 1936 for service across the Pacific. Macao, its moment in history gone, settled again into its state of somnolence. By November, 1936, CNAC's Shanghai-Canton service was extended to the British Crown Colony by November 1936.

American pilots and mechanics operating the S-38s and Dolphins for CNAC thought China was a hardship station. Inflation was soaring, and

The Dolphin was the first aircraft designed and built by Douglas Aircraft Company as a commercial transport. Pan Am flew two of the eight-seat Dolphins in China during the 1930s. This aircraft is in U.S. Army colors.

they were barely able to live on their low pay; they found China unpredictable, ugly, the food strange; conditions were primitive. There was minimal meteorological support, and the weather was often hazardous, with continuous fog and rain and a dense haze often obscuring the ground. One S-38 flew into a fog-shrouded hillside on November 24, 1933, while taking off from Shanghai. Five months later, a second S-38 disappeared on a flight from Shanghai to Canton. Pieces of wreckage and the badly decomposed body of the pilot were subsequently found floating off the coast. Neither aircraft was replaced by Pan American.

The Chinese, fighting their war with Japan, provided little support and were often hostile to the Americans struggling to keep the airline flying. CNAC was soon operating on a shoestring, deficits mounting. But, once he had landing rights to Hong Kong, Trippe was on to other things. Bixby, whose wife and children had joined him in Shanghai, made the long journey back to New York to give Trippe a report on CNAC and to argue for more support from the home office. He had to wait for weeks before he could get in to see his boss. Trippe gave him 10 minutes, then Bixby returned to China.

The passionate belief of Bixby and other so-called "China hands" in the airline somehow got through to Trippe. CNAC began to receive better equipment and more personnel. Despite China's war with Japan, it went on to prosper, actually earning a profit in 1935. The airline had its finest hour during World War II flying DC-2s and DC-3s over the Hump, bringing supplies into China from India.

Trippe sold out Pan Am's share of CNAC to the Nationalists in 1949 when it became obvious to the company that the Reds were going to win the Chinese civil war. All in all, CNAC had, over the years, proved to be one of the best investments Trippe ever made. As for Bixby, he was eventually brought home from China and went on to become a vice president of Pan American and managed several divisions.

Meanwhile, Trippe's attention was once again focused on the Atlantic.

Performance data
Douglas Dolphin

Type	Amphibian
Length	43 feet
Span	60 feet
Height	15 feet
Gross weight	7,800 pounds
Engines	P & W Wasp SC-1×2
Horsepower	450
Range	650 miles
Fuel capacity	90 gallons
Useful load	2,400 pounds
Cruising speed	108 mph
Service ceiling	14,000 feet
Climb rate	700 feet/minute
Passengers	7-8
Crew	1

Lindbergh does it again:

The Atlantic race

Another northward route beckoned. This time, across the North Atlantic: Labrador, Greenland, Iceland. Others had flown the route and pronounced it feasible. But flying a light plane was different than establishing a regular commercial service. Again, Trippe turned to his friend, Charles Lindbergh, now 31 years old.

The Lindbergh's baby, Charles Jr., had been kidnapped and killed in 1932, a case that had literally rocked the country. Another baby had been born, a son, Jon. Anne left him with her mother and again prepared to climb into the rear cockpit of the same red-and-black Lockheed Sirius that the Lindberghs had flown across the Pacific. For this flight, the aircraft was equipped with a new engine, a 710-hp Wright Cyclone.

Much of the Lindberghs' 1933 flight is beautifully described in Anne Morrow Lindbergh's book, *Listen, the Wind*. A gifted writer, she describes the power and grace of flight with lyrical passion, invoking an almost mystical communion between man, machine, and the elements. According to Joseph Corn in *The Winged Gospel*, Charles and Anne Lindbergh perhaps did more to further the cause of aviation among the public than any other flyers of their day.

> There was diminutive Anne relieving her husband at the controls or operating the plane's shortwave radio. She did not look afraid. On the ground, acting the cultured and well-bred lady she was, Anne further exorcised the intrepid birdman image. In interviews she always deferred to

her husband's aviation expertise and, playing the mechanically inept female, falsely denied any knowledge of what she called flight's "cleancut and steely technicalities." Although she privately resented questions about where she kept the "lunchboxes" on the plane, in a sense she asked for them by rhapsodizing over maternity and housekeeping . . . (it) all helped purge flight of manly terror and thus further the aviation cause. . . .

Once again Charles and Anne went through the painstaking preparations for an extended aerial journey: the same crucial decisions on weight (package of needles, ½ ounce; clothing, 18 ounces; Allen wrench, 1 ounce . . .) and a meticulously planned itinerary. Pan American had much more control on this flight. Lindbergh's mission was to survey the three major airways across the North Atlantic, beginning with the route across Greenland. A Danish supply ship, the *Jelling*, carrying a physician, a radio operator and mechanics, was commissioned to sail after the Sirius as it flew through the frigid Arctic skies. The famous couple were not going to be subjected to any unnecessary risks, although they carried no parachutes on the aircraft.*

The Lindberghs departed from Flushing Bay, New York, on July 9, 1933, and once more pointed the Sirius northward. Again, their trip drew a worldwide radio and newspaper audience. Movietone camera crews filmed the departure, while giant headlines blazed the news.

That summer, they surveyed Greenland along the west coast to 70°N and along the east coast to 74°N, discovering uncharted mountain ranges and a fjord 100 miles long. Here, in the icy waters off a rock-and-ice-bound coast, an Eskimo boy carefully painted the name *Tingmissartoq* ["The one who flies like a big bird."] on the aircraft's engine cowling. It was later discovered that the name was at an odd angle; the boy had carefully aligned the lettering with the water, not with the lines of the aircraft.

From the west coast of Iceland, the Lindberghs then flew on to visit the Faroe Islands, the Shetlands, and then western Norway. Continuing east, they flew across the Baltic to Russia, visiting Leningrad and Moscow, where cheering throngs watched as they landed on the Moskva River between two bridges, and then back once more to the Scandinavian countries and around the British Isles.

Southward now, the Sirius cruised along at 145 mph. It touched down in Spain, Portugal, the Azores, the Canary Islands, and then flew on, with

---

*Lindbergh's explanation was that the same weight in fuel or food and water provided better safety. Besides, most of the flight would be over the ocean or over desolate territory where getting down with the right emergency equipment would give them a greater chance of survival. Parachuting down into the frigid sea or onto the Greenland ice cap meant certain death anyway.

Anne looking over the side of the Sirius at long white streamers in the water below that were, Anne noted, "pointing in the direction" of the Cape Verde Islands. At Villa Cisneros, capital of the colony of Spanish Sahara, West Africa, they prepared to spend the night at a small hotel and discovered the bed was filled with bedbugs; they slept on the aircraft: "Lying there quietly in the dark, we were acutely conscious of the wind; a many-stranded stream of sound, a river that had its deep current and its small eddies."

There is no doubt that Anne was often afraid, and her books discuss this frankly. She writes about taking off from Bathurst in British Gambia at night, facing the long trip across the Atlantic to Natal in Brazil, was like "walking through the dark passage as a child . . . this *was* the dark passage and we must go ahead with only a hand brushing the side of the wall." Later, she blurts out, "What was there in the dark out there?"

She also confessed to a constant dread of losing the ball-weight on the end of the antenna — once, it had broken off during an emergency landing at night in Alaska, and she was always been afraid that somehow the ball would snap off by a sudden impact with the water if they flew too low before she could reel it in. Even though they carried a spare ball, they could still lose the use of their radio during a critical period, such as the long flight across the Atlantic.

Once, she allowed herself a rare complaint. Pan American shore stations, she wrote, could be "stone-deaf" to KHCAL, their call sign. But if she sent the signal, LINDBERGH PLANE, it would get immediate attention.

The Sirius droned on across the vast Atlantic. It was almost daylight now, somewhere ahead was South America, but were they on course? "CQ . . . CQ [call to all stations]," she sent, 'LISTENING 28 TO 48 [meters] LINDBERGH PLANE" The radio crackled, and almost immediately came a response. "DDEA SS CAPARCONA BOUND RIO QRK [I receive you well]."

After giving the Lindberghs their position, the ship asked, "WHERE BOUND?", which startled Anne because for hours her whole concentration had been on their destination, and for a moment, it was impossible to think that other people were going about their lives completely unconcerned about the Lindberghs. "BOUND NATAL," she sent.

They flew closer to South America and Anne managed to raise Miami, more than 4,000 miles away. While she might have found some of the Pan Am operators inattentive, those in the towns and cities scattered along the coast of the Americas had remained at their keys throughout the night.

Pan Am's New York headquarters, meanwhile, was pumping out a full-blown publicity effort. Reports came in from the company's distant stations and were retyped and handed out to waiting reporters on the hour. Finally, after some 16 hours in the air, they saw the coast of Brazil ahead "spread low and green in the slight haze." They came in over the town, circled, and landed. It was their longest period spent in the air. With an unsteady hand, Anne wrote in the log: "Landed Natal 17:55 GMT." The usual parade and banquet followed.

The Lindberghs flew north to Belem. The night they landed, John Younkins, who represented the interests of the Ford Rubber Plantation, drove the famous couple to the Grande Hotel, where they would attend a dinner given by the American consul and the American colony in the city. Belem's streets were paved with cobblestones, brought from Europe as ballast for ships, which would drop off the ballast and take on a cargo of rubber during the days of Brazil's rubber boom. The cobblestones made rough riding, but Younkins had driven the streets for some years, and in his words, "was driving along at a good clip." Lindbergh, to Younkins the pilot with nerves of steel, seemed to be nervous about the speed. Younkins laughed and made some remark about whether this was worse than flying the South Atlantic. Lindbergh laughed too, but he appeared so uneasy that Younkins slowed down.

The Lindberghs flew up the Amazon from Belem to the river town of Manaus and turned for home. Port of Spain and San Juan in the Carribbean passed beneath their wings, and then the United States once more, at Miami, the scene of many past Pan Am triumphs.

The Sirius splashed down in Flushing Bay on December 19, 1933, after a trip encompassing five months and 30,000 miles. The Lindberghs had visited 21 countries on four continents. They had largely flown with little weather data, no radio stations, and primitive landing fields. The closest they had come to an accident was a near-collision with a planeload of photographers soon after they had departed from Flushing Bay. Several times, however, heavy swells and the lack of wind, which was necessary for a floatplane to break from the surface, had prevented a departure for several days.

They had flown through hours of fog, rain and snow. It was a "sheer physical terror the whole time," Anne Lindbergh wrote. They had found an outbreak of "island fever" in the Cape Verde Islands and a yellow fever epidemic in Dakar. They had become well-acquainted with the discomforts of spending the night sleeping in an airplane. On the other hand, they had had their share of luxury hotels, banquets with kings and prime ministers and parades past cheering throngs. The Lindberghs had effectively become the goodwill ambassadors of the United States.

Altogether, it was a magnificent effort. Lindbergh had been sending letters to Trippe all through the journey, and his final report on his spectacular flight, made in 1934, covered all aspects of airports, harbors, meteorology, emergency landing fields, and terrain. Lindbergh concluded that the difficulties of the northern route to Europe had been greatly exaggerated, although strong contrary winds and bad weather often occurred.

Trippe, now 33 years old, was ready to fly the Atlantic. Pan Am applied to Paris on December 16, 1935, for a 15-year permit to operate two services a week to points in France to be designated by the French government. Meanwhile, the airline had established a marine terminal at Port Washington, Long Island, similar to its terminal at Dinner Key, Miami, in readiness for Atlantic operations. Was it feasible to fly commercial aircraft across the Atlantic Ocean? Yes, said Lindbergh, "even with existing equipment, it should be possible to compete . . . with the Atlantic steamship schedules." Still, there were enormous problems.*

The great circle route from Newfoundland to Ireland was the most direct, but that meant flying 2,000 miles nonstop, an exploit that no aircraft could do in the early 1930s with a worthwhile commercial payload. Flying west to the Azores and then over to Portugal, meanwhile, would cut the longest flight over water to 1,500 miles, but it would increase the overall distance. The far northern, subarctic route, Labrador-Greenland-Iceland-Northern Europe, was probably the most feasible in terms of distances and safety, but the problems here were a frigid climate and winter nights 20 hours long. This route was favored by Trippe for political as well as technical reasons. For one thing, Iceland and Greenland were under the sovereignty of Denmark, a nation that held no transatlantic goals of its own. Trippe had already purchased landing rights in Iceland for $55,000 and Danish cooperation with Greenland looked promising. The difficulty was Newfoundland, where it was absolutely essential to acquire a stopover point.

Newfoundland was a self-governing dominion, like Canada, but the British were exerting pressure to keep Pan American from gaining a foothold. Imperial Airways was a competitor, but Pan American was far ahead in aircraft design and cross-ocean capability. A reciprocal agreement

---

*This was not Pan American's first experience in the North Atlantic. Pan Am operated a service between Boston and Halifax, Nova Scotia, under a contract with Boston-Maine Airways for two months in 1931. Fokker F-10s flew the Boston-Portland-Bangor segment, while two Sikorsky S-41s, an improved version of the S-38, flew the Bangor-Halifax route via St. Andrews, New Brunswick.

could be worked out. Then, an apparently insurmountable problem occurred.

The start of the Great Depression had been devastating for Newfoundland. Riots and economic turmoil, during which mobs charged the dominion's government buildings, caused the British to revoke independent rule, and Newfoundland became, once again, a crown colony. The colonial office in London then flatly refused to make any agreement with Pan American Airways. The result was a stalemate.

Trippe would continue to push for a route across the Atlantic, but Pan Am would not receive landing rights in Newfoundland until 1937. By then, the airline would already be flying the Pacific.

As for the Sirius, although it had served Lindbergh well, the Lone Eagle became convinced that land planes, not those with pontoons or floats, were the future of transoceanic flight. Seaplane design diminished performance, he argued. As for forced landings, putting down on water in an emergency, where you did not know what was below you, was exceedingly difficult and dangerous, especially at night or in bad weather. Better, said Lindbergh, it build bigger aircraft with the range and power to cross the oceans of the world.

But the *Tingmissartoq*'s day in the sun was still not over. After some years being displayed in the Hall of Ocean Life at the American Museum of Natural History in New York, it was stored at Wright-Patterson Air Force Base in Ohio and then at the Smithsonian's storage facility at Suitland, Maryland. It was then shown, after some 1,500 hours of restoration, in the U.S. pavilion at Expo '70 in Osaka, Japan. Today, visitors can see the Sirius, the only one of its type in existence, at the National Air and Space Museum in Washington. Nearby hangs the *Spirit of St. Louis*.

Igor Sikorsky's marvelous S-42

Above the Caribbean and in the coastal cities of South America, Igor Sikorsky and Charles Lindbergh had long talks during the first commercial flight of the S-40. They discussed the "next step," an airplane that would be bigger, more streamlined and more powerful than anything yet in the skies.

What was needed, said Lindbergh was an aircraft that could, in short, fly 2,500 miles nonstop, about the distance from San Francisco to Hawaii. Each night they discussed the problem over dinner, going over every new innovation, each practical and radical idea, accepting some, dismissing others. They talked and flipped ideas back and forth and Lindbergh would sketch them out on the back of the menu. The aircraft already seemed to take on form and shape. Sikorsky meticulously collected these menus and carried them off the aircraft under his arm at the end of the trip.

Pan American placed an order with Sikorsky on October 1, 1932, for 10 aircraft, designated the S-42. It would be a machine incorporating all the technical refinements that the S-40 lacked. Although Lindbergh did not get the range he wanted with the S-42, 1,200 statute miles with normal payload, it was still one of the most impressive aircraft of its time, and even today, its classic beauty is undeniable.

When the first S-42 was introduced on the Miami-Rio de Janeiro route on August 16, 1934, Juan Trippe had an aircraft that could carry twice the number of passengers twice as far and certainly as fast as the Douglas DC-3, the airplane that many experts feel was the first to justify the term airliner.

The whale

Lindbergh was earning $10,000 a year in 1931 as Pan Am's technical consultant. The Lone Eagle, Trippe, and Priester pored over maps and charts in Pan Am's offices on the 42nd floor of Manhattan's Chanin Building and plotted out the most daring air transportation routes the world had ever seen. Then they decided on what type of aircraft the airline would need to fly those routes.

Trippe's letter to his board of directors on June 26 stated: "Pan American Airways System will presently require additional flying equipment for long-distance, high-speed, over-water air mail transportation." He knew only two aircraft manufacturers could meet that requirement: Igor Sikorsky and Glenn L. Martin. Letters from Pan Am were sent to both, and they began work on designing a flying boat that could span the oceans.

First off the boards was Sikorsky's S-42. When a friend of the aircraft manufacturer first saw the S-42, he asked if Sikorsky had copied it from the shape of a whale.

As Sikorsky explained in his book, *The Winged S*: A flying boat must have the characteristics of a surface vessel while afloat on the water and moving at speeds up to 25 mph. Between 40 mph and 60 mph, however, the craft takes on entirely different characteristics. At these speeds, the aircraft is supported not by the displacement of water but by the striking force of the water, buoying it aerodynamically. The load on the wing increases as the aircraft accelerates, and when takeoff speed is reached, the wings carry the entire weight of the aircraft and its payload.

Sikorsky S-42 *Brazilian Clipper* was renamed *Columbia Clipper* in 1937.

Initially, Pan American's requirements were so high that Sikorsky had doubts he could meet them. The airline wanted an aircraft that could economically fly 1.95 round trips per week. Not only did it have to have sea and airworthiness, but it also had to have extraordinarily long range and a load capacity greater than any other aircraft then flying.

Payload determines the aircraft. According to technology historian Richard K. Smith:

> Contrary to what many aero historians like to believe, one of the last concerns of an airplane designer is what the airplane will look like. The first thing a designer must do . . . is to determine the machine's payload . . . In an airliner of the 1930s, payload consisted of a number of 225-pound units representing each passenger and . . . baggage. [Payload] is the sine qua non of a useful airplane, and without it, the machine is only an expensive plaything.*

Once payload is determined, the next decision for the airplane designer is how far the weight must be lifted and carried. The greater the range, the more fuel must be lifted at takeoff, and, consequently, the more weight that must be carried. It all boils down to a balance. In the end, as with so many things, the final design of an aircraft is a compromise of a thousand decisions.

Smith says in the early 1930s American aircraft manufacturers such as Sikorsky and Martin developed techniques that made them superior to any foreign company in producing long-range aircraft. Their secret was mastery of weight control, a strange, and continually evolving, mix of art and science. Historians such as Smith, believe the S-42 is an outstanding example of this blend. Although there is little to distinguish this flying boat as the sort of streamlined airplane that we have come to expect today, the S-42 — as well as the Martin M-130 that was also in production — not only had sensational performance for their age but remained superior to other British and European aircraft of the same weight, size, and mission for years to come. (By way of example, Smith cites the technical data on the M-130, which were sent to Imperial Airways in Britain as part of a routine exchange of information. The data were greeted with widespread disbelief and dismissed as "ridiculously optimistic.")

Sikorsky started designing the S-42 with extensive wind tunnel tests, producing a structural analysis that ran 939 pages, with the aerodynamic analysis running another 250 pages. All this information, together with piles

---

*The Intercontinental Airliner and the Essence of Airplane Performance, 1929-1939," *Technology and Culture*, July, 1983.

of drawings and charts, were minutely scrutinized by Sikorsky, Lindbergh, and Andre Priester. The discussions and arguments went on for hours.

Wing loading was the key to meeting Pan American demands. Sikorsky Aircraft designed an entirely new wing shape, tapered at each tip instead of the conventional rounding, under the direction of Michael Gluhareff. Each square foot of the S-42's wing could lift more weight than any other wing then in commercial service, 28.5 pounds per square foot, which was a staggering feat at that the time, when a typical wing loading was 15 pounds per square foot. A more conservative 10 pounds per square foot was normal in England.

The monoplane wing was made completely in one piece and had a span four feet longer than that of the S-40, yet the wing area of the S-42 was only 1,330 square feet against the S-40's 1,875 square feet. A new wing flap was incorporated into the trailing edge of the rectangular panel of the wing, providing additional lift for takeoff and a braking action for landing. Thus, the S-42 could land at the same 65 mph as the S-40. The huge trailing edge flap, with a span of more than 68 feet and a surface area of 185 square feet, also amazed the aviation community of 1934.

The 11½-foot-diameter, three-blade propellers were Hamilton Standard *pitch-controlled* models, the brainchild of Frank Caldwell, who won the Collier Trophy in 1934 for his efforts. Pitch control meant the pilot could manipulate the propeller blade angle in flight for better efficiency, much like changing gears in a car. (When the aircraft was taking off, for example, the propeller was set somewhat flattish in relation to the leading edge of the wing for full power. In flight, a greater angle to the wing took bigger bites of air and reduced fuel consumption: less fuel burned, greater range.)

Sikorsky S-42 takeoff.

Windmilling was a problem. When a propeller stops turning in flight it windmills, blocking off air from anything behind it. Sling an engine beneath the wing, and there is no problem, but incorporate it directly into the leading edge of the wing — demanded by Lindbergh and Pan American — and a windmilling propeller will cut down on the wing's lift. What about propeller brakes? They were tried and worked.

Each S-42 propeller was driven by a 700-hp Pratt & Whitney Hornet S5D1-G engine mounted on welded chrome molybdenum tubular engine mounts cantilevered out from the front spar. Refinements included automatic carburetors and engine synchronization indicators that were also used on the S-40. These powerplants did not hang like those of previous Sikorsky aircraft, so the multitude of struts could also be largely eliminated. The few that remained on the S-42 were outboard struts made of duralumin to brace the wing as well as a wing-mounting pylon called a *cabane strut.* Twin booms of the previous Sikorskys were also eliminated. Tail members were attached directly to the hull, although the dual rudders remained. Extensive flush riveting was also used.

Fuel capacity was normally 1,240 gallons carried in eight elliptical-shaped tanks located between the wing spars. The S-42 had a pressure-type refueling system, and four of the tanks were equipped with self-closing dump valves. The valve outlets were flush with the underside of the wing, perhaps too close to the engine exhausts, according to certain critics.

The new flying boat provided seating for 32 passengers (some configurations would carry 38) and was 68 feet long, 114 feet wide, and 17 feet high. Gross takeoff weight was 38,000 pounds, 19 tons, and the S-42's useful load, 18,000 pounds, was 46 percent of gross. It could cruise at 150 mph for 1,250 miles at 75 percent of its rated horsepower.

Passenger appointments were not as grand as the S-40, they were, nevertheless, comfortable, with upholstered seats, each with an adjustable headrest, paired on each side of a spacious aisle 50 feet long and carpeted in dark green. Draperies could be adjusted over each window. Five doorways separated six watertight compartments, any two of which could keep the airplane afloat. The passengers, however, sat in four compartments, eight seats in each.

Walls and ceilings were lined, according to company literature, with "American figured walnut balsa wood veneer panels." Perhaps this was why the cabin walls were painted blue-green. Small metal plates not seen on the S-40 were over the compartment doorways and read "No Smoking" in English and Spanish. Another said, "Life Jackets Under Floor" in both languages.

The crews' quarters included a navigation office with a big chart table running the length of the cabin and two big portholes above the table for light; stashed conveniently nearby were books, charts, and papers. The flight deck had 187 instruments, a far cry from the old S-38. The center of the panel featured an automatic pilot, one of the first installed on a transport aircraft. Radio gear included two radio receivers and two transmitters. The S-42's tail section contained a life raft, drift-sight bombs, flares, water kegs, signal flags, sails, oars, oar-locks, rations, and Manila rope. Also at the rear were two lavatories.

Despite a design based upon payload and despite a surprisingly shallow hull and the deceptively pointed wings, Sikorsky had performed one of those rare industrial miracles. He built a machine that had a clear and honest beauty. The S-42 would be known as the most beautiful aircraft of its time.

Price of the S-42 per copy was initially $242,000, or more than $3.5 million in today's money. All but one of the 10 ships would be given the name Clipper.

The first S-42 was completed shortly after Christmas 1933, but the Housatonic River was frozen solid, and testing was postponed until spring. The aircraft was taxied down the river and out onto Long Island Sound in March. Captain Boris Sergievsky began a series of record-breaking test flights on April 26 with Raymond Quick as copilot. Sergievsky set a world

The *Pan American Clipper* (NC-823M) flies over the unfinished Golden Gate Bridge on its first survey flight to Hawaii.

record, carrying a load of 16,608 pounds to an altitude of 6,561 feet. Takeoff time was 18 seconds, and the aircraft reached 16,000 feet in 47 minutes. The official test flight also exceeded 200 mph.

The pace and number of flight tests increased, with sometimes as many as 30 flights a day. Sergievsky discovered that takeoff time could be considerably reduced with the flaps 10° down, averaging about 20 seconds with a gross weight of 36,000 pounds. Sikorsky also moved the water planing step toward the tail to improve handling characteristics.

A pilot named "Music"

Captain Ed Musick arrived at the Sikorsky facility at Bridgeport in the summer of 1934 to continue the flight testing program. When he saw the first true flying boat designed in the United States, he looked at it with joy: "Cleanest lines I ever saw."

Musick was by now the senior captain with Pan American. He had been a exhibition flyer known as "Daredevil Musick" in the early days of flying before World War I, a past he always tried to live down. He was booked for a night fireworks flight in Venice, California in 1916. Thousands of people stared up into the sky as Musick and a helper, who was supposed to handle the fireworks, took off. High over the fairgrounds, Musick circled, waiting for the fireworks expert to begin the show. The bouncing aircraft made the passenger fumble with the pyrotechnics and

Sikorsky S-42 *Brazilian Clipper* (NC-822M) at Pan Am's Dinner Key Base, Miami.

suddenly, a rocket tore through one of the wings. The wing began to glow and sparks scattered in the slipstream. Musick dived the aircraft for the ground, trailing fire. The crowd went wild; thinking it was a stunt; cheers and clapping filled the air.

Musick arrived over the field where he was supposed to land, but it was dark because he was not expected back so quickly. This was no time for hesitation; Musick pancaked down and the burning wing collapsed.

Clothes smoldering, Musick and his helper dived over the side of the airplane and ran, moments before the fuel tank exploded. Musick was not a man to hold a grudge because an hour later, he was drinking with his fireworks helper and laughing over the whole incident.

He was a pilot in the Marine Corps in World War I, then flew the Atlantic City run for the Aeromarine Company at the foot of 79th Street in New York City. There have been other tales told about his activities during those lean years of the early 1920s. A former bootlegger interviewed years later for a story in the *New York Times* mentioned that they had a pilot who transported the booze. "He called himself Music," said the bootlegger, "we never knew his real name."

Musick, nevertheless, gained a reputation as a serious, professional pilot, and he went to work for Trippe's airline at the Dinner Key terminal in Miami. Dinner Key had become one of the busiest marine terminals anywhere. A long spectators' gallery was packed whenever an aircraft arrived from some distant part of the Americas. Thanks to Priester, Pan American had one of the smoothest operations of any airline in the world. Coming off the aircraft, passengers were first led to the health authorities office to complete the appropriate forms. Next was a visit to immigration and by the time they reached the customs shed, their baggage had already been laid out on racks for inspection. Trippe was determined to fly the oceans, so Priester picked Musick to help set up a transocean flying school and to select pilots for the airline. The course was destined to be one of the most exacting in the airline industry. Musick knew what he wanted: qualified, serious pilots who could be trained to perform at a higher state of the art, playboys and daredevils need not apply. Most of his pilots Musick found in the naval reserve. New pilots were taught navigation, engineering, Spanish and international law.

Musick looked long and hard for a navigation instructor, and finally found Fred Noonan, who was managing the Pan American station at Martinique. Noonan was a Merchant Marine skipper and navigator who had found himself beached when the Great Depression dried up berths on ships. Years later, Noonan would earn his place in history as Amelia Earhart's navigator on her last doomed flight. His boss, Musick, was not content to merely establish the school, however; Musick went through the course himself and graduated as the top man in his class, earning the Pan American title of master pilot. Musick studied the S-42 for several weeks at Sikorsky's plant on the Housatonic River. August I the aircraft was readied for a flight test that would include attempts at several seaplane records. The course was laid out over three states: New York, Connecticut, and Rhode Island, a distance of more than 1,200 miles. At 4:30 in the morning, Sikorsky mechanics were loading and fueling the ship with 1,580 gallons of fuel and 555 pounds of oil. Sand ballast weighed 10,000 pounds. The flying boat was then launched and moored off the Sikorsky ramp at 5:30. Lindbergh arrived at 6 after driving all night to meet the test schedule.

Musick with copilot Lindbergh taxied the aircraft out onto Long Island Sound at 9 a.m. The aircraft behaved perfectly. Musick headed the ship into the wind and opened the throttles. Lindbergh snapped his stopwatch. The S-42 left the water in 18 seconds. In less than a minute, they had climbed to 1,000 feet.

"Boy! Has she got stuff!" Musick yelled.

The aircraft roared across the starting line at Stratford Light. Aviation officials checked their watches. Musick flew four laps: the first averaged 160.4 mph; second, 155.2 mph; third, 156.1 mph; and fourth, 158.1 mph. Roaring back over the finish line, the flying boat had been in the air for 7 hours, 54 minutes, and had flown 1,244 miles. Each time it had crossed the finishing line it had broken a record.

Altogether, the S-42 established eight world records during its flight testing program. But once again, the goal of a long-range aircraft that could carry a useful payload seemed to have evaded Sikorsky. Honolulu was reachable, but only if the aircraft was stripped down and extra fuel tanks installed. Trippe, however, was ready. Almost immediately after the record-breaking acceptance trials, the S-42 was flown to Miami for shake-down flights over the Caribbean, involving more weeks of testing.

The first official commercial flight of the S-42 (NC-822M) began on August 16, from Miami to Rio de Janeiro. The party of 19 passengers and eight crewmembers included Juan Trippe, Colonel Charles Lindbergh, Andre Priester, Eugene Vidal, who headed air transport for America's Department of Commerce, prominent newspaper executives, and other officials of Pan American Airways. Ed Musick was at the controls and Wally Culbertson was copilot when NC-822M lifted off from Dinner Key and began the 15,000 mile trip.

The flight touched 12 countries and colonies, and the run to Rio was timed for five days. One hitch developed in Pan American's best laid plans. The aircraft approached Rio while thick clouds piled up on the horizon.

The weather worsened with drizzle and heavy cloud. Musick made a pilot's decision and put the S-42 down in a lagoon outside Rio. Trippe, knowing the extensive preparations that had been made to receive them, was aghast. Musick came back into the cabin and made a mild remark that it was too bad that they had not been able to make Rio that day. Nobody said a word.

When the flying boat reached the Brazilian capital the next day, however, all seemed to be forgiven. NC-822M was christened *Brazilian Clipper* by Senõra Getulie Vargas, wife of the president of Brazil, and would go on to fly extensively throughout Latin America.

Musick proceeded with Pan Am's Caribbean testing program flying NC-823M, which had been returned to the factory and stripped of all its furnishings. Extra fuel tanks had also been installed to increase its range. Musick flew the Sikorsky for hours with successive motors dead. Engineering data were gathered at various speeds and altitudes. Celestial navigation was perfected. Radio bearings were taken over and over. Special meters were installed to accurately measure fuel consumption. Then came the finale.

Captain Ed Musick boards the S-42 *Pan American Clipper* for the first survey flight to Hawaı

Musick lifted NC-823M off from Miami on March 23, 1935, to start the first long-range flying boat flight in the history of commercial aviation. Copilot was Rod Sullivan; W.T. Jarboe handled the radio; Vic Wright watched the engine instruments, and a few paces behind him, in the rather pretentiously named chart room, was navigator Fred Noonan.

Celestial navigation on board an aircraft that was 4,000 feet in the air was a new and inexact science. One critical problem was the actual speed of the airplane. Sights had to be taken five or six times to check and recheck the figures, but between each sight, the aircraft could have flown 50 miles or more. Musick and Noonan stared at a blinking light on the horizon where nothing should have been. Were they that far off course? It turned out to be the planet Jupiter. All night, the S-42 flew on.

A hundred miles north of St. Thomas in the Virgin Islands, Musick banked the Sikorsky into a turn. Hours later, they were flying over the Florida peninsula far out into the gulf. Back once more: Key West, Biscayne Bay. Musick eased the aircraft down onto the water. They had been in the air for more than 17 hours and had flown 2,500 miles, more than the distance between San Francisco and Hawaii.

Pan Am was threatened by severe financial losses in 1934. President Roosevelt had cancelled the mail contracts on all domestic airlines. Almost all of them promptly stopped operating, and it was months, even years, before many of them could resume operations. The Army Air Corps — with pilots inexperienced in night and bad weather flying — operated a barely functional airmail service, but for all intents and purposes, airmail in the United States came to a halt. The reason for Roosevelt's action was simply that he felt too many airlines were charging too much for their services based on contracts they had received too easily.

Pan American was not a domestic carrier and continued to fly the mail overseas. It was not forgotten by the government and was invited to state its case before a senate committee on January 3, 1935, along with all the other airlines. Chaired by Hugo Black, an Alabama democrat, the committee soon enlarged its investigation to cover the entire airline industry and a string of industry executives and bankers found themselves being grilled about profits and stock manipulations.

Former Postmaster General Walter Brown was forced to appear to defend his policies on awarding contracts, against charges of collusion brought by his successor, James A. Farley.

Lindbergh then jumped to the defense of the airlines and sent a telegram to the White House, protesting that cancellation of the airmail contracts "condemns the largest portion of our commercial aviation without just trial." He then made sure the telegram received a wide distribution to the press. Lindy was a public hero and could not be wrong. There was a public outcry in favor of the airlines. Although there was White House grumbling about Lindbergh courting publicity, the wily Roosevelt knew when he had to back down.

Postmaster Farley reopened the contracts for bidding in April and by May many of the airlines were back in business, flying the mail. New contracts forced competitive bidding at much lower rates, and air transportation companies suffered heavy losses for the next two years. According to a report from the New York-based Council on Foreign Relations, the industry as a whole did not actually return to profitability until 1939.

Pan Am, holder of the monopoly in American international air travel, however, was still on the hot seat. The post office had sent a letter to the president advising him that all Pan Am contracts could be cancelled because they were awarded by "negotiation," rather than by the competitive bidding required by law. The post office went on to say that it did not believe "cancellation of these contracts would be in the public interest" because it would "probably disrupt American air service to the Latin American countries. . . . There is no other air company in the United States that can immediately render comparable service in these countries."

Instead, the post office recommended an immediate reduction of 25 percent in Pan Am mail-carrying rates. This reduction was never executed, although the company did have an overall reduction of about 10 percent in mail revenues. "Pan American and Pan American-Grace's escape from cancellation and from serious loss of revenue in a critical period," concludes the Council on Foreign Relations, "was not only a tribute to adroit management but a recognition of the vital part in our foreign policy which these companies had already assumed."

Pan American Airways, in other words, remained America's "chosen instrument." By 1934, Pan Am was operating 54.5 percent of all Latin American airline traffic. During the 1936-1940 period, it would add some 1,700 route miles of *local* services in Brazil alone, an increase of forty percent. What's more, Pan Am and PANAGRA continued to charge the highest tariffs of almost every airline operating in South America and the Caribbean. In 1937, for example, Pan Am charged 10.5 U.S. cents per passenger mile against 7.6 cents by the German-owned Condor line. (PANAGRA's charge: 10.7 cents.)

For the moment, Juan Trippe had weathered the storm. His next round was about to take place on tiny coral atolls far out into the Pacific.

The *North Haven* expedition

Strangely, it was easier for Pan Am to forge a route across the Pacific than across the Atlantic simply because there was very little there. The obvious route was from California to Hawaii and then across the vast ocean to another American possession: Guam. But Pan American needed island stepping-stones where aircraft could set down and be refueled and where passengers could rest before flying on. Trippe looked at a large globe he kept in his office. He measured distances with a piece of string. He knew Martin was building another aircraft for Pan American, a true wonder of the air age with more range and a greater payload than even the S-42, which was an aircraft before its time. He gazed at the globe, puffed on his pipe, and made a decision.

More Sikorsky S-42s were being built in Connecticut and a new Clipper flying boat was taking shape at the Martin Company factory at Middle River, Maryland, when a 15,000-ton steamer, the *North Haven*, slipped its moorings on San Francisco Bay and headed out into the Pacific. It sailed through the fog-shrouded Golden Gate strait on March 2, 1935, passing under the unfinished Golden Gate Bridge. There was little to distinguish the freighter from the hundreds of other ships that made San Francisco their port of call. But the *North Haven* was unique because this ship was making airline history. Trippe had decided that if the bases in the central Pacific were not there, he would build them on Midway, Wake, and Guam.

Trippe was able to establish his bases through an "informal" working arrangement between Pan American Airways and the U.S. Navy. The reason for this agreement could be summed up in one word: Japan. Tensions between the United States and Japanese empire were rising. Militaristic nationalists had seized control of the Japanese government, which became increasingly belligerent and aggressive in the Far East, China, and the Pacific, the area where the United States and Japan would obviously have opposing interests.

Trippe notified the Navy Department October 3, 1934, that Pan American was ready to start Pacific service and needed suitable marine bases at Wake, Guam, and possibly Midway. Secretary of the Navy Claude Swanson saw the Pan American move as an ideal way for the United States to block threatening Japanese encroachment upon Wake and other islands in the Central Pacific and yet not establish an overly provocative military presence. The bases, developed largely at Pan American's expense, could also be used by the Navy in a wartime emergency.

Trippe had irrevocable leases for the three islands by March 1935 and within a year, Pan American was granted a marine terminal at Subic Bay in the Philippines.

Japan, however, immediately objected to Pan Am's plans as a "concealed military operation" that was aimed at establishing American military airports all the way to the "the gates of Japan." Despite these protests, a solid partnership was established between Pan American Airways and the U.S. Navy.*

William Grooch, the man chosen by Pan American to head its base-building operation, was an ex-navy pilot who had once flown Commodores for Pan Am's rival, NYRBA. Grooch had flown S-38s around South America, until he "became a bit bored with checking lighthouses between the Amazon River and Buenos Aires" and requested a change of duty. Trippe had just the place for him: China.

Grooch found himself aboard the Maersk Line's *Gertrude Maersk* bound from Los Angeles to Shanghai. He would spend the next five years as CNAC's operations manager. Back in Alameda as manager of Pan Am's new Pacific Division terminal, Grooch was astounded to learn that Pan American planned to fly the Pacific. What's more, he was going to be in charge of building the needed bases on remote Pacific islands.

The job was immense. Soon, Grooch was working literally night and day readying the *North Haven* for its voyage. Pier 22, where the ship was docked, was active around-the-clock for weeks. One thing Grooch did not lack was men willing to go out to the Pacific. Indeed, it seemed every seaman temporarily on the beach, every unemployed carpenter and plumber, as well as dozens of college students who seemed to regard the enterprise as something like a 1930s Peace Corps, were all ready to go.

Word quickly got around the waterfront, and soon the airline's terminal and Pier 22 were besieged with scores of applicants. A call went out to all Pan Am stations in the Caribbean and Mexico for experienced construction workers, radio operators, waiters, cooks, electricians, carpenters and so on, and men began to pour in from every direction. A lot of them had knocked around the odd corners of the world for years and believed in travelling light. One man showed up with nothing but a ukulele.

Captain Borklund, master of the *North Haven*, proved to be from "Sweden or Norway," according to Grooch.

"What sort of crew did you sign on?" he asked.

---

*This "partnership" became a very close working relationship. According to Marylin Bender and Selig Altschul in their lively book, *The Chosen Instrument*, "Navy personnel repaired and maintained airline equipment, tested its planes, rode on its survey flights and many of them . . . retired from the service into Pan American's employ."

The skipper thought for a moment, forming his words carefully, "Vell, som of dem could pe petter but dey vas de bess I could get."

Grooch felt that he might be embarking on something close to the *Sea Wolf* or some other hellship of the Seven Seas, but he gave orders for the vessel to sail at midnight March 2. Newspapers, which for days had been referring to Pan Am's "secret" operation, would say the hour fitted in with the airline's nefarious schemes. Grooch actually had a much more mundane reason for picking the time: There was a bitter oil company strike in progress and he was concerned about the safety of the cargo.

What the *North Haven* actually carried in its hold and on its decks when it left San Francisco was also somewhat exaggerated by the press, but it was the equivalent of two complete air bases: 10-ton tractors, barrels of fuel, radio towers, launches, diesel engines, 10-ton electric generators, prefabricated plywood buildings, channel buoys, water storage tanks, and an assortment of food that ranged from frozen steaks to candy bars. It was a $500,000 cargo. There were 118 souls on board, including technicians and construction workers, many them husky young college students who had volunteered for the adventure. Three naval officers would survey Midway and Wake for the flying boat landing sites.

Grooch ordered something close to military discipline for his workers while at sea. A man with a trombone blew reveille, and then every man had 15 minutes to make up his bunk, clean up, and get ready for calisthenics or one of the numerous classes in seamanship, navigation, motor maintenance, construction, and the like that would be held throughout the day.

The crew of the ship turned out not to be the sweepings of the waterfront, after all, but a strongly unionized group who kept to themselves and saw to it that they received union scale pay rates for every additional bit work they were called upon to do.

There was nothing on Midway in 1935 except a tiny station that handled cable traffic between Hawaii and the Philippines. Technically an atoll, it consisted of two small, sandy strips of land, Sand and Eastern Islands, surrounded by a coral reef. The beach of Sand Island became the site of a small tent village, as tons of material were brought ashore by launch from the ship riding at anchor about a half-mile out. The work crews quickly found out that lowering a 10-ten tractor over the side of a ship onto a lighter, with 10-foot swells a common occurrence, was no easy task.

When enough cargo was ashore at Midway for the working party to live fairly comfortably while constructing the terminal, the *North Haven* sailed to Wake, which was an even remoter spot in the Pacific. Wake consisted of Wake, Wilkes, and Peale Islands, all arranged roughly in the shape of a horseshoe and separated by shallow channels. The ship could not come close to shore at Midway because of coral reefs lying near the surface, but the lagoon at Wake was so deep that there was no anchorage.

Peale, with a coral breakwater and a reef that bore the brunt of heavy seas, was selected as the station site, but supplies had to first be landed on Wake, hauled across the island, and then taken across a lagoon to Peale. Then someone got the bright idea of a railroad. Two hundred yards long and constructed from truck wheels without tires and iron stock for the rails, they called it "the shortest railroad in the world."

These problems were not encountered at Guam, which was well-settled and had been a naval base since 1917. Here, Grooch simply took over an abandoned Marine Corps base at Sumay for Pan American's base of operations. Work at Manila was merely improvements to an existing base. Retracing its route, the *North Haven* arrived back in San Francisco on July 28, 1935. Meanwhile, the work parties on Midway and Wake had literally carved marine aviation bases out of the coral. Coral heads at Wake were blasted one by one by the expedition's demolitions expert, Columbia University swim team member Bill Mullahey, 24, who had little more than goggles as diving gear because scuba equipment had not been invented; Mullahey had never handled explosives.

Gradually, the bases took shape. The tent villages were replaced by huts. Pipelines linked underground fuel tanks to offshore refueling barges. Tall antennas for the radio direction finders rose above the sandy islands. Blasting the coral heads was slow going, however; after weeks of work, Mullahey was still only half-way across the lagoon.

The *North Haven* would put to sea a second time during the following winter to deliver construction equipment for passenger accommodations.

Not surprisingly, an S-42 was already over the Pacific Ocean during the first voyage.

The proving flight

On March 27, 1935, Musick lifted NC-823M, formerly called the *West Indies Clipper* and now called the *Pan American Clipper*, off from Biscayne Bay and headed it west across the Gulf of Mexico on the first stage of the long flight to California. The aircraft had been stripped for the flight; apart from two beds in the rear, all seats and furniture had been removed. The center compartment held additional gas tanks that were braced to take the shock of takeoffs and landings.

Oddly, Musick was full of misgivings about flying the Pacific.

"I don't think we're ready for it," he confided to his wife, Cleo, as he sipped what was perhaps his favorite drink, tea. Most of the other Pan Am pilots were also nervous about flying the ocean, even considering it suicidal. It was not that the jump from San Francisco to Honolulu had not been flown because in the Dole Race of 1927 two aircraft had made it, but seven others had either crashed, killing the pilots, or had disappeared at sea. Still, a navy team had made it across in 1934, and other daredevils had managed to reach Hawaii in one piece. Yet these *were* daredevil stunts; establishing a regular passenger service was something else.

Noonan was tracking the route with radio bearings and sunsights as the S-42 flew across Mexico and came in to land at Acapulco, where a ground crew from Pan Am's Mexico City office was waiting to service the aircraft. Turning north, Musick brought the aircraft down at the San Diego Naval Air Station where tanks were refilled.

That night Musick and his crew had a noisy dinner at the Coronado Hotel; it was the scene of many parties when Musick was a young, footloose pilot, and the hotel must have brought back a host of memories.

Temporary headquarters for the Pacific Division had been established at Alameda on San Francisco Bay, across from San Francisco. A large and expectant crowd was waiting for the *Pan American Clipper* to land. The S-42 dropped down and taxied up to a mooring buoy. Musick hated crowds. The self-conscious crew waited as a battery of cameras were turned on them. Officials made long speeches about the opening of a new era in transportation. When it was Musick's turn to speak, he walked up to a microphone: "We're glad to be here."

Musick couldn't get away that easily. His photo was on the front page of all the newspapers. The San Francisco *News* headlined,

GIANT SILVER CLIPPER SHIP ARRIVES FOR
TRANS-PACIFIC SERVICE

Whenever Musick was spotted on the street, a horde of small boys materialized to dog his heels. His desk at the airport was piled high with requests to sponsor shaving cream, liquor, cigarettes, and the like.

The crew settled down again to more weeks of flight tests. Every bay and lighthouse on the coast was sighted and identified from the air. They practiced night flying, approaching Alameda from various angles. Once they flew under sealed orders far out to sea to intercept the freighter *Malolo* and then returned to Alameda using the radio direction finder alone. Noonan hit it right on the nose.

Other skills were gradually being developed by the airlines, but were very rudimentary by today's standards. Pacific meteorology, for example, amounted to little more than hearsay. Such essentials as regional weather maps simply did not exist. There was even an old flyer's tale that straying aircraft could be sucked into a vortex off California.

No one knew at the time that thunderstorms could erupt 40,000 feet in the air, that a cumulus cloud could tower 25,000 feet high, its top shaped into a dark, threatening anvil. No one knew that inside those clouds, fierce winds and enormous pressures waited with crushing menace. Weather stations across the Pacific were particularly sparse: Honolulu, Midway, the Aleutians.

Pan American was practically starting from scratch, like the Caribbean. Apprentice pilots at Pan Am's school were required to take a course in meteorology, which was also included in Andrew Priester's ongoing correspondence courses for the airline's aircrews. Information was shared with the U.S. Navy and foreign weather services. The Japanese were reluctant to make data from their Pacific weather stations available to the Americans, but Pan Am was able to get a lot of their information through some navy sleuthing and cryptoanalysis.

Eight routes, *tracks*, were specified between Alameda and Honolulu based on Caribbean and South American experience. Pilots would select a particular route at departure time, depending on the most favorable combination of weather and schedule commensurate with safety and the most economical fuel consumption.

Pan American's pioneering work added two new phrases to the lexicon of aviation: the *point of no return*, the spot beyond which there was no turning back, crucial when determining payload, and the even more scientifically named *howgozit curve*, actually a graph on which the captain draws several solid lines; three solid lines from the lower left-hand corner: one represents the hours flown as opposed to miles covered; another, the gallons of fuel used versus the hours in flight; the third shows how many miles should be covered for the gallons of fuel consumed. The first officer keeps a constant performance record during flight.

Besides the three solid lines, he inscribes broken lines to contrast the actual course of the flight with the expected normal flight. Any deviation, or other factor, such as wind, must account for the change.

A fourth line on the howgozit curve runs from the upper left and bisects the miles-versus-gallons line. That bisection is the point of no return.

Brooklyn-born Hugo Leuteritz, who devised much of Pan Am's early radio network, was able to extend the range of radio navigation to approximately 1,000 miles by improving on the British-invented Adcock system: an antenna strung between four poles aligned according to the points of compass. The *North Haven* sufficiently filled the void between Honolulu and Guam. By using two stations, an aircraft could be covered by the overlap.

All Pan Pacific stations were manned by ex-navy personnel with top secret clearances. Leuteritz, in fact, never had a problem getting the navy to fill a vacancy for an operator or a technician. It was no secret, moreover, that besides their work for Pan Am, operators on the Pacific islands also monitored Japanese shipping.

The day arrived for the *Pan American Clipper* to leave on its proving flight to Honolulu at 3 p.m. on April 16, 1935, witnessed by a large crowd. The aircraft soared into the air over San Francisco Bay and disappeared into a cloud bank beyond the Golden Gate. High above the ocean, the temperature hovered near freezing and the crew donned fleece-lined boots and padded flying suits to ward off the chill. The S-42 passed over steamers stationed along the route, with Noonan constantly checking radio bearings and marking off checkpoints on his charts. They droned on through the night, and just after dawn saw the Hawaiian islands rise out of the sea. The Clipper was ahead of schedule and the meticulous Musick circled until it was exactly 8 a.m. before he landed. The 2,300 miles from Alameda had taken 18 hours, 9 minutes.

The return flight held more suspense. Fighting a strong head wind that pushed unceasingly against the nose of the aircraft, the S-42 averaged less than 100 mph for almost the entire trip. A crowd, including the wives of the crew, stood waiting expectantly in Alameda as the hours dragged by. Trippe stared at a wall map in New York, waiting for word.

Fuel was rapidly disappearing as the Clipper plowed through a solid overcast. Soon, there was only 30 minutes fuel left and still the California coast was not in sight. Then, at 5:21 p.m., the S-42 broke into the clear. The hills surrounding San Francisco Bay were just ahead. More than five hours overdue, the *Pan American Clipper* dropped straight down onto the water. Musick had forgone the usual circle. When the flight engineer tested the tanks with a stick, he found them "just about damp at the bottom." Trippe went to dinner.

Commentators and newspaper editorials announced that the Pacific had been conquered, but Trippe and others at Pan American Airways knew the real work was yet to come. The Clipper brought back 14,000 letters from Honolulu, the first time mail had been carried by air over the Pacific. Trippe had also spent, for the first time, an enormous amount of money developing the route before the mail contract was in hand, yet FAM-14 had not been awarded to the airline.

The postmaster general was under fire from congress for playing favorites with Pan American Airways. There were accusations that Pan Am had overcharged the government, but it was almost impossible to substantiate the charges. Each Pan Am division manager ran his own operation like an independent kingdom. Data on costs were scattered throughout nine divisions and dozens of field offices in as many countries. Pan Am, the post office and congress became embroiled in argument, with Trippe running the course like a linebacker through a broken field.

Musick made another flight from Alameda to Honolulu on June 12 again at the controls of the *Pan American Clipper*. A few days later, he flew on to Midway Island, following a chain of reefs and atolls that stretched more than 1,300 miles northwest from Oahu. Far to the west, almost on the other side of the ocean, the *North Haven* was approaching Manila.

Reaching Midway in 9 hours, 13 minutes, Musick eyed the rough water around the island apprehensively, but he put the S-42 down on the lagoon without a mishap. Work was still going on to get Midway ready for commercial operations. The construction crew had erected a powerhouse for the two diesel generators. A machine shop and store room had been constructed. Nearby, two steel towers, topped by water tanks, and a windmill, stood stark against the brilliant blue sky.

The *Pan American Clipper* returned to Alameda and was promptly readied for the next stage. This time it would be flown by Rod Sullivan because Musick was returning to Baltimore to test the Martin M-130. Grooch, back from base-building in the Pacific and assigned to Alemeda's operations department, went with the pilot to inspect the S-42. They found a swarm of workers getting it ready. All the seats had been re-moved, and Grooch would recall later that it was "packed full of gas tanks."

Sullivan and John Tilton, copilot, left August 9, 1935, and flew the 1,260 miles from Midway to Wake Island. The two dozen men working on Wake had not yet completed the landing area. There were too many coral heads and even though they had marked the landing area with two lines of buoys, it was still slightly short.

Sullivan flew over the island, peering down apprehensively at what appeared to be an enormous number of coral heads, plainly seen in the clear water. He radioed the island that the water in the lagoon appeared to be only six inches deep. Don't worry was the answer, it's 15 feet. The crew held its collective breath and the pilot eased the ship down and barely got it stopped in time. Sullivan was not very happy about the whole thing, but he cooled off somewhat when he was greeted with an iced cake that spelled out "Welcome to Wake Island."

When Sullivan arrived back at Alameda, FAM-14, at the inevitable $2 per mile, was awarded to Pan Am by the post office. Trippe must have sighed with relief. The next flight, reaching Guam on October 5, again carried thousands of letters on board the *Pan American Clipper*.

Sikorsky S-42 *Brazilian Clipper* (NC-822M) was used exclusively in Latin America.

Pan American was ready to begin regular air service by November across the Pacific from California to the Philippines, but the Sikorsky S-42 would be cheated out of the final glory. The aircraft that would actually fly the Pacific and, forever linked to the Orient, in the public mind, would be the Martin M-130.

Captain Ed Musick was awarded the Harmon Trophy as outstanding aviator in 1935, the third American to win it after Lindbergh and Wiley Post. The honor did not come without a price. The crew of the *Pan American Clipper* was tired and worn out from the long, tension-filled flights. They were averaging 125 hours a month in the air, which was far more than allowed by Department of Commerce regulations. Tempers were short. Some of the crew members took refuge in excessive drinking. Noonan, in particular, was known to literally disappear for a weekend and then show up badly hungover. The crews needed relief, with junior pilots notably resentful of the long hours and low pay. All requests for pay raises went to New York, where they were inevitably ignored.

'Short Snorters'

Pan Am's South American routes remained active; NC-822M was flying from Miami to Rio, a distance of 5,400 miles in five days. Cruising at around 160 mph and carrying an average of 32 passengers, the S-42 would fly 900 miles nonstop.

Radio Officer Chapman, now flying the S-42s, would report in to WKDL or to San Juan Radio every 15 minutes, and would give the aircraft's exact longitude and latitude every hour. His equipment consisted of a 15-watt radio and 150 feet of antenna wire weighted with a three-pound lead ball that was reeled out for every transmission. Cruising en route, Chapman transmitted in Morse on such frequencies as 1638 kHz and 3285 kHz. Closer to a landing area, he used voice and transmitted on 2870 kHz. If there was no control tower, Chapman, who would go on to fly DC-3s, contacted the Pan Am motor launches directly, which cleared the landing area.

Trippe's vision had by now established Pan Am in the public conscious. Flying to South America or the Caribbean? There was only one airline that mattered. The Pan Am flight even became routine enough to develop traditions. Whenever a Pan American aircraft crossed the equator, for example, the skipper pulled back on the yoke. The aircraft would climb abruptly, and the pilot would then push the stick forward gently, causing a quick sinking sensation. Another way to celebrate crossing the equator was the Short-Snorters Club. Pilots, crewmembers, and passengers would sign each others' dollar bills and then tape them together, the Short-Snorter. Many airline crews and travelers would cross the equator often enough to develop quite a string. Some say that Pan American pilots originated this idea, while others argue that it began with the Alaskan bush pilots. Short-Snorters were carried by many aircrews and servicemen right through World War II.

Modifications

Three S-42s were built and the next four to come out of the Sikorsky factory were designated S-42A. This model had improved aerodynamics and the wing span increased by about four inches. Wing loading was actually enhanced by about a pound. A change to the S1E-G Hornet engine boosted horsepower to 750, producing a higher allowable gross weight of 40,000 pounds, increasing speed to 160 mph, but not appreciably altering range. The service ceiling was enhanced by about 4,000 feet. The final three Sikorskys bore the S-42B designation. This was, again, an improved aircraft, with a higher gross weight of 42,000 pounds and a range increased to 1,800 statute miles. Wing loading was a remarkable 31.3 pounds. The tradeoff for increased range, however, was a reduced payload to 24 seats and a slight drop in overall speed from that of the S-42A.

Atlantic competition

The United States and the European nations realized that the Atlantic Ocean remained the crucial prize in the quest for world air supremacy.

The Germans entered the contest with their DO-X, a monstrous 12-engine aircraft that had once flown with 169 people on board. Its flight deck closely resembled that of a ship right down to an immense control wheel. The DO-X crossed the South Atlantic in 1932, then flew north to New York, where it made a triumphant circuit of Manhattan. It barely made it back to Berlin, however, and was not developed further.

The airship *Hindenburg* made 10 round trips across the Atlantic in 1936, only to be destroyed the following year at Lakehurst, N.J. The Germans would make other transoceanic flights using floatplanes and depot ships, but would not seriously consider a trans-Atlantic service until they had put the Focke-Wulf Fw 200 *Condor* into service in 1938, with a nonstop Deutsche Lufthansa flight from Berlin to New York. By then, aviation was on the doorstep of World War II.

The British airship R100, with its "olde English" dining room and waitresses in starched aprons, made a round trip journey to Montreal in July 1930. The British aviation public thrilled at the thought of trans-Atlantic service by airship, then the R101 crashed in northern France on October 4, 1930, killing, among others, the British secretary of state. The airship idea also died.

Then there were those who would cross the Atlantic for reasons of prestige and national honor. General Balbo of the Italian Air Force led a formation of 24 Savoia-Marchetti warplanes across the Atlantic in July 1933 via Holland, Ireland, Iceland, and Labrador. Twenty-three of the aircraft made it back to Italy. Twin-engine warplanes are seldom viable machines in the commercial world, and Italy retired from the contest, content that it had shown the flag.

The French entered the game with *Lieutenant de Vaisseau Paris*, a massive 37-ton machine with six Hispano-Suiza water-cooled engines and a top speed of 162 mph. It crossed the South Atlantic and made its way up the Caribbean islands to the United States in 1935. Fate would not be kind to the French on this trip, however; at Pensacola, a furious storm wrecked the aircraft at its moorings, and it was taken apart and shipped back to France in pieces. The *Vaisseau* would cross the Atlantic again, but by then it would be nine years old, requiring 36,000 pounds of fuel to hoist it across the ocean. Its builders would finally admit that it was without commercial possibilities.

By 1937, therefore, the competition among those who were going to begin a viable airline service across the Atlantic had narrowed to two main contenders: Juan Trippe of Pan American and George Woods-Humpherey of Imperial Airways. Each had a different attitude toward an Atlantic route. Pan American Airways wanted to fly the Atlantic because it was a commercial airline. The British, however, had more complicated reasons. They saw it as a lifeline to Canada, part of the All-Red Route to link the British Commonwealth and Empire around the world. To Trippe, it was hard cash; to Woods-Humpherey, imperial bonds. They decided to work together.

The director of Imperial Airways, however, was also known for his definite ideas about doing business; one of his pet hates seemed to be pilots. There was something about pilots that really irked Woods-Humphery. He detested their independent and undisciplined ways, their constant complaints about their low wages and their cavalier treatment by the airline. There is a story that one day Woods-Humphery saw an individual lolling about the passenger lounge who he took to be a pilot. It was too much. He'd had enough of these lackadaisical pilots with their constant whining. He marched over to the man and fired him on the spot, but it turned out that the man was a passenger waiting for an aircraft.

Pan Am had 133 aircraft going to 165 airports in 1934 and it was showing a profit. Although the airline had been denied landing rights in Newfoundland after its dominion status had been revoked, Trippe was not going to give up. He sent businessman Harold Long to Portugal to successfully negotiate with the Salazar regime for landing rights in the Azores. The agreement was signed in Lisbon on April 4, 1937, and granted Pan Am the right to operate between North America and Lisbon via the Azores and between Lisbon and London.

The fact that Pan American Airways was in many instances almost conducting foreign policy was not lost on the State Department, but an international air policy for the United States was yet to be defined, and state had to content itself with a request for Pan Am to keep it "fully informed." Out of a sense of noblesse oblige, Trippe obliged.

Whenever American and British diplomatic officials did get into discussions about airline policy, at least one difference between the two countries on commercial matters was readily apparent. The British would openly refer to the government-subsidized Imperial Airways, while American government officials would go to great lengths to avoid appearing to be negotiating for Pan American, which also happened to be government subsidized, primarily by airmail rates, referring always in conversation and correspondence to "a United States airline company."

Hundreds of trans-Atlantic telephone calls and reams of correspondence produced some progress. Pan American and Imperial obtained landing rights at Foynes Island, Republic of Ireland. Both airlines then agreed that one would not start trans-Atlantic service without the other, and they also agreed to share trans-Atlantic mail between them.

Trippe's British partners were undergoing a severe pounding in the British press, which was taking Imperial Airways to task for its inferior aircraft. Matters for Imperial were not helped by the 1934 London to Melbourne air race. Although the winner of the 11,000-mile competition had been a one-of-a-kind de Havilland, specially built for the event, second place had gone to a KLM Douglas DC-2, one of the standard aircraft used on the airline's regularly scheduled flights to the East Indies. A Boeing 247 had come in third.

Two American aircraft out of three was too close for British comfort. Everyone agreed that Imperial would have to do better. One Imperial pilot, motivated less by national prestige than by the desire for a safe operation, would note in his report on a reciprocal flight with Pan Am, "Every opportunity should be taken to find out about ideas that are being taken up *now* by Pan American, as they are two years of practical work ahead of us in this field."

Ireland, meanwhile, insisted on being a part of any international agreement involving trans-Atlantic flight, and aviation representatives of Ireland, Canada, and Britain met in Montreal. They formed the North Atlantic Company on December 2, 1935, and a key provision of its charter was that all Atlantic eastbound and westbound air traffic would stop in Ireland.

Joint meteorological reporting arrangements were set up, and the British established a major radio station in Newfoundland. The North Atlantic Company then petitioned the U.S. Department of Commerce for landing rights in the United States and joint mail operations with American airlines flying the Atlantic. A Pan American-Imperial Airways agreement was then signed on January 25, 1936. Pan Am would operate a trans-Atlantic service in conjunction with the British and under the same terms as the North Atlantic Company pact.

Pan Am established its Atlantic Division in the spring of 1937 as an autonomous operating unit, and by June the division's terminal at Port Washington, New York, had a staff of 113. Captain Harold E. Gray piloted the *Pan American Clipper III* (NC-16736) on May 25, 1937, for an initial survey flight from Port Washington to Bermuda. The last of the line from the factory, the *Clipper III* was a stripped down S-42B, with a range increased to 2,800 miles but space for only about a dozen seats.

An Imperial Airways Short C Class flying boat, the *Cavalier*, which had been crated and sent to Bermuda by ship, simultaneously made the reciprocal flight. Full commercial service between New York and Bermuda was established in June.

Captain Gray, who would go on to become Pan Am's executive vice president in charge of the Atlantic Division and then successively president and board chairman of the company, then flew a series of five Atlantic survey flights. He departed Port Washington in the *Clipper III* on June 25 and reached Shediac, New Brunswick, before returning home without landing. Flight number two, departing on June 27, flew as far as Botwood, Newfoundland. The third flight left on July 3 and reached Southhampton via Foynes Island, Ireland. The Imperial Airways' Short S.23 Empire flying boat *Caledonia* took off from Foynes westbound, timed with the *Clipper III*'s departure.

Somewhere in the mid-Atlantic, the two airliners exchanged radio messages. The more experienced Americans were flying at 10,000 feet in cloud, while the British airplane stayed at approximately 1,000 feet fighting strong west winds. The *Clipper III* winged into Foynes after a flight of 12 hours, 30 minutes, touching down in such a routine manner that one Irish onlooker described it as "a messenger boy arriving on a bicycle." Eamon de Valera, president of the Irish Free State, congratulated Captain Gray on the flight. Gray, who had joined Pan Am in 1929, flying trimotors between Mexico and Texas, said it was an "enjoyable trip."

The Imperial Airways flight took three hours longer to reach Newfoundland after battling strong winds, rain, and fog. Flight number four on August 22 followed the same route, while a final survey flight was made across the southern route via Bermuda, Azores, Lisbon, Marseilles, and Southhampton on August 16.

The Atlantic Division moved its base of operations to Baltimore in November 1937 and the *Bermuda Clipper* (NC-16735) made its first flight to Bermuda from this new base on November 17. These flights to Bermuda and across the Atlantic were not without hazards. The fickle North Atlantic weather could change in a matter of minutes. Wind speed often averaged 35 knots, cutting aircraft ground speed to as low as 100 mph.

Ice was a particular problem. On an eastbound flight on September 21, 1937, Captain Wilcockson, the pilot of the *Caledonia*, noted ice forming rapidly on the wings of the airplane at 4,000 feet even though outside temperature was a moderate 27°F. The ice crusted on the *Caledonia*'s windshield and formed a ball on the radio antenna. Incoming radio signals weakened, making it difficult for them to contact Botwood. A dead area for radio was also noted about 300 to 500 miles off the Newfoundland coast. Ice would cause the January 21, 1939, crash of the *Cavalier*, which flew the Imperial Airways half of the Bermuda–New York run. Pan American's S-42Bs were soon equipped with retrofitted de-icer boots and other de-icing equipment.

Flying the North Atlantic regularly, however, did not mean that passenger service was available or even feasible. Imperial made five round trips over the Atlantic in 1937, but the British aircraft were stripped to the bare ribs. When one British aviation official asked if he could fly across on one of the Imperial flights, sitting "on the floor" if necessary, he was tersely told that there was no floor. Here again, the differences between the British and American designs were revealing. The S.23s were "bare" aircraft and flew with a crew of four. The S-42Bs, on the other hand, operated with a crew of eight, and only one of its four passenger compartments were ripped out to create space for extra tankage.

On its first crossing to Britain, the *Clipper III* also carried 1,995 pounds of spare parts for maintenance support on the other side of the ocean. The Short S.23 had a more modern and uncluttered appearance than the S-42B, but the American airplane was equal in speed.

Crews of the S.23 and the S-42B flying the joint schedule between New York and Bermuda competed, unofficially, to see who could fly the 770 miles the fastest. A comparison of flight times proved that the American aircraft could fly the route faster than the Short. The S-42B's antiquated appearance was deceptive and a comparison of the two aircrafts' technical data, shown below, reveals why. Except for the undesirable feature of a higher power loading, Pan Am's S-42B was the superior airplane on almost every count.

Sikorsky S-42B versus Short S.23
(Both aircraft modified for Atlantic service)

	S-42B	S.23
Mtow*	45,500	45,000
Tare	24,300	24,595**
Disposable load	21,200	20,405
Load: Tare	46:54	45:55
Full fuel	14,484	17,864
Wing area, sq. ft.	1,340	1,500
Wing loading, lbs/sq. ft.	33.9	30.0
Engines × horsepower	4 × 750	4 × 940
Power loading, lbs/hp	15.1	11.9

*See glossary for definitions.

**Less than standard tare because about 5,000 pounds of cabin furnishings were removed.

If Imperial was not ready to begin carrying passengers, Pan Am could not start a service. Trippe, however, always continued to push hard, always ahead of everyone else, always with new ideas, always a new service to begin. He negotiated with everybody: the French, the Norwegians, the Spanish, even the Egyptians. The new Boeings were on the way, ideal for the Atlantic run, but Woods-Humpherey was also waiting for better aircraft, the De Havilland Albatross and the Short-Mayo Composite, and commercial trans-Atlantic service did not start for another two years.

The S-42, meanwhile, continued to give exceptional service around the world. The first aircraft out of the factory, the NC-822M, was not scrapped until July 1946. The two other S-42s, NC-823M and NC-824M, were both destroyed in accidents in the Caribbean, but not before the venerable 823M made survey flights across the South Pacific and opened service from Hong Kong to Manila.

All S-42As were assigned to Caribbean and South American routes. Three, the *Jamaica Clipper*, the *Antilles Clipper* and the *Brazilian Clipper* (not the S-42 that made the inaugural flight to South America, which was renamed the *Colombia Clipper* in 1937), performed years of service before also being scrapped in July 1946. The *Dominican Clipper* (NC-15376) was lost in an accident in San Juan, Puerto Rico, on March 10, 1941.

The S-42Bs, however, were the model that added the most laurels to the type. As we shall see later, NC-16734 made survey flights and initiated service across the South Pacific. The *Bermuda Clipper* (NC-16735), later called the *Hong Kong Clipper II*, opened the Baltimore-Bermuda run before it was transferred to the Far East. It was destroyed by Japanese bombing on December 8, 1941. As for the *Pan American Clipper III*, after its Atlantic survey flights it was flown on the Bermuda route and then transferred to South America. It was destroyed 1,000 miles up the Amazon River at Manaus, Brazil, on July 27, 1943.

Performance Data
Sikorsky S-42

	S-42	S-42A	S-42B
Type	Boat	———	———
Length	68 feet	———	———
Span	114 feet	118 feet	118 feet
Wing loading	28.5 lb/sq. ft.	29.9 lbs/sf	31.3 lbs/sf
Height	17 feet	17 feet	22 feet
Gross weight	38,000 lbs.	40,000 lbs	42,000 lbs
Engines	P&W Hornet × 4	———	———
Horsepower	700	750	750
Range	1,200 miles	1,200 miles	1,800 miles
Fuel capacity	1,240 gals.	———	———
Useful load	18,000 lbs.		
Cruising speed	150 mph	160 mph	155 mph
Service ceiling	16,000 ft.	20,000 ft	15,000 ft
Climb rate	800 fpm	———	———
Passengers	38	38	24
Crew	5	5	5

Pan American's Sikorsky S-42s
(in order of construction)

Model	Reg. No.	Original Name	Area of Use	Remarks
S-42	NC-822M	*Brazilian Clipper*	So. Am.	Renamed *Columbia Clipper* in 1937; scrapped 7/15/46.
S-42	NC-823M	*West Indies Clipper*	So. Am.	Renamed *Pan American Clipper*; renamed *Hong Kong Clipper* in 1937. Sank Antilla, Cuba, 8/7/44.
S-42	NC-824M	None	So. Am.	Destroyed Port of Spain, Trinidad. 12/20/35.

Model	Reg. No.	Original Name	Area of Use	Remarks
S-42A	NC-15373	*Jamaica Clipper*	So. Am.	Scrapped 7/15/46.
S-42A	NC-15374	*Antilles Clipper*	So. Am.	Scrapped 7/15/46.
S-42A	NC-15375	*Brazilian Clipper*	So. Am.	Scrapped 7/15/46.
S-42A	NC-15376	*Dominican Clipper*	So. Am.	Destroyed, Juan Harbor, Puerto Rico, 3/10/41.
S-42B	NC-16734	*Pan Am Clipper II*	So. Pac.	Renamed *Samoan Clipper*. Lost Pago Pago, Samoa, 1/11/38.
S-42B	NC-16735	*Bermuda Clipper*	Atlantic	Renamed *Alaska Clipper* In 1940; renamed *Hong Kong Clipper II* in 1941. Destroyed by Japanese bombing, 12/8/41.
S-42B	NC-16736	*Pan Am Clipper II*	Atlantic	Renamed *Bermuda Clipper* in 1940. Destroyed Manaus, Brazil, 7/27/43.

The Sikorsky S-43:

The baby Clipper

Igor Sikorsky sat at the controls of a small, 18-seat amphibian for the maiden flight. It was his 43rd design since he had left Russia 25 years earlier. Sikorsky revved the engines and turned the aircraft in preparation for the takeoff run on Long Island Sound on a crisp autumn morning in 1935. A group of reporters, government aviation experts, and airline officials watched. The twin engines roared and the amphibian commenced its run.

Then it happened.

One of the engines cut out because the fuel supply had failed.

But with the other engine wide open, Sikorsky kept flying and, incredibly, the aircraft rose into the air. Two hundred feet up, a mechanic succeeded in restoring fuel pressure to the failed engine and it fired.

Sikorsky subsequently grinned at the reporters and observers. "Gentlemen," he said, "I am going to tell you a funny story. Believe it or not, you have just seen a multi-engined amphibian take off from the water, for the first time in history, on only one engine. And if I hadn't done it myself, I wouldn't have believed it."

The idea for the S-43 was simple enough: replace the aging Consolidated Commodores in South America with a better-performing aircraft that could also serve as a backup for the S-42s. Sikorsky's answer: a scaled-down, amphibious version of the S-42 that inevitably earned the sobriquet Baby Clipper. Powered by two Pratt & Whitney S1E-G Hornet engines instead of four, each rated at 750 hp, the S-43 had a gross weight of 20,000 pounds, which was quite heavy for that size of aircraft. It was only 20 percent lighter than the DC-3, which went into service a few months after the first S-43 was delivered in January 1936.

The S-43 was constructed entirely of metal. It had Hamilton-Standard constant-speed propellers and a semi-cantilever monoplane wing with a single, box-type spar and a flush-type duralumin skin. The wing also incorporated a fabric-covered duralumin structure flap that was hydraulically operated to reduce landing speed and allow shorter takeoff runs. Wing loading was 25 pounds per square foot. The hull was of duralumin, semi-monocoque construction with four bulkheads providing five watertight compartments. The cabin had a minimum roof height of six feet. Seating was provided for 16 or 18 passengers, depending on the configuration.

Flight tests showed that the Baby Clipper could cruise at 166 mph at a height of 7,000 feet. Service ceiling was 19,000 feet, with a climb rate of one thousand feet per minute. But S-43 was a lot more aircraft than many assumed. Captain Boris Sergievsky flew a Baby Clipper to a height of 27,950 feet on April 15, 1936, breaking the former altitude record by almost 10,000 feet. The outside temperature was 40 below. When the aircraft landed, ice an inch thick still coated part of the wings.

One problem that pilots encountered with the S-43 occurred when they attempted to take off with the wing flaps down. Landing gear retraction would cause the wing flaps to rise, causing loss of lift and several near disasters. Certain pilots theorized that the problem was caused by leaking hydraulic fluid. Pan Am pilot Art Peters experimented with the flap control handle in various positions and found that when he left it in the down position, fluid would leak, bringing the flaps up. Flaps stayed down with the handle in the neutral position. This method was later adopted in the operating manual.

Pan American Airways would order 13 of the ships; seven were delivered to Panair do Brasil, two were assigned to Panagra, and the remainder were flown by Pan Am in the Çaribbean. The aircraft never received the notice it deserved because Trippe's interest in a northern, subarctic route across the Atlantic waned as better aircraft came on line.

After Lindbergh's flight in the Sirius across Greenland and Iceland, Pan Am seriously considered starting a service from Copenhagen and Stavanger, Norway, to Reykjavik, Iceland, via the Shetland and Faroe Islands using the S-43. Originally, Pan Am's plans called for commencement of the service by the summer of 1936; a radio station was set up in Iceland, and cooperative agreements were signed with the Danish airline, Det Danske Luftfartselskab (DDL), and the Norwegian carrier Det Norske Luftfartselskap (DNL). As part of this agreement, DNL actually or-

Thirteen of the 18-seat Sikorsky S-43 "Baby Clippers" went into service with Pan Am, Panair do Brasil, and PANAGRA. Almost all aircraft were assigned to South America; several additional aircraft were delivered to European airlines.

dered an S-43, Sikorsky construction number 4312, which was delivered with the S2E-G Hornet engine. But the service never materialized, and the S-43 was used for internal operations.

Sikorsky Aircraft built 53 S-43s and besides those sold to Pan Am delivered them to such airlines as KLM, Inter-Island Airways, and Chargeurs Rennis of Paris. But the S-43 remains a curiously forgotten aircraft, overshadowed by its big brother, the S-42, and by the technological wonders that had already begun to fly the air routes of the world.

Performance Data
Sikorsky S-43

Type	Amphibian
Length	51 feet
Span	86 feet
Wing loading	25 pounds/square foot
Height	18 feet
Gross weight	20,000 pounds
Engines	P&W Hornet×2
Horsepower	750
Range	775 statute miles
Fuel capacity	690 gallons
Useful load	6,750 pounds
Cruising speed	166 mph
Service ceiling	19,000 feet
Climb rate	1,000 fpm
Passengers	16/18
Crew	3

Pan American's Sikorsky S-43s
(in order of construction)

Reg. No.	User	Area of Use	Remarks
NC-15063	P. do B.	So. Am.	Crashed.
NC-15064	P. do B.	So. Am.	
NC-15065	Panagra	So. Am.	
NC-15066	Pan Am	Carib.	Destroyed at Fort de France, Martinique, 8/3/45.
NC-15067	P. do B.	So. Am.	Crashed.
NC-15068	P. do B.	So. Am.	Crashed.
NC-16926	P. do B.	So. Am.	Destroyed at Sao Paulo, Brazil, 1/3/47.
NC-16927	P. do B.	So. Am.	Crashed 7/28/40 but rebuilt.
NC-16928	Panagra	So. Am.	Crashed.
NC-16930	Pan Am	Carib.	
NC-16931	P. do B.	So. Am.	
NC-16933	Pan Am	Carib.	
NC-16932	Pan Am	Carib.	

Martin M-130:

Pacific conquest

Millions of people around the world were glued to their radios on November 22, 1935. Commentators were describing the scene in Alameda, California, where a crowd of more than 25,000 people stood in bright sunshine listening to speeches; thousands more were crowded onto the docks overlooking San Francisco Bay. Crowds watched from rooftops and from the ferries that churned slowly across the water from San Francisco, the surrounding hills a brilliant backdrop. Streams of water arched into the blue sky from fire boats, rockets were bursting overhead, and sirens shrilled.

The object of everyone's attention was a giant flying boat that had been drawn up to a dock that now doubled as a flag-draped reviewing stand. The aircraft was named the *China Clipper*, and it was going to fly the inaugural mail route across the Pacific, from San Francisco to Manila. It would mark one of the most important events in air transportation history.

Today, it is hard to appreciate the technological wonder that this flying boat represented. It was a time when the nation was struggling to lift itself out of a severe economic depression, and the flight of the *China Clipper* seemed a psychological wonder, as well, practically representing hope. Things just couldn't be as bad as they looked when America could build and fly a machine so majestic, so perfect, as to almost defy description. Over and over, the speeches marking the rite of inauguration would contain such phrases as "a new era." Not only did the *China Clipper* evoke the spell of distant, exotic lands — in a way, it also carried the hopes of a depressed nation yearning for a brighter future.

Ed Musick attended a luncheon that day in his honor at San Francisco's Palace Hotel. The pilot had not had a good night's rest and was chain-smoking one cigarette after another. He sat restlessly through a succession of speeches that described him as something close to the greatest pilot of the age. One after the other, the dignitaries stood up to heap on the accolades: Postmaster General James Farley, Mayor Angelo Rossi of San Francisco, Governor Frank Merriam of California (who had declared November 22 Pan American Airways Day) Pan Am Pacific Division Manager Clarence Young, and, of course, the president of Pan American Airways, Juan Trippe.

Musick looked composed under all the attention but his thoughts had a tendency to stray. The S-42 had made it to Hawaii only four times. Wake? Twice. Guam? A lonely once. Manila? Zero.

There was even more that made him uneasy. Only days before, an editorial in a leading Japanese newspaper described the coming inaugural flight as "military preparations in the guise of civilian enterprise." It went on to say that the closeness of the projected route to Japanese-held islands merited "serious consideration."

Musick also knew that the day before, two Japanese nationals had been arrested by the FBI for trying to get on board the *China Clipper*, moored across the Bay. Apparently, they were trying to tamper with the radio direction equipment.

None of this was reported in American newspapers, which preferred to focus on the drama of the flight rather than discuss other implications that might raise some slightly embarrassing questions. Why, for example, did the U.S. Navy maintain jurisdiction over Wake? And why did the navy and Pan American Airlines have such a close connection?

Musick and his crew and the entire assemblage of officials and their entourages were taken by launch over to Alameda. The *China Clipper* loomed above them. A public relations genius had come up with an imaginative way to load the mail sacks that the aircraft would carry across the Pacific. The first sack of mail was rigged to fall into the Clipper's hold automatically. A switch was triggered by an electrical impulse transmitted to the Pan Am terminal from Mount Wilson Observatory; the impulse was picked up from the star Betelguese in the constellation of Orion. The last bag was delivered to the aircraft by a Wells Fargo stagecoach, an actual relic of the 19th century. The whole act, almost pure showbiz, struck a responsive chord in the mind of the public everywhere.

Radio announcers had been giving a minute by minute description of events for hours, carried live across the nation over NBC and CBS.

"Sweet Sixteen," the Martin M-130 *China Clipper*, on its inaugural airmail flight to the Orient, flies over the unfinished Golden Gate Bridge.

"We are here on the shores of historic old San Francisco Bay," one reporter intoned.

"In a few minutes now, we will bring you the sailing of the first China Clipper in eighty years, from this grand old Bay from which the original Clipper ships set sail; we realize that, since time began, this vast Pacific Ocean at our feet stood as an unconquerable barrier between East and West. Now, at last, this barrier is to be no more." He began to get into his stride.

"And it is America, whose dynamic energy and courage to pioneer, whose aeronautical genius, whose far-sighted government, has alone of all nations on the face of the earth, made this tremendous achievement possible. Within a few feet of our platform, the *China Clipper* , studded with powerful engines, her great glistening whale-like hull resting gently in the water, stands ready. What drama is packed into the hold of this tremendous airliner, the largest ever developed in America where the airplane was born, the most outstanding aircraft ever developed in the

The Old and the New

The China Clipper, seen for the first time in Macau showing Chinese fishing junks, a marked contrast between the ancient Chinese mode of transportation, still in use, and the most modern of all travel ships.   April 27, 1937.

Wavy flag is noticeable on the *China Clipper* during arrival at Macau.

world; what years of pioneering have preceded her!" Winding up with a flourish, he left home audiences with a vision of the future.

"On the wings of these sturdy Clipper ships are pinned the hopes of America's commerce for a rightful standing in the teeming markets of the Orient. In no other section of the United States is that feeling more keen than here on the Pacific coast. . . ."

Now Juan Trippe stepped to the microphone on the flag-draped platform and doffed his brown fedora; he was 36, a successful business-man: "It is significant and appropriate that the first scheduled air service over a major ocean route is being started under the auspices of the American government, by an American company operating aircraft de-signed and built in the United States and in the charge of American captains and crews." The crowd cheered wildly.

Next, the postmaster general read a message from President Roose-velt: "Even at this distance, I thrill to the wonder of it all. They tell me the inauguration of the trans-Pacific sky mail also celebrates the hundredth anniversary of the arrival of the first clipper ship in San Francisco. The years between the two events mark a century of progress that is without parallel, and it is our just pride that America and Americans have played no minor part in the blazing of new trails. There can be no higher hope than this heritage of courage, daring, initiative and enterprise will be conserved and intensified."*

Seven men in smart blue uniforms now appeared on the platform. Their names and ranks were read out to the audience as they went aboard: R.O.D. Sullivan, first officer; Fred Noonan, navigator; George King, sec-ond officer; C.D. Wright, first engineering officer; Victor Wright, second engineering officer; William Jarboe Jr., radio officer; finally Captain Edwin C. Musick. (The two Wrights were not related.)

Still more dignitaries had their say over the radio hookup: President Manuel Quezon of the Philippines, the governors of Hawaii and California, and California's Senator William McAdoo.

The announcer's voice broke in again on the radio. "The China Clipper, a beautiful sight resting on the quiet waters of Pan American's enclosed base here, is turned towards the opening in the breakwater. Ground crews stand at their posts, ready to cast off their lines at the captain's signal. By radio now, Mr. Trippe will get the report from the Clipper and from the far-flung airways's bases across the vast Pacific to the other side of the world. Here is Mr. Trippe now, speaking to the Clipper."

---

*The president was misinformed because the first clipper ship to stand in through the Golden Gate was the Samuel Russell in 1850.

Trippe:	*China Clipper*, are you ready?"
Musick:	Pan American Airways *China Clipper*, Captain Musick, standing by for orders, sir."
Trippe:	Stand by, Captain Musick, for station reports.

Five Pan Am bases across the Pacific then reported in with code signals.

KNBF, Honolulu:	"Pan American Airways ocean air base Number One—Honolulu, Hawaii. Standing by for orders."
KNBH, Midway:	"Pan American Airways mid-ocean air base Number Two—Midway Islands. Standing by for orders."
KNBI, Wake:	"Pan American Airways trans-Pacific airways Number Three—Wake Island. Standing by for orders."
KNBG, Guam:	"Pan American Airways mid-ocean air base Number Four—Guam. Standing by for orders."
KZBQ, Manila:	"Pan American Airways trans-Pacific air terminal, Manila, Commonwealth of the Philippines. Ready and standing by, sir."
Trippe:	Stand by all stations. Postmaster General Farley, I have the honor to report, sir, that the trans-Pacific airway is ready to inaugurate airmail service of the United States Post Office from the mainland across the Pacific to the Philippines, by way of Hawaii, Midway, Wake and, Guam islands.
Farley:	Mr. Trippe, it is an honor and a privilege for me, as postmaster general of the United States of America, to hereby order the inauguration of the first scheduled service on Foreign Air Mail Route Number Fourteen at 3:28 p.m., Pacific standard time, on this day which will forever mark a new chapter in the glorious history of our nation, a new era in world transportation, a new and binding bond that will link, for the first time in history, the peoples of the East and the West.

All that remained for Trippe to do now was to give the final order. He stepped again to the microphone.

| Trippe: | Captain Musick, you have your sailing orders. Cast off and depart for Manila in accordance therewith. |

White-clad ground crews ran forward. Lines were cast off. A band broke into "The Star-Spangled Banner."

Musick opened the throttles, and, engines roaring, the Martin M-130 taxied out into the Bay. Hundreds of small watercraft jockeyed nearby. High above, 22 aerial bombs exploded in salute. Small American flags floated down. Dozens of other aircraft circled, most of them filled with reporters, while hundreds of automobile horns added to the racket.

The Clipper was heavily loaded with fuel and 1,837 pounds of mail: 58 sacks filled with 111,000 letters. Musick gunned the engines, commenced his run, and lifted the airplane smoothly into the air. Official takeoff time was 3:46 p.m.

But he was not climbing fast enough.

The San Francisco-Oakland Bay Bridge loomed ahead, a maze of cables. Reflexes came into play, and Musick ducked underneath, skimming the water. The swarm of small aircraft obediently followed like a line of ducklings tailing their mother. It was a sight never seen since. Trippe, who had realized what happened, almost visibly flinched.

Climbing higher, the Clipper was cheered by thousands and thousands of schoolchildren lining the marina along San Francisco's waterfront. The aircraft was rising steadily now, clearing the towers of the unfinished Golden Gate Bridge, engines roaring. Musick kept the back pressure on the wheel, heartbeat slowing, one could almost see him grin.

San Francisco fell away, the cheers of the crowd finally muted, lost in the bright sunshine. In a minute, the *China Clipper* was a speck on the horizon, climbing into silver-toned clouds. Then it was gone.

The Dude's gamble

Glenn L. Martin, once a barnstormer known as "The Flying Dude," had made aviation history in May 1912 when he was the first to make a round-trip flight between Newport Beach, California, and Catalina Island. He went on to form his own aircraft manufacturing company and in the early thirties, Major Billy Mitchell flew the Martin MB-2 bomber to ring the death knell of the battleship when he sank the "unsinkable" *Ostfriesland*.

Glenn Martin purchased 1,200 acres just outside Baltimore for a new factory in 1928, as a leading aircraft manufacturer. Succeeding years were not kind to Martin Aircraft. A series of bad decisions had caused heavy financial losses. The company had gambled a fortune on the development of a new bomber, only to see the Army Air Corps reject it. (It was finally

Captain Ed Musick stands at the top of stairs while preparations are underway to load the Martin M-130 *China Clipper* with the first Pacific airmail. Postmaster General James Farley is behind the mailbags and Juan Trippe is in profile looking at Farley.

accepted and became the B-10.) The company's employees were even having trouble cashing their payroll checks.

Then a savior appeared in the person of Juan Trippe. A letter arrived from Pan American Airways, asking the company to bid on a flying boat that would be the absolute state-of-the-art. Glenn Martin cut an odd figure in the often rough-and-tumble aircraft manufacturing community. The third man to fly a heavier-than-air machine of his own design, he was a tall, wavy-haired Kansan who was always well-dressed, even dapper. He was never known to drink, smoke, or to utter profanities. Although a lifelong bachelor, he often liked to be seen in the company of beautiful women.

Trippe and Martin haggled for days over the contract, with Martin first making a bid to build three aircraft for two million dollars. Trippe countered with one million. They finally settled on a price of $417,000 each. It was almost a steal for Pan American. As it turned out, Martin lost money on the deal, but the popularity of the M-130 and subsequent government work would make up for it. For Trippe, the aircraft would be worth every penny.

The contract between the Martin Company and Pan American Airways was signed in 1931, at the same time that Sikorsky began work on the S-42, but on the face of it, the airline's demands seemed like a jump into the future: build an aircraft that could cruise at 150 mph and carry 52 passengers nonstop for more than 3,200 miles. In 1931, 10-passenger

The *China Clipper* anchored at Manila Harbor before 1938 with the Manila Hotel in the background.

transports stayed in the air for no more than a few hours and were straining if they reached 120 mph. To top it all, the aircraft had to lift more than its own deadweight.

"Don't do it," said Martin's associates. But there was something else that was notable about the Dude, he was a born gambler, and the challenge to build an aircraft for Pan Am fired his imagination like nothing had ever done before. "I'm going to build a large passenger-carrying flying boat," he insisted, "even at the risk of everything I have."

The first keel, laid in May 1933 was Construction Number 556. It eventually became an aircraft registered as NC-14714 and would bear the name *Hawaiian Clipper*. Construction Number 557 was registered as NC-14715 and named *Philippine Clipper*. The third ship, destined to be the most famous, and actually the first delivered to the airline, was Construction Number 558, NC-14716. It was called the *China Clipper*, known forever to Pam Am people as "Sweet Sixteen."

A high-wing monoplane flying boat, the design of the Martin M-130 grew under the direction of the manufacturer's chief engineer Lassiter Milburn, assisted by engineer and test pilot Ken Ebel. If there was a driving force behind the aircraft, it surely must have been Andre Priester, Pam Am's operations chief. Priester insisted on every advanced engineering concept, tried or untried, that could be incorporated into an aircraft: dual electrical system, dual hydraulic system, extra bulkheads in the hull, new wing flaps, better engine cowling that could conserve heat. The ideas poured out from the small, bald Dutchman.

At the Martin plant, the massive hull soon towered above the scaffolding, wings spanning 130 feet; many who came through the facility thought it would be too big to fly. The M-130 was the second largest flying boat in existence, after the Dornier-X. It was an aircraft built for a maximum gross takeoff weight of 51,000 pounds, twice its structural weight, 24,611 pounds, with a basic operating ratio of 51:49. Uprated engines were installed in 1936 and MTOW was boosted to 52,000 pounds and the ratio improved to 45:55.

Martin's M-130 was made mainly with 24ST aluminum alloy, riveted and braced, with two cantilever outer panels for wings of box girder construction. The wing area aft of the rear spar was fabric-covered. Tail surfaces were monoplane type with a single fin and rudder. Tabs were attached to the rudder, elevator, and ailerons for trimming the ship in flight. A wing area of 2,315 square feet yielded a relatively conservative wing loading of 22 pounds per square foot. Martin preferred not to build an aircraft with a complicated flap, such as that on the S-42.

The M-130 had the first double-row radial engines on a commercial airplane: four 14-cylinder Pratt & Whitney Twin Wasps, each pumping out 830 horsepower and driving a Hamilton Standard constant-speed, three-bladed propeller with brakes. The engines were set into the leading edge of each wing, which were mounted on a vertical extension above the combination hull and fuselage. Later, the engines would be upgraded to 900 horsepower behemoths. Consuming fuel at an average rate of one gallon a mile, the M-130's fuel capacity was 12 tons, or about 4,000 gallons. Thousands of pounds of weight were saved by simply doing away with heavy fuel tanks because gas was carried in the double bottoms of the sea wings, *sponsons*, which also provided lateral buoyancy and replaced the wing float pontoons used on former flying boats.

The aircraft's radio station housed two transmitters, both with fixed antennas and trailing wire, as well as a direction-finding receiver and a specially designed goniometer loop to take radio bearings on signals from coastal stations and ships.

Elegance found in the S-40, or even the S-42, had passed, but passenger accommodation in the M-130 was certainly spacious. The cabin interior, 45 feet long, was divided into eight compartments, the largest was a 16-foot-long lounge. Company literature described the compartments as follows (from the nose):

a — forward anchor compartment.

b — "control room" for the pilots, plus the radio operator's station; beneath the flooring on the starboard side was a mail and cargo compartment.

c — forward baggage compartment on the starboard side with an entrance hatch; on the port side, a galley.

d — forward passenger compartment.

e — flight mechanic's station located immediately forward of the wing and above the forward passenger compartment.

f — lounge compartment accommodating 16 passengers.

g — two aft compartments accommodating 10 passengers each.

h — "toilet room" (with two lavatories) located on the starboard side and a steward's office on the port side.

i — aft baggage compartment and entrance hatch.

Compartments were about 11 feet wide, with settees that were convertible to bunks. Ten large square windows, which could be opened in flight, were spaced along the hull. The galley was equipped with a refriger-

Interior details of Martin M-130, which probably was not as comfortable as the illustration.

ator, sink, and electric grill for preparing hot meals. For the seven-man crew there was little in the way of amenities, but they could rest, two at a time, in bunks in the tail of the aircraft.

The Pan American M-130 was rated to carry 43 passenger, but this was no more than self-serving airline fiction. It actually meant there were, potentially, 43 *seats.* In practice, the aircraft would often fly the Pacific with more crew than passengers, and, despite the ingenious use of the sponsoons, much of the cabin space would be taken up with extra fuel tanks. What, in fact, was Pan American to do with these expensive airplanes? The obvious answer was not trans-Pacific service.

On the Atlantic route, the critical distance was the 2,000-mile gap between Newfoundland and Ireland; in the Pacific it was the 2,410 miles between California and Hawaii, 17 percent longer.

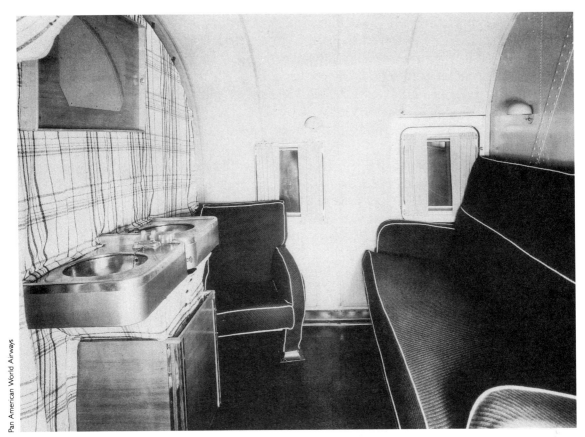

State Room of the Martin M-130.

If you assumed a cruising speed of 130 mph, all other things being equal, the Newfoundland-Ireland hop takes 15.3 hours. With fuel consumption at, say, 850 pounds per hour, 13,855 pounds would be needed for the trip with a one-hour reserve.

The California-Hawaii flight, on the other hand, would take 18.5 hours and 16,575 pounds of fuel, about one-and-a-half tons more than the Atlantic trip. Fly from California to Hawaii and you have the capability to fly to any point on the globe. You can stretch these figures out for any headwind you care to calculate, but while the M-130 could fly these distances, it was not going to lift much of a payload. The Martins "were close to marginal as to load," stated William Masland, a Pan Am captain who flew the M-130. No airplane in the 1930s, in fact, flying those routes, was going to carry 43 passengers. The mail contracts were going to be the only thing that would keep Pam Am and its Martins financially afloat.

On December 20, 1934, "Sweet Sixteen" was the first aircraft ready for its flight trials and was towed down the Middle River to Chesapeake Bay; modifications while the three aircraft were still under construction had reversed the order of completion. There was a brisk northwest wind of about 30 mph. Pilot Ken Ebel taxied upwind and downwind, getting a feel of the aircraft.

Taxiing back to a launch moored at a buoy, he let off the six men of the mooring crew. Then, with L.C. McCarty as copilot and Otto Jent, the flight mechanic, Ebel opened the throttles. The mighty aircraft churned forward, throwing up clouds of spray. It was only intended to be a taxiing test at full throttle, but the M-130 twice left the water, spending a total of a dozen seconds in the air. After some consternation in the cockpit, it was discovered that trim tabs had worked themselves into the climbing position.

Now came the planned first flight. Ebel taxied the ship three miles out into Chesapeake Bay. With a roar, the M-130 took off. Ebel climbed to 2,000 feet and made two flights of 20 and 18 minutes each. The M-130 would attain a top speed of 181 mph at 8,000 feet, a cruising speed of 157 mph, and a service ceiling of 20,000 feet.

The acceptance ceremony for the first M-130 took place in Baltimore on October 9, 1935. Martin could not appear because of illness, so Trippe presided with Lindbergh by his side. The audience was packed with Washington officials. NC-14716 was commissioned and handed over to the airline, and 12 days later Pan Am was awarded the trans-Pacific mail contract; there were no other bidders. Significantly, it was granted to Pan American by a special panel that included the secretaries of war and the navy; war was rumbling below the horizon of the Pacific, like an approaching storm, gathering strength.

This was Pan Am's first aircraft that the Lone Eagle did not have a significant role in flight testing. Only months before had been the sensational trial of the kidnapper and killer of the infant Charles Lindbergh Jr. Hounded by the press, Lindbergh and his wife had practically gone into hiding. The tragic kidnapping and the carnival atmosphere of the trial were corroding their spirit. In a few weeks, the Lindberghs would leave to take up residence in England.

Again, the new aircraft was flown to Pan Am's Caribbean proving ground, where it put in 10,000 miles flying between Miami and Puerto Rico. Then, once more, Musick flew west across the Gulf of Mexico and then across Mexico to Acapulco. Following in the footsteps of the S-42, the Martin turned north and landed at Alameda, where it was to be gussied up for its maiden flight across the Pacific.

Jones corner

Once in the air on November 22, the crew settled down for a long flight and took off their uniforms; Second Officer George King put on red pajamas and bedroom slippers. Eight hours later, the Clipper was 1,200 miles out over the Pacific. It was a magnificently clear night. Radio contact with the Pam Am stations at Alameda, Los Angeles, Honolulu, and Midway came in loud and clear. Along the way, greetings were picked up from the Coast Guard cutter *Itasca*, the Norwegian motorship *Roseville*, and the U.S.S. *Wright*.

About 300 miles out from Hawaii, they saw the first layers of cloud above the islands, and 200 miles out, they sighted the smoke from Mount Moloki. Musick ordered the crew to get into uniform and shave with cold water. The sun was already high when they came gliding into Honolulu. Landing time was 10:19 a.m., and the flight had taken 21 hours, 4 minutes.

The *China Clipper* was loaded and checked during the night for a dawn takeoff. Twenty-one crates of food, including Thanksgiving turkeys, cranberries, and sweet potatoes were loaded. More mail sacks went into the hold, and then 14 passengers, complete base staffs to replace those on Midway and Wake, plus four Chinese cooks and a waiter for Wake Island, came on board.

At 6:35 a.m., to the accompaniment of cheers from hundreds of people watching from pleasure craft, the Clipper was off again. Squall lines barred the way to Midway, but the Clipper roared on at 2,000 feet, staying beneath the clouds. It flew on over Perouse Pinnacle and French Frigate Shoals, sharp points of rock jutting from the sea, and then, at 2 p.m., it circled the barren island and landed, only one minute behind schedule after a flight of eight hours.

Daylight, Sunday, November 24: The Clipper was already loaded and checked out. This time it would carry only nine non-revenue passengers and three tons of cargo; airborne at 6:12 a.m. Like a stone skipped across the Pacific Ocean by a huge hand, the M-130 winged toward Wake. The international date line was coming up. They crossed the line 203 miles west of Midway, flying on instruments, in heavy cloud; a goodwill message was received from the Matson liner, S.S. *President Lincoln*.

Soon after 1 p.m., they were coming up on Wake, and at 1:38 p.m. local time, Tuesday, November 26, the Clipper landed in the lagoon, loosing one day due to the date line. They had covered the 1,252 miles from Midway at an average speed of 148.7 mph. Musick and his crew was given a tour of the island by a happy George Bicknell, Pam Am's base manager. The facilities were identical to those at Midway except for a pavilion at the pier head.

The *China Clipper* departed Wake at dawn on Wednesday, November 27. Cloud base was 2,000 feet and for the first three hours of the flight they stayed below it. They passed over the U.S.S. *Chester*; more greetings were exchanged. Approaching Guam, navigator Noonan took radio bearings from nine stations, including the Japanese radio station on Rota, an island about 50 miles north of Guam. They sighted Mount Tejoe, and the Clipper landed at Apra Harbor at 3:05 p.m. Guam time.

They were now on the last leg of the journey. Musick taxied out into the harbor on a rather rough sea at 6:12 a.m. on November 29 and eased the M-130 into the air. They had stayed an extra day in Guam to keep on the original schedule. Above the clouds, they found a tailwind that boosted the ground speed to 200 mph.

Most of the day the Clipper stayed between 6,000 and 8,000 feet, and then descended, dodging squalls. Ahead, the high mountains of Luzon rose above the sea, and with an enthusiastic escort of Army planes, they dropped down into Manila harbor at 3:32 p.m., November 29.

The entire crossing of 8,210 miles of ocean had taken the Clipper 59:48, 12 minutes early according to the original schedule of 60 hours.

The Clipper taxied toward the Pan Am landing float and was surrounded by swarms of pleasure watercraft; one high mast tore away an antenna wire. The crew stepped ashore to thunderous cheers from the crowd. Musick was asked to comment on the flight. He stepped to the microphone and looked off toward something on the horizon.

"Without incident," he said.

The prolonged roar of the crowd forced officials to cut short their speeches, and Harold Bixby, Pan Am's Far East manager, took Musick to the Manila Hotel, overlooking the harbor. Hordes of reporters still hung around him, but all they got from him was, "We're glad to be here."

On Monday, December 2 at 2:53 a.m., the *China Clipper* left Manila for the return trip. A heavy load and a treacherous 21-knot crosswind forced it to fly out to sea at barely three hundred feet off the water, but gradually it pulled up to a 3,000 foot cruising altitude. Suddenly, the number four engine began losing oil and Musick shut it down. Squall after squall hit the huge airplane, but Musick brought it into Guam toward evening. Storms were hammering at the island, and Pam Am mechanics worked through a wild night to repair the engine.

The Martin was airborne again at 6:11 the next morning, racing out of Guam ahead of a squall line. But the weather was deteriorating. They rode out a storm with winds clocked at 70 mph, in one hour passing through eight separate rain squalls. Yet the big Clipper seemed impervious, winging on above the storm-churned ocean. By the time they landed at

Wake at 8:57 p.m., however, the weather had improved and flying was smooth.

The Wake-Midway hop was uneventful, and soon they were taking off for Honolulu, carrying 18 Pam Am employees on their way home. To make sure they arrived in San Francisco during daylight hours, the Clipper left Honolulu at 3:02 a.m. Hawaii time on Thursday, December 5, for the last leg of its historic flight. The Martin flew from Pearl Harbor on a northwesterly course that brought it to a point some three hundred miles north· of the halfway point between Hawaii and California. Here, they picked up tailwinds and rode them east. For future reference, the crew named the point Jones Corner. When asked why later, the crew looked perplexed, no one knew. But it's been Jones Corner ever since.

As they winged across the sky toward California, navigator Noonan, probably at the urging of Pan Am's public relations department, sent a long message:

EXCLUSIVE BY NOONAN NAVIGATOR CHINA CLIPPER, NEVER IN MY LIFE HAVE I SEEN SO MANY STARS OR BEEN SO CLOSE TO THEM . . . WE ARE UP TEN THOUSAND FEET A MILE BELOW US THERES A MATTRESS OF BLUE WHITE CLOUDS HALF A MILE THICK STOP THE MATE OF A SURFACE SHIP WOULD REPORT QUOTE SKY OVERCAST UNQUOTE BUT ITS CLEAR AS MOUNTAIN AIR UP HERE AND ABOUT AS COLD . . . WRITING THIS IN AN EASY CHAIR IN CABIN RELIEVED IN CHART ROOM BY JUNIOR FLIGHT OFFICER GEORGE KING STOP COMMANDER MUSICK AND FIRST OFFICER SULLIVAN LEANING BACK IN THEIR SEATS IN COCKPIT CHECKING OPERATION OF AUTOMATIC PILOT CONNECTED WITH CONTROLS STOP FIRST ENGINEER C D WRIGHT BACK IN HIS MAZE DIALS AND GADGETS IN UPPER FLIGHT DECK TAKING NUMEROUS READINGS DOWN ON CHART STOP RADIO OFFICER JARBOE SEATED BACK OF PILOTS EARPHONES ON HEAD DRAWING RADIO BEELINE ON GOLDEN GATE THOUSAND MILES AWAY STOP SECOND ENGINEER IN AFT COMPARTMENT TAKING OFFWATCH SIESTA ONLY MAN NOT ON DUTY . . . ITS A GLORIOUS NIGHT COULD SEE OCEAN AND LIGHTS OF THREE SHIPS AT VARIOUS TIMES COMMA AND ROLLING BANK CLOUDS MILE BELOW UNTIL MOON WENT DOWN AFTER THAT FLASHED ALONG AT ONE HUNDRED FIFTY TO ONE HUNDRED SEVENTY MILES HOUR OVER BLUEBLACK CUSHION AIR AND UNDER SPARKLING ARRAY BILLION STARS IN DARK BLUE VELVET SKY. . . .

The engineer probably deserved his sleep. The two engineers, in fact, were the unsung heroes of the trip. Both had averaged less than four hours sleep a night. They had managed to leave the aircraft only at Honolulu and Manila and had spent the rest of the time constantly monitoring the engines and checking cargo loading.

As they approached San Francisco, Radio Officer Jarboe was busy giving their position to the Pan Am stations as far away as Shanghai and Miami. A hundred miles off the coast, the Clipper plowed into heavy overcast. Sullivan, at the controls, dropped lower, trying to find cloud base.

After 17 hours in the air, the *China Clipper* completed an instrument landing on San Francisco Bay, arriving at 10:36 a.m., December 6. The eastward crossing of the Pacific had been flown in 63 hours, 24 minutes. The entire round trip of 16,420 miles had taken the Clipper 123 hours, 12 minutes, at an average speed of 133.2 mph.

The flight of the *China Clipper* set 19 world records and became part of air transportation history. Now a letter could be sent from the Philippines and be in Washington or New York within a week. Mail from Honolulu could reach its destination within 24 hours after leaving the islands. The world had suddenly grown smaller.

Back in Baltimore, meanwhile, the other two Martins were being readied for service. The *Philippine Clipper* was accepted by Pan Am on November 14, 1935, and flown to Alameda by Captain Ralph A. Dahlstrom. On the 715's first flight to Manila, it was commanded by Captain John Tilton, a somewhat dashing, handsome man who everyone called Dad from his habit of calling everyone else son. Tilton had flown the Pacific before, having captained the *Pan American Clipper* to Guam back in August. Following the *China Clipper*'s first flight to the Orient, Musick had time to instruct both Tilton and Dahlstrom, who was going to act as first officer on the *Philippine Clipper*'s inaugural flight, and to bring them up-to-date on conditions at the Pan Am bases across the Pacific.

The *Philippine Clipper* left for Manila on December 9, 1935, carrying three non-revenue Pan Am passengers. Five days later, after 58 hours, 37 minutes, in the air, NC-14715 landed on Manila Bay. A typhoon kept the ship anchored until December 23 before it could head for home. As Tilton positioned the Clipper for take off and pushed the throttles forward, a sailboat suddenly cut across the aircraft's path, and it was only by cutting power and swerving violently that Tilton avoided a collision. Another hazard of flying boat travel.

The return trip was routine until the hop from Honolulu to Alameda, when an engine overheated. Tilton was forced to dump fuel and return to Pearl Harbor. The problem fixed, he again started for California, but the gremlins seemed to have it in for the *Philippine Clipper* on this flight. About

800 miles off the California coast, the outboard left engine had to be shut down. The old problem of overheating again. The Clipper landed at Alameda December 26; flying time from Manila was 58 hours, 43 minutes.

Tilton went on to fly the *Philippine Clipper* regularly and became the senior pilot of the Pan Am's Pacific Division; later, he was the airline's chief pilot. It was Tilton who flew the NC-14715 to Hong Kong to link with CNAC service before an S-42B was permanently assigned to the Hong Kong-Manila hop. Taking an average of about 120 to 125 hours flying time, the Alameda-Manila-Alameda runs settled down to a fairly routine operation, enlivened now and then by moments of terror. On one flight to Manila, for example, the *Philippine Clipper* lost an engine past the point of no return out of Guam. Still hundreds of miles from the coast of Luzon, a second engine quit. Tilton started to get worried. Then, just as the Clipper crossed the mountains east of Manila, a third engine packed up. Tilton was now hanging on the wheel, sweating it out. Still a few hundred feet up from the surface of the water, the fourth engine suddenly quit. They got down safely.

The third Martin to leave the factory, meanwhile, was flown to Miami for flight testing. One of the early passengers allowed to take a flight on the 714 was John A. Vianna, a jovial businessman from Rio de Janeiro. Although his comments on the flight were later written into a publicity release by Pan Am's busy public relations department, Vianna was obviously thrilled with the experience.

"When you ride in Uncle Sam's largest airplane," enthused the Brazilian, "you are sitting in big easy chairs in a lounge almost as large as some sitting rooms. As this ship's interior is arranged, 50 people would 'rattle around' in it." In contrast to what we shall see later, Vianna also found the Martin amazingly quiet. "The most striking thing about the aircraft is its silence in the air," he goes on, "we easily conversed from one compartment to another."

NC-14714 joined its sisters at Alameda on December 24, and Musick flew it to Honolulu, where he arrived with an escort of 20 Air Corps airplanes from Wheeler Field. Three thousand people, including the territorial governor, were waiting to greet him, and the 714 was christened the *Hawaiian Clipper* by pouring coconut milk over her snub nose.

By early-1936, all three Martin Clippers were in service in the Pacific. The $417,000 that Trippe had paid for each aircraft, against $242,000 for the S-42s, represented a fortune. In comparison, the Douglas DC-2, the largest and most modern landplane then in service with Pan Am, cost $78,000. But perhaps Trippe consoled himself with the thought that with the Martin Clippers, he had bought the acknowledged queen of the skies.

The chartered *North Haven* once again, sailed for the Pacific in January 1936, this time to build luxurious passenger accommodations on Midway, Wake, and Guam. A flight to the Orient on a Pan Am Clipper was expensive: round trip to Honolulu was $648; round trip to Manila, $1,438.20 — one way, $799. The equivalent today would be a fare of around $10,000, about twice what it costs to fly the Concorde. Only the rich were going to fly the Clippers, and the accommodations were built accordingly.

Hotels were designed by the architectural firm of Delano & Aldrich, constructed with two sections projecting from a central lobby. Each of the hotel's 45 rooms came with a wide, screened veranda and a bathroom with hot-water shower. Lobbies were decorated with aquariums filled with brilliant fish native to the atolls.

Meals were served in a spacious, plant-bedecked dining room by Chamorro waiters (natives of Guam) in spotless white jackets, and strict rules required that all Pan Am employees wear coats and ties when eating in the dining room with passengers present. Surrounding the hotels were palm-lined gardens, every shrub and tree brought in by the *North Haven*, creating a tropical, if somewhat artificial, ambience.

Far across the Pacific, meanwhile, the Japanese were making their displeasure over the *China Clipper* flight known to Pan American Airways. Even while the Clipper's inaugural flight was still in progress, a CNAC transport flying from Hong Kong to Tientsin was forced down by two Japanese fighter planes. Somehow, the Japanese seemed to have troops right on the spot, and the aircraft was immediately surrounded by Japanese soldiers with fixed bayonets. The American pilot and the passengers were accused of spying and photographing Japanese troop movements from the air. It looked as though nothing would calm the irate Japanese. Then, a few hours later, the tension seemed to dissipate, and the CNAC aircraft was allowed to proceed. But Japan had made its point. There was a limit to which it would tolerate an American presence in the Pacific and the Far East.

Even uglier was an incident that occurred on January 5, 1936. Captain Sullivan spent the morning taking the *China Clipper* on a short test flight over San Francisco Bay. Satisfied that all was in order, the aircraft was readied for an afternoon departure for Honolulu. Sullivan revved the engines at 4:50 p.m. and guided the giant ship out from the dock at Alameda toward the takeoff point. Suddenly, there was a jarring thump and the aircraft shuddered. Sullivan's first thought was that he had hit a shifting sandbar, and he returned to base.

When the Clipper was hauled out of the water, the ground crew was astonished to find 10 long gashes in the hull. Pan Am apparently clamped a news blackout on the incident, but after investigating the bottom of the Bay around the Pan Am base, Karl Leuder, the Alameda base manager, reported a discovery: several concrete pedestals with iron rods embedded in them had been placed so that they stuck up to within a few feet of the surface. The FBI and Pan Am investigators apparently never found the origin of the objects, or if they did, the information has never been released. But to some, looking for darker reasons, it pointed to a coming confrontation with the growing Japanese Empire.

The *Hawaiian Clipper* had the honor of opening passenger service to the Orient on October 21, 1936. The first trip carried nine passengers, including Mr. and Mrs. Cornelius V. Whitney; Sonny was now chairman of Pan American Airways. On November 2, the *Philippine Clipper* set down in Hong Kong, although an S-42B eventually linked China and Manila.

The *China Clipper*, in the meantime, was a leading attraction at the International Exposition held on Treasure Island in San Francisco Bay. The Sweet Sixteen was also kept busy flying in fresh orchids and other tropical blossoms to keep the Pacific island exhibits well supplied.

A year after passenger service opened, the Clippers had logged 2,731,312 miles in the air and had carried 1,986 passengers and 506,000 pounds of cargo. Between November 22, 1935, and December 13, 1937, the *China Clipper* alone made 30 round-trips between San Francisco and Manila. The following year, the 716 would make 12 round trip-flights between San Francisco and Hong Kong, plus two round-trips between San Francisco and Manila.

The Clippers were a magnet for publicity, and Pan Am's New York headquarters beat the drums at every opportunity. A deal was struck with Warner Brothers to produce the movie *China Clipper*, making sure that the airline had the right to censor technical details and any part of the story that related to winning mail contracts. As far as the public was concerned, Pan Am wanted everyone to believe that passenger travel was at the heart of its operation. It was, certainly, more glamorous than hauling letters, and a happy public meant happy congressmen.

The Musick-like pilot was played by stony-faced Humphrey Bogart, working for a driving, visionary chief, a sort of American Riviere, the tough manager in Antoine de Saint-Exupery's *Night Flight*. After battling through a typhoon to reach the Clipper's destination on time, Bogart grumbles "how swell it would be if he'd said thanks." Those who worked for Trippe must have thought the line glorious.

China Clipper came out to rave reviews and was the hit of the year, although it somehow left the impression that the Clipper was flying all the way to China, when, in fact, negotiations were still in progress. On August 6, 1937, Trippe stood in the Oval Office at the White House and received the Collier Trophy for distinguished service to aviation from the hands of President Roosevelt: "You well deserve it."

Those who watched said Trippe's usually bland features suddenly flashed with that "devilish" smile. But afterward, he gave no sign of being satisfied with the honor. He still had much more to do.

Performance Data
Martin M-130

Type	Boat
Length	90 feet
Wing span	130 feet (sponsoon span: 34 feet)
Height	25 feet
Gross weight	51,000 pounds (later 52,000 pounds)
Engines	P&W Twin Wasp × 4
Horsepower	800 (later 900)
Range	3,000 statute miles (passenger)/ 4,000 (mail only)
Fuel capacity	4,000 gallons
Useful load	22,784 pounds
High speed	180 mph
Crusing speed	157 mph
Service ceiling	20,000 feet
Passengers	43 (as a sleeper: 18)
Crew	7

Pan American Martin M-130s
(in order of construction number)

Reg. No.	Name	Remarks
NC-14714	Hawaiian Clipper	Began world's first transocean scheduled air service, 10/21/36. Name changed to *Hawaii Clipper*. Lost Pacific Ocean, 7/28/38.
NC-14715	Philippine Clipper	Destroyed in crash, Boonville, Calif., 1/21/43.
NC-14716	China Clipper	Began world's first trans-Pacific mail service, 11/22/35. Destroyed Port of Spain, Trinidad, 1/8/45.

Call of
the South Seas

Trippe and his family made a journey around the world in October 1936. They took along a party of seven, including Senator William McAdoo, chairman of the senate commerce committee; Wallace Alexander, chairman of Matson Steamship Company; Cornelius ("Sonny") Whitney, the rich socialite who was Trippe's figurehead as chairman of Pan American Airways; and Roy Howard, chairman of Scripps-Howard newspapers.

Weight requirements meant that only eight could be taken on the M-130 Clipper on the San Francisco-Honolulu hop, and the rest travelled on the Matson liner *Lurline*, a popular sight on the California-to-Hawaii run during those years. As the ship approached Honolulu at dawn, a tiny speck on the horizon grew rapidly until the Martin Clipper roared over the ship, Captain John Tilton banking the aircraft. Betty Trippe, standing on the ship's bridge next to her husband, had tears of joy running down her face.

The group attended a Hawaiian luau with hula dancers and roasted pig and the Trippes went surfing. The next day at 4 a.m., the entire party assembled to board the *Philippine Clipper* for the rest of the trip across the Pacific. On each island — Midway, Wake, and Guam — they were welcomed at the newly constructed hotels; the Pan Am service was faultless. When the airliner landed at Wake, everyone insisted that Betty Trippe step ashore first so that she could claim to be the first "white woman" to set foot on the island.* The path to the hotel, she noted later, was made of crushed coral lined with newly planted trees, and the party staggered into the building almost wilting from the island's furnace-like heat.

Arriving at Manila, the Trippes dined with President Quezon of the Philippines before flying to Hong Kong. En route, Trippe sent a message to the White House:

> FEW MINUTES WE ARE LANDING AT MACAO AND HONG KONG COMPLETING THE FIRST TRANSPACIFIC PASSENGER FLIGHT TO ASIA FROM THE U.S. WE ARE GLAD TO INFORM YOU THAT THIS FIRST FLIGHT WAS MADE DURING YOUR ADMINISTRATION BY AN AMERICAN COMPANY WITH AIRCRAFT BUILT IN U.S. AND IN CHARGE AMERICAN CAPTAIN AND HIS FIVE FLIGHT OFFICERS.

The touched down in Macao to greet a flag-waving crowd and then attended a three-hour banquet. In Hong Kong the next day, escorted by Harold Bixby, they transferred to a CNAC Douglas Dolphin amphibian for an eight-hour flight to Shanghai. By this time, CNAC aircraft were flying a north-south trunk line connecting Shanghai and Nanking with Canton and Hong Kong; they also flew an east-west route from Nanking to Chungking. Beyond Chungking, a spur line went to Chengtu.

Pan American representatives had assiduously promoted the idea of air travel among rich Chinese merchants and government officials. China had no railroads to the interior, and air transportation offered practically the only means of unifying the country, if you didn't count camel caravans and sedan chairs. Airfields were still primitive, but more of them were being built. The small Loening amphibians, handy to land on lake or river, were being replaced by DC-2 landplanes carrying 14 passengers and a crew of three.

The Trippes were received with a round of cordial formalities by Chinese officials; they met Generalissimo and Madame Chiang Kai-shek, and Trippe was pleased to see that CNAC, and by association, Pan Am, enjoyed very close connections with the Nationalist Chinese government.

Back in Hong Kong once more, some of the party returned to the

---

*The businessmen and flight crew were wrong. Betty was not the first of either her race or gender to find herself on Wake Island. On March 4, 1866, the ship *Libelle*, en route to Hong Kong out of the Sandwich Islands, struck the reef surrounding Wake and was lost. Among the 29 who made it to the shore, was Madame Anna Bishop Schultz, an opera singer of note, and her husband, Martin Schultz. For twenty-one days they lived on the island, and then Madame Schultz and twenty-one others decided to chance the open sea in the ship's longboat and make for Guam, 1,500 miles away. They buried $300,000 worth of quicksilver, part of the ship's cargo, and set sail. Apparently the boat reached Guam, and Madame Schultz continued with her world tour. The quicksilver was never recovered.

United States, while the Trippes continued their journey on foreign craft. They boarded an Imperial Airways landplane for the long journey to Europe across India, Arabia, Egypt, the Mediterranean countries and, finally, France, where they stayed at the Ritz in Paris.

Next stop was London and a reunion with the Lindberghs before flying on to Berlin. In Hitler's Germany, they visited the impressive Air Ministry, lunched with aviation officials brimming with small courtesies (Goering was not present), and noted with alarm the frank preparations for war.

Whatever civilian aircraft they saw, however, from French flying boats to German landplanes, Trippe was happy to observe that they were inferior to the Clippers. The Trippes then boarded the airship *Hindenburg* for a flight to Rio de Janeiro and made the last leg home on a Pan Am Sikorsky. Trippe could now claim another first because they were the first travelers to fly entirely around the world by civilian aircraft.

Trippe's imagination was fired to even greater heights after his long, impressive tour of some 36,500 miles in almost two months. More routes had to be added so that his airline could girdle the globe. The next time he went on a world trip, it would be Pan American all the way. One opportunity that presented itself was a commercial route from Honolulu south to Australia and New Zealand.

New Zealand joins the system

As in the Atlantic, opposition to Pan American landing rights in Australia came primarily from Britain's Imperial Airways. Imperial linked up with Queensland and Northern Territory Aerial Services, better known as QANTAS, at Singapore. The British hoped to extend this service across the Pacific to Canada, using British-owned Fiji as a refueling point. But without landing rights in Hawaii, its plans were stopped.

On this point, however, the United States government was adamant, no foreign airlines landing at Honolulu. Trippe needed Fiji, too, but if there was no Hawaii for Imperial, there was no Fiji for Pan Am. For once, the president of Pan Am could do nothing, and it looked like there would be another impasse like the Atlantic.

New Zealand had always self-consciously viewed itself as a back-water, and its government was concerned that it would be left out of the British Empire's world-girdling airline service, the All-Red Route. It was the opening Trippe wanted. If he could not get to Australia, he would settle for New Zealand, and perhaps he didn't need Fiji, either.

Pan Am began a series of negotiations with the New Zealand government, with Harold Gatty, Trippe's representative in Australasia, at one point writing directly to the country's prime minister. The British got wind of the negotiations and exerted tremendous pressure on the New Zealand government, but Gatty, the former navigator for Wiley Post on his round-the-world flight in 1931, hung on tenaciously. Get New Zealand into the mainstream of the world was his siren song. It worked. Although Pan Am's unilateral negotiations with foreign governments again did not go down well in Washington, Gatty secured landing rights for Pan Am at Auckland on March 11, 1937. Pan Am had been ready for weeks.

The airline's Martin M-130s were totally committed to the Alameda-Manila route, and Trippe assigned the pioneering work in the South Pacific to the Sikorsky S-42s. For the first survey flight to Auckland, Ed Musick once again took the controls of NC-823M, the *Pan American Clipper*. (This aircraft would later be given yet a third name, the *Hong Kong Clipper*, and would be the first Sikorsky used on the Hong Kong-Manila route.)

Pilot's luck

Musick was no longer the exuberant, young pilot who saw every flight as an adventure. He was aging from the strain of Pacific flying and overwork. Pan Am was engaged in a worldwide struggle for routes. The enormous costs of operating the *North Haven* and building bases across the Pacific had drastically eaten into profits. The answer, as Trippe saw it, was more and longer routes.

As senior pilot, Musick was loaded with more responsibilities than just flying airplanes. The operations manager at Alameda was transferred to the Atlantic Division, and Musick had to take over his workload. His desk piled high with paper, he often went home too tired to eat. Cleo urged him to give up the pioneering flights, perhaps retire or transfer to an easier job. But Musick kept going.

By now he had logged more than 10,000 hours in the air and had flown more than one million miles. He had become a slight, round-shouldered man, almost old at 44. His face was usually set in an inscrutable mask, crows' feet furrowing out from brown eyes searching for something in the distance. He fretted about the publicity chores that the company's public relations department constantly loaded on him.

With Lindbergh now living in England, Musick was boosted as the Number One pilot in the country. They had told him to transmit good copy during his first flight to Honolulu. "Say something about the sunset," they said. He sent, "SUNSET, 6:39."

Once again, the insides of the S-42 were ripped out and filled with pipes and valves. The odor of raw fuel was so strong inside the aircraft that the flight crew had to fly with the windows open, huddled inside heavy clothing to keep warm. The Sikorsky, in fact, was almost a flying gasoline bomb. On the flight to Honolulu, the flight engineer noticed one of the engines was running hot, and Musick decided to dump some gas out of the wings to lighten the ship enough to shut down the engine. The dump valves opened and hundreds of gallons spilled into the sky.

A little later, a worried navigator came forward with the news that he had seen drops of gasoline inside the aircraft. Everyone practically froze. It meant that some of the dumped gas had blown back into the ship. A spark could blow them up like a fireball. They pushed open as many windows as they could, shut down everything electrical including the radio, and flew on. No explosion occurred, but everyone sighed with relief when the hull of the S-42 touched water at Hawaii.

At Honolulu, Musick met Amelia Earhart on her way around the world. Her plane had crashed while landing in Hawaii.

"Rotten luck," he said to her. "Don't let it whip you."

She had only a few more months to live. Flying east from New Guinea on her second try, Earhart and her navigator, Fred Noonan, would disappear in July 1937 somewhere near the Japanese-held Micronesian Islands in the Central Pacific.* Although later there were rumors that she was on some sort of intelligence mission, the mystery has never been solved.

The *North Haven* had sailed throughout the region in early 1935, taking soundings and weather readings and surveying a number of islands, including Jarvis, Baker, and Howland, the latter only 400 miles from the Micronesias. One tiny spot the ship had surveyed was Kingman's Reef, a dot in the ocean some 1,100 miles southwest of Hawaii. Trippe had done some creative thinking. It would be the Sikorsky's first stop. Here, the chartered steamer *North Wind* with a radio direction finder was positioned as a floating base. On St. Patrick's Day, 1937 Musick took off for the South Pacific.

Reaching Kingman's Reef, the S-42 swept in over the tiny atoll, while the *North Wind's* siren blew continuously. Pago Pago in Samoa, however, was another matter. As Musick flew over the lagoon, he saw that it was no more than a beautiful bathtub, a perfect stretch of water — surrounded by steep mountains reaching to 1,500 feet. It took Musick two tries, the second time he dove straight down the side of a mountain with flaps full down and hit the water hard.

As soon as the Clipper came to a stop, dozens of outrigger canoes

---

*Noonan had left Pan American somewhat under a cloud. Some would say his drinking was the cause.

and praus put out and gathered around the aircraft like a strange cluster of chicks around their mother. The Pan Am crew waited for three days at Samoa for a gale to blow itself out and conditions were good enough for a safe takeoff. They then flew the 1,800 miles to Auckland, where a crowd of 30,000 waited to greet them. The Pan Am crew was cheered again and again. Even Musick was overwhelmed and grinned back.

But Imperial Airways could not be ignored. Shortly after the S-42 landed, a Short Brothers flying boat, the *Centaurus*, dropped down and anchored nearby. The two pilots shook each other's hand somewhat cautiously.

On the way home, the lagoon at Pago Pago looked even smaller than before. Once they had landed, Musick ordered all excess weight, even the souvenirs the crew had picked up from here and there, to be dumped overboard. He was becoming tired of taking chances.

Back at Alameda once more, Musick was surprised to hear from New York that regular service to New Zealand would be flown by the Sikorskys. The company was not waiting for the new Boeings (the 314) to come into service, and the Martins were being flown practically around the clock. Extra tanks were installed on NC-16734, an S-42B now named the *Samoan Clipper*, in Honolulu. After more than a week of tinkering with engines and fuel flows, the Pan Am crew took off on the inaugural commercial flight on December 3. Musick landed at Auckland several days later. He would make one more trip out to the South Pacific.

Canton Island

The dangers of missing Kingman's Reef and the difficult landing site at Pago Pago caused enough misgivings among Pan Am's aircrews that the company now looked into an alternative route. This was via an even remoter speck in the Pacific, Canton Island, but it presented a problem for Pan Am because there was some dispute over the title. The island was claimed by both the British and the United States.

Trippe made his usual visit to Washington and presented his standard argument, which normally went along the lines of patriotism; "If we don't do it now, the foreigners will beat us." One of his arguments for building a terminal on Wake Island was that he had "heard" that the Japanese were planning to build a base there.

With Canton, he also pushed the idea that it was one of the "keys" to the defense of the Panama Canal, even though Canton is closer to Australia than Central America. Whether Trippe actually believed these arguments himself or not is conjecture, but he found many Capitol Hill ears willing to listen to him and he soon received firm, but "unofficial," approval.

On May 18, 1937, a stormy day, the *North Haven* hove to off Canton Island. The island was no more than a white blur in the driving rain. In a few days the weather cleared, and the crew began offloading supplies. The British, however, had somehow caught wind of the enterprise, and as supplies were being lightered ashore and shacks were being built, the cruiser *Essex* appeared, determined to enforce the Empire's sovereignty.

They found a party of Yanks digging guano for shipment to the United States, claiming immunity under an old law that gave them right to any such activity provided the island was uninhabited. The Brits raised a doubtful eyebrow, and then built a postal shack on their half of the island and garrisoned it with one stalwart Briton. Possession established, the cruiser sailed away.

The lonely Briton stayed there for some years, apparently forgotten by his countrymen. When his supplies ran out, the Americans took him under their wing. It was not until 1942 that someone remembered him and took him back home. Meanwhile, in March 1938 President Roosevelt issued an executive order claiming Canton Island and Enderbury Island, another atoll in the Phoenix Group, for commercial aviation needs. Roosevelt insisted that this had "nothing to do with war."

Trippe asked for a navy supply ship to transport Pan American engineers to the island, which was granted. In December, Pan Am was also given permission to establish a base in New Caledonia, a French colony. Trippe had bypassed Fiji. As for Canton, he was content to lease the property rights of the United States half of the island from the government for $1 a year.

Death of an aviator

Before Canton Island and New Caledonia could become operational, Musick made his third trip to the South Pacific: Pago Pago, January 11, 1938, dawn.

Seven men filed on board the *Samoan Clipper* for the final leg of the flight to New Zealand. Musick was flying with a new crew. He went through his usual meticulous preparations for taking off, even carefully wiping the seat and controls with a rag. He would never take off an aircraft until he felt perfectly comfortable; even the creases in his pants had to be right. The sky was clear, and the aircraft was loaded with 2,300 gallons of gasoline. The engines fired, and Musick maneuvered the aircraft into position for the takeoff run. He pushed the throttles forward, and they were away.

Two hours later, the ground operator received a message.

OIL LEAK IN NUMBER FOUR ENGINE AM TURNING BACK TO PAGO PAGO MUSICK.

Another message, about 50 minutes later, said they were going to jettison most of the fuel. Musick would not land the Clipper on the restricted lagoon at Pago Pago with a full fuel load. At 7:59 a.m. came another message that the Clipper was 70 miles out from the harbor. More fuel was being dumped. Then silence.

A search by the U.S. Navy minesweeper *Avocet* found an oil slick, clothing, and debris. They picked up the remains of a coat with the radio officer's wings pinned to it. Pages from an engineering log floated on the water. Nearby were parts of the navigator's desk, still with pieces of chart attached. But there was not much else.

A Samoan woman out fishing in a canoe reported later that she had seen the aircraft pass low overhead. She saw liquid spouting from its wings. Then, she said, there was a flash of fire and an immense bang. The airplane had fallen into the sea.

A message went out to all Pan American divisions:

ALL DEPARTMENTS STOP IT IS WITH INEXPRESSIBLE REGRET WE MUST CONFIRM TO YOU THE LOSS OF THE NC-34 WITH ITS ENTIRE CREW IN THE IMMEDIATE VICINITY OF AMERICAN SAMOA AT APPROXIMATELY 1903Z (11:30 A.M. PST) JANUARY ELEVENTH PRESUMABLY FROM A SUDDEN FIRE OF UNDETER- MINED ORIGIN STOP CREW MEMBERS WERE CAPTAIN MUSICK COMMANDING COMMA CAPTAIN CECIL G. SELLARS FIRST OF- FICER COMMA JUNIOR OFFICER PAUL BRUNK COMMA NAVIGA- TION OFFICER FRED MACLEAN COMMA FLIGHT ENGINEERING OFFICERS JACK BROOKS AND JOHN STICKROD COMMA FLIGHT RADIO OPERATOR TOM FINDLEY STOP AT ELEVEN AM LOCAL TIME YOUR STATION . . . PLEASE ARRANGE MEMORIAL TRIB- UTE TO CAPTAIN MUSICK.

It was the first loss of a Pan Am Clipper at sea.

Theorizing about the cause of the explosion eventually pointed to the flap motors igniting gas vapors. Aviation engineers pointed out that Musick would have lowered the flaps in preparation for landing and that he had also just dumped a quantity of fuel. Fumes had most likely collected at the point where the wings joined the hull — where the flap motor was located. As soon as Musick moved the switch. . . .

Three days after the accident, a steamer sailed to the spot where the aircraft went down, its engines stopped. The captain read the burial service as the crew stood silently. A wreath was lowered, and then they sang the hymn, "Abide with Me."

Trippe called the death of Musick and his crew an irreplaceable loss. The U.S. Department of Commerce suspended Pan Am's authority to use Pago Pago. All over the world, the disaster was front-page news. Musick had been the most famous transport pilot in the world, a legend. There was a huge public outcry about cross-ocean routes that were neither desirable nor necessary. Yet Trippe pushed on with his vision, ignoring the charges. Considering aviation today, it is hard to say that he was wrong.

In New Zealand, a country where Musick is especially remembered, there is one memorial to him, at least, that will always live on. The New Zealand government awards the Edwin C. Musick Trophy to "pioneers in advancing safety in aviation." Ed Musick would not have asked for anything more.

10

The golden age of flying

Helen Gierding was on her way to Manila to marry her fiancé Stephen Hagerman, plus she was going to fly there on a Pan American Clipper. She resolved to write it all down, a journal that she could go back to and read one day when it had all faded into history.

She traveled across country by train from her home in New Jersey and she was met in San Francisco by friends, Mr. and Mrs. Victor Savale. They went with her to see her off at the Alameda Clipper terminal. It was January 25, 1937 and at the small, white Pan Am building, the pre-boarding process was a hive of controlled confusion. People were arguing with stewards who were sealing all cameras, which was required by navy regulations passengers were told. Luggage was being weighed and Helen was relieved to see that she was two pounds under the 50-pound limit.

There was a stir as a Pan Am ground crewman chalked something on a board. Passengers strained to see. They would be flying on the *Philippine Clipper*, it announced; Captain Ralph Dahlstrom was the pilot. It was the Pan Am Clipper's 83rd flight across the Pacific.

One bell sounded. The crew, smartly dressed in Pan Am's blue uniforms with white-covered caps, filed on board.

Gierding began to say her good-byes to the Savales and other friends.

Two bells. It was time for the passengers to board. Inside the cabin, the steward was busy getting everyone settled, offering them packets of gum to chew and cotton to place in their ears, "which no one took except for one timid gentleman." There were 13 passengers on the Alameda-Honolulu leg of the trip — two more, Helen later found out, than had ever been carried by the Martin Clipper.

Everyone appeared stiff and a little self-conscious, looking around at each other and grinning "foolishly." Each of the women were assigned one of the bunks, which were arranged in two compartments. The steward showed them how to get in and out, which could be quite a trick, he explained, in rough air.

Finally, the baggage was loaded, the tanks filled, and the last ground crewman jumped ashore. Hatches were clamped shut. The passengers settled into their green lounge chairs, and the steward went around saying, "Fasten the seat belt, please." At 3 p.m., the *Philippine Clipper* taxied out past the breakwater and began its takeoff run, white spray flashing past the windows. It roared up into the sky, circled once, and began the long flight to Hawaii.

Nearly seven months later, a writer and lecturer named Dorothy Kaucher, from Southern California, arranged a loan from a friendly bank manager and followed Helen Gierding to the Orient. Kaucher flew on the *Hawaii Clipper* piloted by Captain Ed Musick, departing from Alameda on August 11, 1937, the 135th Clipper crossing. In the seven months between the trips of these two women, Pan Am had expanded its services in the Far east. On April 21, 1937, the *China Clipper*, piloted this time by Captain William Cluthe, had left the United States carrying 1,200 pounds of mail destined for China and other parts of the Orient. At Manila, the mail was transferred to a Sikorsky S-42 (the *Hong Kong Clipper*), which sped it on to Hong Kong. Eight days later, the first passengers were on their way on a Pan Am Clipper from San Francisco to China.

Traveling with Kaucher that August day in 1937 was an assortment of passengers, including a New York businessman, a Princeton sophomore, an officer in the Chinese Air Force, and a Merchant Marine captain, on his way somewhere, who hammered the side of the cabin with his fist and shouted, "And they call this thing a ship!" Only Kaucher and the Chinese Air Force officer had tickets through to Hong Kong.

Gierding, meanwhile, found the cabin of the Martin chilly and would complain later that she "nearly froze to death." Most of the passengers wore their hats and coats, and some had blankets wrapped around them. One, Helen found out, was Kenneth Parker, president of the Parker Pen Company, who was "very young looking" and a "grand" person. Mining engineer Harry Burmeister, on the other hand, reminded her of the comedian Joe E. Brown.

The passengers chattered on while the steward served a meal that, contrary to Pan Am publicity shots of the "sumptuous dinner hour," Helen found was less than adequate. (Perhaps she was also considering the expense of the flight.) Nevertheless, the indomitable steward worked hard, and she noticed he did not seem to finish his duties until well past midnight.

Kaucher was also chilled; "it seemed too lonely above the sun's warm rays", but, on the other hand, she found the meal "sustaining," a careful choice of word. Later, she watched in fascination as the navigator aft, sitting on the top of a ladder, shot the stars through a hatch. She talked the navigator into letting her take a look and spent several minutes gazing up at the star-filled sky. Both sides of the aisle were lined with canvas-covered compartments for luggage.

A few hours after her dinner, Helen Gierding, hungry and cold, decided to turn in. Trying to undress in the 2X4 foot space between the bunk and the cabin roof was an ordeal, but at last she was between the sheets, only to find herself frying. The bunk was "like a Turkish bath!" A blast of heated air beat down on her from an overhead ventilator. Throwing off the covers, she finally drifted off to sleep, lulled by the dull, shuddering roar of the engines.

Toward dawn, she awoke, dressed, and went to the main cabin. The men had spent the night there, and it was now a mess, with blankets and newspapers thrown together on the floor and empty cups scattered around. The men looked rumpled, their ties loosened, suits creased. They glimpsed the pink and white, sea-edged buildings of Honolulu at 10 a.m., and half an hour later they landed near Diamond Head after a flight of 22 hours, 45 minutes. Ground crewmen pulled the aircraft into the dock, and the steward performed his last passenger rite of the trip, spraying each of them with disinfectant before they went ashore.

After a day of sight-seeing in Honolulu and one night in a hotel, Helen boarded the Clipper again the next morning for the next leg of the trip. Over Kauai, they looked down at "puffy white clouds," and whenever an excited passenger saw something "that looked the least bit interesting," there would be a shout, and everyone would immediately crowd to the windows.

Passengers made the tricky transit from aircraft to shore at Midway by launch, bouncing unsteadily on a choppy sea, and were then driven to the Pan American Hotel in a Ford station wagon. Ready to greet them, on the wide, screened porch of the hotel, were Mr. and Mrs. Clark, the hotel managers. Helen noted it was a one-story building with about 24 rooms. She showered in salty-tasting water from the island's well, later relieved to find that water used for drinking was collected from the rainfall.

Later, she walked around the island among the immense number of strange-looking gooney birds, none of which seemed the slightest bit afraid of humans. She noticed about a half-dozen Orientals and was told that they were Japanese nationals who worked as technicians for the Commercial Pacific Cable Company, which had cable traffic facilities on the island.

To Kaucher, approaching Midway and looking down at the formations of coral in the blue-green water was like seeing grottoes at the bottom of fish bowls. She, too, rode up to the hotel in the battered station wagon, noting the patches of green lawn on either side of the path, constantly watered by lazily turning sprinklers. She later climbed the 92-foot lighthouse tower.

Up at 4:30 the next morning, passengers on the 83rd flight once more rode the launch out to the Clipper, officially departing at 6:30 a.m. Helen was allowed to see the control room while en route to Wake. The navigator, she noted, was as busy as a "one-armed paperhanger," constantly "looking at things and writing things down." Her Clipper landed at Wake at 1:45 p.m. Wake time, January 29, 1937. It was intensely hot, and the passengers went swimming in the remarkably clear water, paddling around the Clipper and watching the ground crew perform its duties.

Kaucher celebrated her crossing of the International Date Line by following the advice of another passenger and "calling today tomorrow." She was also given a certificate signed by the captain:

"From the Domain of Phoebus Apollo, Ruler of the Sun and Heavens. Know all Peoples that Dorothy Kaucher, once earthbound and time-laden, is now declared a subject of the Realm of the Sun and of the Heavens, with the Freedom of our Sacred Eagle. . . ."

A heavy rain was falling when her flight reached Wake, an island, she found, that looked like a narrow horsehoe with the Stars and Stripes and the blue and white flag of Pan American Airways flying over it. The airport manager, wearing starched whites, shook hands with everyone and handed out raincapes. The hotel looked like a "miniature Mt. Vernon on a rock pile," she said. But inside, it was comfortable, with deep wicker chairs, soft lighting, and electric fans — almost a scene, she felt, from *Better Homes and Gardens*. She discovered that the Pan Am base and hotel was actually on Peale Island, but somehow the name of Wake Island had been attached to the base and the entire island group. The island-based Pan Am physician explained to her that Peale was the naturalist on Commodore Wilke's expedition of 1841, but Wake received its name from an English sea captain, Sir William Wake, who sighted the atoll in the 18th century.

She braved the hot sun to try to explore the island, walking through scrubby patches of magnolia and surrounded by clouds of screeching fork-tailed terns. Amid the sand dunes she came across acres of oil and gasoline drums, an immense fuel dump. Soon, she was glad to be back inside the cool hotel. "This Wake sun," said one of the maintenance men, "is no joke."

While the food may have been a little light on the aircraft, Pan Am evidently did not starve its passengers on land. She scanned the handwritten dinner menu reading:

Relishes

Beef Broth   Hearts Lettuce & Asp Tips

Swiss Steak

New Potatoes   Cut String Beans

Sliced Peaches

Asst. Cookies

Cream Cheese & Crackers

Tea   Cocoa   Iced Tea   Coffee   Lemonade

The hotel manager walked down the hall knocking on each door at 4:30 a.m. Kaucher found the early hour "like a 4 a.m. call to go duck hunting." Tables had been set the night before for breakfast in the dining room, coffee cups turned neatly upside down and rolls and fruit placed in the center of the table. The aircraft's crew had already eaten and had left to prepare for the flight.

They had already read the weather reports: scattered showers, chance of a thunderstorm, visibility good, cloud tops at 8,000 to 11,000 feet, barometer steady. It looked like a good day. Kaucher noticed a silver mist hung over the lagoon. Someone handed her a typed sheet of radio news; Shanghai had been bombed. There was not much talk among the five passengers who filed on board for the flight to Guam.

The hours droned away. Helen Gierding on the 83rd flight across the Pacific felt tired, and she spent most of the time eating and dozing or thumbing through week-old magazines. Soon, the bulk of Mount Tejoe was on the horizon, and the Clipper circled and landed at Guam at 3:24 in the afternoon.

In the dining room that evening, which on Guam was in a separate building from the rest of the hotel, some of the passengers became boisterous. One man, wearing a spotless white suit, decided he was going to get a coconut from one of the nearby trees; a crowd of diners followed him outside. He was finally able to climb to the top, said Helen later, but only after he had fallen several times.

Dorothy Kaucher, on her flight to Guam, again enjoyed the "sustaining" meal served for lunch and noticed they had more of the menu's "Asst. Cookies." The 135th flight landed at Guam's Apra Harbor in gray rain. Later that day, Kaucher took a cab out to the Naval Lookout Station to watch the *China Clipper* arrive from Manila. Almost two years earlier, she had stood on the promontory of Land's End at San Francisco and watched the *China Clipper* return from its first flight to the Orient. Kaucher was surprised to feel tears in her eyes as she now watched it land at Guam.

That night, she met white-faced passengers who had just arrived from Manila. They told tales of Japanese bombing, Japanese ships shelling the docks of Shanghai. *The Guam Eagle*, a half-dozen mimeographed pages published by the Associated Press and the cable company, reported that the State Department was warning all Americans of the impending danger in China. The U.S. Navy said it had enough ships in Chinese waters to remove 3,000 Americans immediately.

Tree-climbing high jinks or not, Pan Am had all the passengers on Helen Gierding's flight up for an early departure the next day. The Clipper took off from Guam harbor at 8:22 a.m., and at 2:15 p.m., they saw Calagua Island in the Philippines. Over Cavite, the aircraft shuddered and creaked from severe air pockets, but Captain Dahlstrom brought the seaplane in for a smooth landing.

Helen caught sight of Stephen at the terminal. They waved wildly to each other, but she was told she could not go outside the customs area until her bags had been inspected. A little later, someone relented, and Helen rushed out to where her future husband waited.

When Dorothy Kaucher arrived at Cavite seven months later, the scene was very different. The Japanese onslaught in China seemed to have left Manila filled with tension, heavy with a strange foreboding. Everyone seemed to be hurrying somewhere. A small group waited to board the Pan Am Sikorsky to Hong Kong. Of those who had departed San Francisco on the 135th Clipper flight across the Pacific, only her and the Chinese Air Force officer were going on.

They boarded the Sikorsky S-42, the *Hong Kong Clipper*, which seemed remarkably narrow after the Martin Clipper. It had portholes instead of windows, and when they took off, the sea seemed to engulf them as if they had sunk. On the flight, they were served a box lunch. Someone announced that 60 people had died of cholera that day in Kowloon.

In Hong Kong, the Chinese officer said a hurried goodbye; he was flying north to Shanghai. She wandered about the chaotic, feverish city, feeling as though she was on the edge of a vast ferment, as if history was closing in on her, about to change her life forever. A few days later it was time for her to leave for home. Almost with a sense of relief, she caught the Sikorsky back to Manila. She and another American woman, looking pale and shaken, seemed to be the only passengers. The woman told her she had been "shot at in the Whangpoo." (Shanghai is at the junction of the Whangpoo River, a tributary of the Yangtze, and the Woosung River.)

Once more, Kaucher checked in at the Manila Hotel near the harbor, all potted palms and wicker chairs, feeling out of place among the "snowy white suits, shimmery dresses." Kaucher paused when she felt someone standing near her table during a 2:30 a.m. breakfast. She looked up. It was Captain Musick. He had strolled across from the table where he was having breakfast with his crew.

"We're glad to see you're going back with us," he said, and then walked on.

She remembered it as a kind greeting, one of the highlights of her trip. Musick would live only a few more months.

Flying for Pan Am

It was hard to become a Pan Am pilot. Andre Priester's exacting standards far exceeded anything else in the industry. Regardless of how much flying time you had in a logbook, if you signed on with Pan Am, you started at the bottom rung: apprentice pilot. At first, merely having flying experience was enough to be considered for employment, although Pan Am hired most of its pilots from the U.S. Naval Aviation Corps.

Later, however, a college degree, preferably in aeronautical engineering, was required. Some pilots even joined the company as stewards and clerks in various departments, finally moving up to supernumerary third pilots or "apprentice" second engineers, often to be bumped off the flight when weight limits were exceeded. More than one would-be Pan Am pilot found himself waiting for the next available flight while marooned in places like Accra, Natal, or Wake Island.

Once hired, you started to learn things the Pan Am way, and not merely flying an aircraft. Maintenance, communications, and traffic management, everything about the Pan Am system, were required study. After becoming licensed in radio operation and mechanics and proving that you knew celestial navigation as well as your hometown avenues, the company promoted you to junior pilot, but you couldn't let this go to your head.

First duty on board a Pan Am airplane was often flight engineer. Only after you had mastered all these duties, plus some foreign languages and international law thrown in, could you receive promotion to senior pilot and became eligible for the left seat in the cockpit. Not that you sat there right away, of course.

Before you could take command of an aircraft for Pan Am you needed a minimum of 2,000 hours flying time — and that was *Pan Am* hours. To make the grade as captain of a Clipper, add five trips to China. Those captains completing correspondence courses, including a required course in ocean meteorology, were eligible for the super grade: Master of Ocean Flying Boats. Actually, as the aircraft became more complicated to operate, pilots were taking courses and studying manuals throughout their whole career.

William Masland's career with Pan Am might serve as a typical example of the process. Masland, who eventually became a captain flying Boeing 314s, started with Pan Am in 1935. A former Navy pilot on the carrier *Langley*, he conceded that he thought himself as something of a hotshot until he went to work for Pan American.

"They put every last one of us into a hangar at Dinner Key . . . and there we stayed until we earned our A and E mechanic licenses," Masland said, "even if it took two years, which in some cases it did." Following this stint they had to earn their radio licenses — "copy twenty words a minute of cipher, know the ins and outs of five different types of equipment, and so forth."

Masland was later assigned to Port of Spain, where he flew S-38s and S-41s, "running across Venezuela to Barranquilla at the mouth of the Magdalena." Everyone serviced and maintained the aircraft as well as flew them, with facilities often no more than "a couple of Indians in a dugout canoe with some five-gallon tins of gas."

Next assignment for Masland was with the trans-Pacific Clippers, first as a junior officer who acted as the understudy to everyone else on the flight deck. Eventually, the junior officer navigated a crossing from Alameda to Manila under the watchful eyes of the navigator. If successful, he was moved up a grade to second officer. Even while this was going on, there was continuous study and exams. Masland's meteorology exam, for example, given by Clover, Pan Am's chief meterologist, lasted three hours. Second officers were usually assigned to flight crews as the navigator.

First officers, then as now, were almost always anxious to build up their hours and make the transition to the left seat. But it was one thing to fly an airplane, another to be responsible for the lives of the crew and passengers and hundreds of thousands of dollars worth of airplane. A few were content to be copilots forever.

Basil Rowe described several instances in which he knew of copilots who conscientiously built up the 2,000 hours of flying time and then decided that because they had been flying as number two for so long, they might as well go the rest of the way. Certain Pan Am captains encouraged their first officers to do as much of the work as possible on a flight to build up hours, and to relieve captains of the work. Basil Rowe always made it a point to take along a mystery thriller because "the copilot needs to build up his time, and I need to build up my rest."

As soon as the ship reached cruising altitude, the pilot often turned the ship over to Filbert, the automatic pilot (called George in other services). Filbert, in fact, was one of the most popular pieces of equipment on board, and there were many stories about its involvement in pilot antics.

On one particular flight that Rowe captained, the air was exceedingly rough. Whenever he or the copilot rang for the stewardess (these were pre-feminist days), she would wait, sometimes for a considerable time, until the air smoothed out before making her way up to the cockpit. After this happened a few times, Rowe rang for her and then switched on Filbert. A few minutes later, the stewardess arrived and found the cockpit empty, the plane on automatic pilot, the side windows open, and a note pinned to a wheel. Crouching in the baggage department, the two pilots watched her horrified reaction as she read:

It's too tough for us. Hope you get down O.K.

For years, flying with Pan Am was the peak of the flying profession, but that's not to say that all Pan Am pilots found the company to be the best of employers. Once the early years of pioneering were past, the hard, long — and dangerous — hours of monotonously flying over the same route could quickly cool the ardor of even the most dedicated of flyers, especially among the younger men. New pilots joining the company, in fact, often complained about the long hours for low pay. As we have seen, overwork was almost expected of you when you joined Pan Am, and there were many complaints from pilots, especially from the younger men, who were abruptly told they were now assigned to the Caribbean or the Pacific Division or South America just as they began raising a family and planning to buy a house and settle down. After some years of discontent, all Pan Am pilots eventually joined the Air Line Pilots Association (the company's clerical employees opted to affiliate with the Brotherhood of Railway Clerks). But if you wanted to fly for the airlines during the 1930s, there was one position that was acknowledged to be the pinnacle of the profession — Clipper captain with Pan American.

The 'Hawaii Clipper' mystery

Captain Leo Terletsky watched a star shell burst over Guam harbor on July 28, 1938. The burst drifted down, showering green sparks, barely visible against the rising sun, a few minutes after six in the morning. The shell was fired from the Pan Am launch and signalled Terletsky that his way was clear for takeoff. He nodded to First Officer M.A. Walker and pushed the power button. The engines coughed, growled, then caught. First the outboard engines, then the two inboard engines. Blue smoke drifted away.

The Clipper's new Hamilton Hydromatic propellers disappeared into an opaque disk. For a few moments, Terletsky, who had once fought in the Russian Revolution before emigrating to the United States, listened to their surging power as they settled down into a pounding beat. He was 43 years old with a wife in Palo Alto, California. He had joined Pan Am in 1936 after making a sparse living as a barnstormer in New England and then flying for Waco Aircraft, Barret Airways, and Maughton Aviation. He was not considered Pan Am's best pilot, with some 9,200 hours of flight time, but he was professional and competent and had gone through the airline's exacting training program. Terletsky was well aware of all the dangers of Pacific flying, from wind and rain to a faulty magneto or a sticky fuel pump.

He turned the wheel, hand on the throttles, easing the *Hawaii Clipper* into position for takeoff. For a moment, it jockeyed there, idling, as if gathering strength. Since early in the year, large wavy American flags had been painted on the bows and wings of the three Pan Am Martin Clippers as a precaution against inadvertent attacks by Chinese and Japanese aircraft in the Orient. The Pan Am insignia had been moved from the bow to a spot just to the rear of the pilot compartment. The captain again nodded at the first officer and then moved the throttles. In a few seconds, the huge ship was pounding across the bay, spray shooting up in a huge rooster tail behind the aircraft. It soared into the air. The time was 6:08 a.m.

The flight looked routine. There was a slight tropical depression near the Philippines, and Terletsky set a course slightly south of the usual route to avoid a thunderstorm. William McCarty, radio officer, tapped out half-hour position reports to KMGB at Guam, KZDY at Panay in the central Philippines, and KXBQ in Manila. The messages began to all look monotonously alike: moderate head winds, scattered showers, speed 105 knots, altitude 10,000 feet. Thirty-three years old, McCarty had once worked as a radio operator aboard the Matson luxury liner *Lurline*.

He tapped out the *Hawaii Clipper's* call letters, KHAZB, at noon, and sent out another report: the air had grown rougher, with winds of 19 knots from 247°; their position was 12° 27' minutes north latitude, 130° 40' east longitude; ground speed was 112 knots; the sky was nearly covered with cloud; it was raining.

Howard Cox, flight engineer, above the bridge in the engineer's cabin, sat surrounded by 180 dials and levers that monitored and controlled the Clipper's four engines. Cox had just returned from Seattle, where he had spent a few weeks acting as the airline's technical advisor on the development of the giant Boeing flying boats, a new generation of aircraft. He was scheduled to go back to New York and temporarily assigned to the *Hawaii Clipper*.

Ivan Parker, cabin steward, making his 26th trip across the Pacific, was passing out lunch to the six passengers. Today it was appetizers, consomme, creamed tuna on toast, peas, and fruit cocktail.

George Davis, second officer, walked through the lounge, checking for any damage to the hull or the wing struts that might have been caused by the takeoff. He paused and spoke for a few moments with Edward Wyman from Bronxville, New York, a vice president with Curtiss-Wright and a former assistant to Juan Trippe, and Kenneth Kennedy, Pan Am's Pacific-Alaska Division traffic manager. Nearby, two other men were quietly chatting together in a corner. They were Dr. Fred Meier, a scientist with the U.S. Department of Agriculture, and Dr. Earl McKinley, dean of the Medical School of George Washington University, traveling together on a grant from the National Research Council. They were on their way to the Philippines, Meier to test a device that took air samples and McKinley to visit the Culion Leprosy Colony. They were both personal friends.

Panay, the closest base to the *Hawaii Clipper*, acknowledged McCarty's report at 12:11 p.m. and requested the Clipper's permission to transmit the noon weather. McCarty signaled: "STAND BY FOR ONE MINUTE BEFORE SENDING AS I AM HAVING TROUBLE WITH RAIN STATIC." After a minute of silence, Panay again came on the air, asking if it could transmit.

The only answer was a crackle of static.

For a while, there was not much concern at the Pan Am station. It was not unusual for aircraft to lose contact. The minutes ticked by . . . 12:30 . . . 1:00. At 1:30 p.m., a worried Panay station manager stared at the clock and decided McCarty had had enough time to repair any problem with the aircraft's radio set. He radioed all Pacific bases, asking them to go to emergency standby. By 10 p.m., Pan American was sure the aircraft's fuel was exhausted, and it was down.

The U.S. Navy organized one of the largest sea searches to that date in an effort to find the *Hawaii Clipper*. Ships and aircraft methodically crisscrossed the Clipper's last reported position and then spread out far across 160,000 square miles of ocean, seeking any sign of the missing flying boat. The army transport *Meigs*, which was only just 70 miles from the aircraft's noon position, sailed back and forth over the area. On the second day, it spotted a 1,500-foot circle of oil on the ocean's surface. Nothing else was found. The *Hawaii Clipper* had disappeared. The search was abandoned on August 5, 1938.

There have been many stories about dark plots to hijack or destroy the Pan Am Clipper. Author Ronald Jackson in his book, *China Clipper*, intertwines historical fact with conjecture and describes a scenario in which two Japanese nationals sneak on board the Pan Am flying boat and then hijack it to Koror Island, an "unknown" Japanese-occupied atoll in the Micronesias, lying fewer than 400 miles to the southwest of the Clipper's route. Some said that the Japanese were anxious to copy the aircraft's Pratt & Whitney engines.

One of the passengers, a Chinese named Wah Sun Choy, was said to have been carrying a bag full of money for Chiang Kai-shek. There are even stories that the *Hawaii Clipper* was on some sort of spy mission. Certainly the United States Navy had been conducting spying operations around the Central Pacific since the 1920s, when the U.S.S. *Milwaukee* had cruised through the Micronesias, obtaining hydrographic and weather data, and did not leave the area until Japan vigorously protested.

In 1921, a Marine Corps lieutenant colonel named Earl Hancock Ellis traveled through the Micronesias disguised as a German trader. He died in 1923 under the proverbial "mysterious circumstances," reportedly in the Palau islands. And then there was the disappearance of Amelia Earhart the year before during her attempted flight around the world, some were already insisting it was actually a spy mission.

But, despite a few rumors of FBI reports that describe suspected sabotage attempts at Alameda, and despite the obviously bellicose stance of the Japanese in the Pacific during those years, there has never been any hard evidence made public of a spying mission or a hijacking. The disappearance of the *Hawaii Clipper* remains a mystery.

Trippe loses control

Pan Am had a rough year in 1938. The loss of Ed Musick and the crew of the *Samoan Clipper*, followed by the disappearance of the *Hawaii Clipper* brought ominous rumblings from both the government and Pan Am's board of directors. Pan Am was also losing money at the rate of $95,000 a month and the board was still complaining over the half million dollar loss posted by the Pacific Division in 1937.

Now, with the *Hawaii Clipper* missing, these losses were bound to increase. The two remaining Clippers simply could not be turned around fast enough and the original schedule was only being flown at 60 percent. The company desperately petitioned the Post Office Department to increase its mail payments.

Ironically, Trippe was at his peak. He was hailed everywhere as the man who "made" Pan American Airways. Yale awarded him an honorary degree. *Look* magazine announced that Carole Lombard, the most starlike of Hollywood stars, found Juan Trippe fascinating and one of the world's most interesting men.

But the growls from the Pan Am board of directors gathered strength. Trippe was too "secretive" they said. They had to make decisions without knowing all the background information. The far-flung affairs of the airline were now too much to be handled by one man. "For years," said one executive, "Trippe kept all the secrets of the business in his head." New aircraft, new routes, war breaking out everywhere — how could a world-wide airline be effectively run by one man?

The company's desperate financial straits only made it worse. When the morbid directors gathered in January 1939, they were forced to forego a dividend for the stockholders. Pan Am, in fact, was starved for capital: debt amounted to $2.5 million in callable bank loans and $3.5 million in what were called equipment trust certificates, actually mortgages on the airline's Boeing 314s.

Working capital was only $300,000, and $200,000 was immediately needed to develop a base at Noumea in French-held New Caledonia. The banks did not like what they saw. They shook their collective heads over the figures and passed the word: As far as Pan Am was concerned, their purse strings were tightly shut.

When the palace coup finally came, Trippe, even though he had been aware of the complaints for years, was still very surprised.

At the boarding meeting of March 15, 1939, Trippe's old friend, Sonny Whitney, now controlling some $4 million worth of Pan Am stock, had himself elected "chief executive officer" as well as chairman of the board. Trippe was left holding the title of president, but the directors made it clear that Whitney now held the reins to the company. As CEO, Sonny made haste to fill the vacancies on the board of directors with men of his choosing: Artemus L. Gates, president of the New York Trust Company, which was suddenly kind enough to purchase one-third of the equipment notes, and William S. Paley, youthful president of Columbia Broadcasting System.

Playboy Sonny Whitney, only a few months older than Juan Trippe, had inherited $20 million and was one of the original angels who bankrolled the company. There seemed to be nothing he did not do or anyplace he did not go — whether it was championship polo or hunting jaguars in Mexico or appearing with beautiful women everywhere.

Sonny's money bankrolled mining in South America, motion pictures in Hollywood (including a gamble, *Gone With the Wind*, getting ready to shoot under the management of a young producer, David O. Selznick), and a variety of other projects, including Marineland near St. Augustine, Florida. Now the largest shareholder in Pan American, Sonny hankered to have his name listed at the top the company's annual report. As one biographer of Pan Am put it, the coup gave him his chance "to shine as a Captain of Industry."

It was an uneasy victory. Trippe confined himself to his office at one end of the Chrysler Building's 58th floor, while Whitney presided from his magnificent suite at the other end. They would pass each other in the hallway without speaking. At the weekly meetings of the airline's top executives, chaired by the new boss, Trippe seethed in silent fury. Realizing this was not going work, and with management procedures in chaos, the directors enforced a sort of peace. Whitney grudgingly backed down.

Management practices, particularly fiscal responsibility, were streamlined and brought up-to-date, and Trippe, after a suitable "public" confession of his sins, was handed the corporate scepter once again. Trippe also vowed that he would be more accessible to the directors and would make a clean breast of things once a week to the directors' executive committee. Peace on mahogany row was restored.

As for Trippe and his former friend Sonny Whitney, they were never reconciled. The day after Pearl Harbor, Whitney resigned from the company and joined the Army Air Forces as a major in a combat intelligence unit. "Our paths don't cross," he would say of Trippe many years later.

Treasure Island

Pan Am began to expand its overseas facilities at the behest of the United States government. Trippe created a special subsidiary, the Pan American Airports Corporation, which secretly entered into a contract with the War Department. The Export-Import Bank lent Pan Am funds, initially estimated to be $12 million, to undertake the work. The money was repaid to the bank by the War Department using funds from "the president's kitty," an emergency appropriation voted by Congress.

The remaining two Martin Clippers, meanwhile, were ranging across the Pacific and, as the tempo of war picked up, began to carry an increasing number of VIPs. Maxim Litvinoff, Russia's ambassador to the United States, chose the Pacific route to reach the United States instead of chancing a flight across war-torn Europe. Major General Claire Chennault was speeded three times across the ocean on missions connected with the Flying Tigers. The Clippers carried oil company engineers on their way to Arabian fields, Chinese government representatives trying to buy airplanes and guns, scrap metal salesmen, arms dealers, and groups of Japanese schoolchildren because Japan's diplomatic personnel were sending their kids home.

The *China Clipper* had a close call with disaster in April 1936 when a refueling barge broke loose on San Francisco Bay and crashed into one of

Navy war paint puts a different face on the *China Clipper*, which perhaps was the most famous of the Martin M-130s.

its wings. Luckily, the aircraft managed to escape with only minor damage. Two years later, when headquarters in New York asked for a photograph of the Clipper silhouetted in the sunset over the Golden Gate Bridge, another brush with catastrophe occurred. As the commercial aircraft containing the photographer came up alongside the Clipper, its pilot saw a stream of gas cascading from one of the Martin's wing tanks. Someone had left the cap off, and the fuel was being sucked out. The camera plane had no radio, but hand signals warned the Clipper's crew. The M-130 streaked for the nearest airport. Just as it was approaching the field, the engines quit, but the *China Clipper* landed safely.

Pan American Airways moved its West Coast facility in February 1939 from Alameda to the new site of the International Exposition on Treasure Island, a man-made island in the middle of San Francisco Bay. "Sweet Sixteen" made the first flight from the new base.

The Clippers were now flying legends, the aircraft that came first to the public mind whenever and wherever aviation was discussed. But an event occurred in 1938 that put the handwriting on the wall for the era of the flying boat. Even as this form of air transportation reached its peak, it was already doomed. A German four-engine Focke-Wulf Fw 200 landed at Floyd Bennett Field in 1938 after a nonstop flight from Berlin. It demonstrated once and for all that landbased aircraft now had the range and the facilities for nonstop transocean service.

The war becomes hot

There didn't seem to be any reason for the delay. No explanation. Just a directive from the New York office that the *Hong Kong Clipper* remain at Hong Kong instead of keeping to its flight schedule and taking off for Manila. Then a Japan Airways flight from Tokyo landed and a diplomat, Saburo Kurusu, hurried aboard the Clipper. In his tightly held briefcase, he carried the final terms that would attempt to forestall a complete diplomatic break between the United States and the Empire of Japan. The Sikorsky departed for the Philippines.

Kurusu quickly transferred at Manila to the *China Clipper*, which roared off across the Pacific, paused for two days at Midway while a balky engine was repaired, and then alighted at Honolulu. The Japanese envoy then hopped aboard a Boeing 314 Clipper departing for San Francisco. In another day or so, he was in Washington, where he immediately took the Japanese terms to Secretary of State Cordell Hull. Either Kurusu was duped by his own government, or he was intimately involved in a fantastic gamble.

Art Peters was piloting a Clipper from Guam to Manila in late 1941. Just before his early morning departure he was called to Marine Headquarters. The Navy had "lost the Japanese fleet," he was told. Fly north from Guam for several hundred miles before turning west for Manila, just to see if he could find it. Later, they were flying "through the scud" at 8,000 feet when Peters looked down. There, stretched out for miles below him were more ships than he had ever seen before or since.

There were ships of all kinds: carriers, battleships, cruisers, knifelike destroyers darting along the edges of the vast fleet. Concerned that there might be Japanese aircraft around somewhere, the Clipper turned for Manila, keeping strict radio silence. Peters arrived in Manila five hours late to face an irate Pan Am station manager. "He was madder than hell," Peters recalled later, "until I told him where we had been and what we had seen."

It was 5:40 a.m., Monday morning, December 8; Clipper time was 18:40 GCT. Inside the Pan Am hotel on Wake, the Chamorro kitchen helpers were cleaning up the breakfast dishes. John Cooke, airport manager, strolled in. He had just seen off the *Philippine Clipper* on its way to Guam. This trip carried five passengers and was being flown by Captain John Hamilton and a crew of eight. The usual bustle around the Pan Am station was routine and normal; Cooke went to his office to sort out some paperwork. Twenty minutes later, his life would never be the same again.

The news flashed across the ocean like an electric whiplash: Pearl Harbor, 2,400 miles to the east, Japanese aircraft had attacked the American fleet. The coded message, "Case 7 Condition A" jarred in the earphones of Donovan McKay, the *Philippine Clipper's* first radio officer. He did not have to be told what it meant. Hamilton immediately wheeled the giant flying boat around, dumping some 3,000 pounds of fuel from its wing tanks to get the Clipper's landing weight down to 48,000 pounds. Nine years a Pan Am pilot, Hamilton was a graduate of navy service and had survived the lean depression years when he had once taken a flying job sowing rice from the air at 10 cents an acre.

The Martin landed at Wake and was immediately prepared to leave again. Hamilton had an urgent request from the island's navy commandant, Commander W.S. Cunningham, to make a patrol, and, according to his wartime orders, Hamilton had to leave for Honolulu immediately. In the next 15 minutes, the Clipper was refueled with sufficient gas for both the patrol and the flight to Midway.

Hamilton and Cooke were driven to the navy commandant's office to discuss the patrol, and left a short time later. The car, driven by a company chauffeur, bounced over the coral on the way back to the Pan Am base. It was a few minutes before noon. Suddenly, they heard the drone of airplanes and the tremendous crash of bombs. A flight of nine Japanese aircraft roared over the island. The three men scrambled out of the car and jumped into the hole of an unfinished foundation.

A bomb screeched down and exploded about 20 feet away, almost burying them in sand and debris. Explosions rocked the sandy soil. Again and again, the Japanese aircraft made passes over the atoll. After some minutes, there was a sudden lull in the bombing. Hamilton jumped up and ran to take cover behind a large drainage pipe. Cooke and the chauffeur started after him, but suddenly there was a chatter of machine gun fire and a line of spurting sand walked toward them. They both dived back into the hole.

The Pan Am base had become a shambles. A bomb hit Cooke's house dead center. The Pan Am hotel was ablaze. Supply buildings, radio headquarters, and fuel tanks all went up in flame and smoke. Aircraft roared overhead. Bombs came down like a shower of hail, and the air was filled with flying debris, rock and sand.

Men buried themselves in sand and dove into the water. An airport clerk, Leo Valiton, dived into a length of dredging pipe lying on the beach.

A bullet seemed to follow him inside, bounded around, and finally wounded him in the leg.

Riding at anchor, the *Philippine Clipper* was drenched with water as a bomb fell barely one hundred feet ahead of it. A line of machine gun holes stitched its way up the fuselage. But no vital spots were hit.

The Japanese airplanes roared away.

Ninety minutes later, Hamilton and his crew had stripped the Clipper of all extraneous equipment and cargo, loaded up the five passengers and as many Pan Am personnel as they could carry, and taxied out for takeoff. The first and second tries failed to break the heavily loaded flying boat free of the water. Hamilton taxied back to the starting point in a series of S turns to create waves. They rose into the air on the third run.

The 1,185-mile hop to Midway was without incident, although they did see two Japanese warships heading for Wake. Navigation was totally celestial because Wake's and Midway's adcock systems had been blown to pieces. After failing to raise Midway on the radio, they got a message through to Pearl Harbor, which then routed it to Midway by submarine cable. Approaching Midway in the darkness, they saw it was fairly easy to spot, buildings blazing. Channel buoy lights were not illuminated, but the landing area was obstructed with small water craft anyway. Hamilton put the Clipper down by almost feeling for the water. He found the Pan Am barge and tied up. Midway was in an uproar. They had been shelled that afternoon. A mob surrounded the Clipper crew yelling questions, but they could tell them little except that Wake was finished.

The *Philippine Clipper* was hurriedly refueled and, still loaded with its Pan Am passengers, was soon on its way to Honolulu. Fewer than 24 hours after departure from Wake Island, they landed at Pearl Harbor and stared in dumb horror at the carnage. Smoke still rose from smoldering buildings and sunken ships. Only two serious casualties on the Clipper required attention: the steward, Charles Relyea, received a bullet in the groin and the radioman, McKay, was wounded in the ankle.

Hamilton flew the *Philippine Clipper* from Pearl Harbor to San Francisco on December 10 under strict radio silence. When the aircraft landed, a horde of newsmen and photographers rushed to interview the Pan Am personnel, and the story of their escape appeared in newspapers all over the country. For the remainder of its war service, the *Philippine Clipper* wore a wound stripe on its bow.

In Hong Kong, it was Monday morning, December 8, still pitch-black. Captain Fred Ralph and his six-man crew were busy at Kai-tek Airport getting the *Hong Kong Clipper* ready for an unusually early return to Manila. Besides its six-man crew, the venerable S-42 workhorse, which the crew called "Myrtle," would be carrying Walter Houghton, a Pan Am meteorologist who was just finishing a vacation in Hong Kong, and Arthur Lawrence, a company accountant who was in Asia on a routine business trip. They had almost readied the ship for takeoff at about 7 a.m. when they learned that there was going to be a delay; the news came five minutes later that Japan was at war with the United States and Great Britain. Air raid sirens were already wailing. Instantly, Ralph ordered his men to remove all their personal belongings from the aircraft. They were just finishing this when the Japanese bombers appeared.

The bombers circled lazily in the pale morning sky, and then came the sound that the world had come to know all too well — the high-pitched whistle of falling bombs. The bombs shattered Kai-tek Airport. Shrapnel riddled dozens of aircraft, huge holes were dug in the runway, the roof of a hangar folded inside with a roar. Ralph and his crew were standing on the dock when they saw Japanese airplanes coming in low, firing. They all jumped into the water.

The enemy aircraft made seven passes on the *Hong Kong Clipper*, leaving it a blazing wreck. Ralph stood in water up to his waist and watched Myrtle die.

Pilots and ground crew scrambled desperately during a pause in the raid to wheel five undamaged CNAC airplanes out of their hangers and into the nearby vegetable fields. The aircraft were hurriedly camouflaged with bamboo and mud just before the Japanese bombers returned to finish the job.

When Japanese bombers struck at Hong Kong, as far as CNAC's pilots were concerned, it was only one more war zone. For years they had been flying far and wide across China on indefinite schedules, mostly at night, to dodge Japanese fighters, and in weather that even made the birds seek shelter. CNAC had become an absolute lifeline of the Chinese Nationalist government. DC-2s and DC-3s, flown by American pilots, were hauling cargoes of tungsten and tin from China to the world markets to earn precious foreign exchange for the almost broke nationalist regime. The Pan Am subsidiary's Douglas Dolphins and aging Commodores were practically the only means of communicating with vast areas of the country's interior.

As soon as the Japanese aircraft had left that Monday morning, CNAC prepared to evacuate all United States citizens and a number of other refugees from the colony. Twice more before sundown the Japanese bombers returned to plaster the airport, but the five aircraft hidden in the vegetable plots escaped unscathed. As soon as it was dark, groups of evacuees were brought to the field and assigned seats. One after another the CNAC airplanes took off and vanished into a heavy overcast that had moved in during the afternoon.

All that night, the shuttle went on, carrying the evacuees to Namyung, 200 miles into the interior of China over Japanese lines. Sixteen trips were made that night. Now and then, fire from a Japanese gun would arch tracers into the sky, but the shuttle went on. The fuel truck operators had fled, and until they found someone who could operate the truck, the refueling had to be done by hand, a painfully slow operation.

CNAC aircraft carried 275 adults and more than a hundred children to safety in two nights. Among those rescued: Madame Sun Yat-Sen, widow of the founder of the Chinese Republic; C.P. Chen, head of the Chinese Currency Stabilization Board; and H. H. Kung, the Chinese finance minister. Also flown out were Captain Ralph, his crew, and his passengers. They would later make it back to the United States by flying over the Hump from China to India.

Three of the eight American CNAC pilots who flew the rescue aircraft went without sleep for more than 50 hours. Among those not rescued were Charles Schafer, Pan American's traffic manager, who tirelessly had helped, first, to disguise the five aircraft, and then had worked on for two days and nights loading and dispatching the aircraft. Just before he could board the last airplane out, Japanese bombers caught it on the ground and destroyed it. It ended his last chance to escape.

Meanwhile, on the other side of the Pacific, the *China Clipper* was flying unarmed reconnaissance missions far out to sea. Military censorship instantly clamped a tight lid on her operations. Almost the first wartime mission of "Sweet Sixteen," however, was to evacuate a group of expectant mothers from Pearl Harbor — it managed to beat the stork to San Francisco Bay. When there was no cloud cover, the Clipper flew most of the way by hugging the water. It became the pattern for Clipper operations throughout the war.

Presidential power to take over the airlines in the event of a national emergency had been on the books for a long time. President Roosevelt delegated this power to the Secretary of War on December 13 and the next day, Robert A. Lovett called a meeting to plan a worldwide supply system for United States and Allied forces. Among those attending the meeting were representatives of Pan American Airways. The army and the navy needed long-range aircraft capable of carrying tons of critical supplies for distances up to 10,000, even 15,000, miles. Ocean-crossing transports were in critically short supply. At the start of the war, the entire United States fleet of long-range, ocean-flying transports consisted of 11 converted B-24s, Pan American's nine Boeing and two Martin flying boats, and five Boeing Stratoliners belonging to TWA. At the meeting, it was agreed that the navy would take the two Pan Am Martins, while the army would take over the Boeing 314s.

Once under Navy control, the two M-130 Clippers were overhauled, given a coat of dark-blue war paint, and flown with Pan American crews on whatever mission the navy needed. During most of 1942, they provided a shuttle service between Hawaii and California. Pan American Airways became, in effect, a branch of the United States government. On military contract flights, the aircrews wore army olive drab or navy greens with gold wings denoting active reserve status. When they switched to routes in South America or across to the neutral airports of Foynes in Ireland or Lisbon in Portugal, they donned their Pan Am blue.

Storm warning

Admiral English, commander of the Pacific Submarine Fleet, was getting very impatient. It was January 20, 1943, and he was due in Richmond, California, to attend an important conference on submarine warfare. His briefcase bulged with top secret data on refinements that should be made to new submarines. But there was a large storm off the coast of California.

Out in Pearl Harbor, the *Philippine Clipper*, now wearing a straight American flag on its bow and dark Navy paint, rode at anchor, temporarily immobilized by the blow off California.

Admiral English decided he couldn't wait any longer. A telephone call went to Pan Am Captain Robert Elzey. Round up your crew, the Clipper is flying. Refueled and made ready, NC-14715 departed Honolulu as Flight V1104 at 5:30 p.m. (Pacific war time) on January 20. On board were a crew of nine, and 10 passengers, including Admiral English and his staff; George Angus, Pan Am's Pacific Division radio superintendent, who would act as the flight's second radio officer; and a navy nurse, Edna Morrow, who had just been told she had cancer and was going home to die.

Estimated time of arrival at San Francisco was 10:18 a.m. the following morning.

The flight proceeded normally. Every few minutes, the two radio officers would send a brief message to the ground stations to confirm their position. There was a brisk tail wind, and at 5:35 a.m., the *Philippine Clipper* notified Treasure Island of a new ETA, 6:35 a.m., more than three hours ahead of schedule. At this point, the Clipper was apparently flying in clear air and confirming its position with celestial observations.

The coast of California, meanwhile, was socked in with moderate to intermittent rain and a ceiling of one thousand feet. Stiff 24-knot winds from the southwest scudded the heavy clouds across the sky. Another front was expected to move through San Francisco at around 8 a.m., with rain and three miles visibility. The wind increased to 40 knots, churning up whitecaps on the bay.

At 6:18, Flight VI104 revised its ETA to 7:10. It was now closing rapidly with the coast.

A little later, the Pan Am station reported the weather as heavy rain, wind south 44 to 48, ceiling 900 to 1,000. Visibility was down to just over one mile. The front had moved in sooner than predicted. Treasure Island suggested San Diego as an alternate.

The Clipper had more than enough fuel on board to make San Diego and could approach very close to San Francisco before deciding to go for the alternate. Treasure Island was not worried, therefore, when the captain seemed to vacillate about his course of action.

At 7 a.m., VI104 advised Treasure Island that it was over the Farallone Islands, about 25 miles off the California coast. But a later position fix seemed to place the Clipper a little farther to the north than its reported position.

At 7:15 a.m., VI104 reported that it was flying due west; apparently the captain had decided to circle and make a decision about the weather. At this point, Elzey might not have realized he was facing a southwest wind of one hundred miles per hour at 10,000 feet.

The last message from the *Philippine Clipper* was at 7:20 a.m. It requested a radio "fix." When Treasure Island tried to raise the aircraft at 7:26 a.m., there was no answer.

About 100 miles north of San Francisco, near the town of Ukiah, a woman came out of her farmhouse when something made her pause and search the sky. It had been raining hard all night, and she had come out to check the creek that ran a few feet from her front door. As she was going back inside, she heard, louder than the noise of the storm, the sound of aircraft engines. Suddenly, through the clouds, she caught a brief glimpse of a large airplane. It was very low, with its running and cabin lights gleaming. It passed over the house and disappeared. Five miles to the north of the farmhouse, at 7:30 a.m., the *Philippine Clipper* slammed into a hillside, just a few feet below its summit.

A massive search was organized, but it was not until 10 days later that a Martin Mariner spotted the wreckage. A party had to go in by foot to reach the spot. Although the searchers covered every inch of ground looking for Admiral English's briefcase, it couldn't be found, but it was finally discovered by a boy not far from the wreck.

Closed hearings by the Civil Aeronautics Board in San Francisco the following month laid the blame for the crash on Captain Elzey for not establishing his position correctly, and Pan Am was also blamed for not having a more formal holding procedure over San Francisco. The immediate cause seemed to be carburetor icing, said the CAB, which forced a descent.

What were the decisions that led to the crash? One can imagine the scene: an irate admiral impatient over the delay, a pilot under navy orders but concerned about the safety of the aircraft.

Did Admiral English pressure Elzey to land at San Francisco regardless of the weather?

The question seems as remote now as the bleak California hill on which the *Philippine Clipper* met its end. Today, pieces of the Martin's wreckage can still be seen on the hillside between Ukiah and the town of Boonville, not far from the present Ukiah VORTAC navigational aide station. Most of the debris lies at the bottom of a ravine. Fragments of metal cover the ground, almost up to the crest of the hill, reflecting the bright sun that never seems to warm the fog that often drifts in from the sea.

Balancing the books

The *China Clipper* had spent an amazing 12,072 hours and 54 minutes in the air by January 1942 and flown more than 1.5 million miles, more than 65 times the circumference of the world at the equator. NC-14716 was beached in March and rolled into a hangar at Treasure Island. A crowd of maintenance mechanics under shop superintendent John Boyle was waiting for her. It was time for the aircraft's first major overhaul, a job that complex had never been attempted before.

First order of business was to inspect the inside surfaces of the wing attachment fittings, which could not be seen during the regular maintenance checks. To do this, the mechanics had to actually remove the aircraft's 130-foot wings, the empennage, and hydro-stabilizers. Although each step required a carefully thought-out procedure — it had never been done before — the maintenance crew accomplished the task in one day. Fittings were stripped of their cadmium plating and magna-fluxed tested for tiny flaws. Those that passed inspection were replated and reinstalled.

While this was going on, the ship was inspected throughout for corroded parts, and all the electrical equipment was revamped. A new electrical panel was installed in the engineer's post, and a whole new electrical network was installed to accommodate new voice radio equipment. The Clipper was going modern. "Sweet Sixteen" finally left the Treasure Island hangar as sound as the day she made her first flight seven years before.

The *China Clipper* continued in Navy service until October 13, 1943, when it was returned to Pan American's control and re-painted with her original colors. For the first time, 716 left the familiar skies of the Pacific and was flown across the United States to Florida, where it was assigned a route between Miami and Leopoldville, on the Congo River in Africa.

In 1944, an attempt was made to balance the books on the Sixteen. After more than seven years flying the Pacific route, the *China Clipper's* logbooks showed it had flown 2.4 million miles and spent 15,769 hours in the air. It had crossed the Pacific 178 times, which equaled 89 round-trips. Its four Pratt & Whitney engines had each used 2.34 million gallons of fuel, worth some $540,000, and 31,200 gallons of oil. The Clipper had used up 104 engines, 5,000 spark plugs (another $15,000), and $2,100 worth of baths to protect it from salt-water corrosion. The major dismantle-over-haul cost $10,000. Conversion to a military transport, say, $1,000. Meals in flight, tack on another $25,000. Then add in the expenses of the aircrews, mechanics, station radio operators, cooks and waiters, traffic aides, and so on.

On the other hand, the total income from the two Martin Clippers and two Boeing Clippers on the Pacific route for the year ending December 31, 1940, was more than $4 million — of which, mail income came to almost $3 million. In 87 months of operation, the *China Clipper* alone carried 370,000 pounds of express goods, 380,000 pounds of mail, and 3,500 passengers.

Boeing 3I4:

world's greatest

Design lines were coming together, taking shape, representing a massive flying boat. The engineer paused for a moment, holding up the sheet of paper. The rest of his family had long since gone to bed, but he was wrapped up in his work, the papers scattered over his dining room table. The house, silent. He bent over the table. The engines were the key. This flying boat would require the most powerful aircraft engines in the world — perhaps as much as 1,500 horsepower each. The hull would be all metal and too big for the sections to be built full length in a jig. Perhaps — but it was late. The engineer stretched and thought of going to bed. Something else occurred to him: fuel tanks. Perhaps . . . they could go here. He worked on into the night.

The engineer was Wellwood Beall, who once sold Boeing's P-26 pursuit planes in China and was now the manufacturer's service engineer. He was designing a flying boat that would be the greatest aircraft of its type in the world.

Boeing gets the nod

Juan Trippe had approached four aircraft manufacturing companies in February 1936 — Douglas, Sikorsky, Consolidated and Boeing — asking them to bid on a long-range, four-engine marine aircraft that would be capable of flying either the Atlantic or the Pacific. It would be required to carry more payload and more passengers than any other aircraft then in the air.

Douglas Aircraft was involved in building the DC-4 for American Airlines and United Airlines and "passed" on the project. Sikorsky Aircraft submitted its design for a flying boat known as the S-44, but it was too small and unable to meet the proposed payload that Pan American sought. Consolidated Aircraft's design was just not up to Pan Am's standards.

When Robert Minshall, Boeing's chief engineer saw Pan Am's requirements, his first thought was that it would stretch his company's facilities to the limit. The airline also insisted on all design approval rights and that meant an unknown. And what an aircraft. It would have to be a machine with a gross weight of more than 80,000 pounds. The engines would be massive. The airline's specifications were for a commercial ship that had never been built nor dreamed of. No, said Minshall, Boeing was going to have to turn this project down. But Wellwood Beall was very interested. Why not a big flying boat? He began working on the project at home.

First, he thought, let's take the wing of the XB-15, the experimental predecessor to the Army's B-17 Flying Fortress, and add a water hull to it. Sketch in a double-decker construction, one deck for, say, around 70 passengers, one for flight crew and baggage. The engines? The new Wright Twin Cyclone 14-cylinder jobs, rated at 1,600 horsepower, should do it. Range? Beall guessed 3,500 miles.

He took his drawings to Minshall. Minshall spread them out, looked them over, and then began to examine them more carefully. After awhile, he looked up at Beall and grinned. Beall recognized the look. Minshall was hooked.

Boeing requested that Pan Am extend the deadline date so complete blueprints and projected performance figures could be worked up. Beall was relieved of all other duties, assigned a team of 11 engineers, and went to work. On July 31, 1936, the two companies signed a contract for six aircraft, designated the B-314, at a unit cost of $618,908, with an additional $756,450 each for engines and spares. Pan Am also took an option for six more airplanes.

The primary design requirements for the B-314 were fourfold:

❖ Transport up to 10,000 pounds of payload, with a range of at least 2,400 statute miles against a 30 mph head wind at a cruising speed of 150 mph at an altitude of 10,000 feet.
❖ Permit efficient operation with a minimum of crew fatigue and a minimum of maintenance.
❖ Provide *unprecedented* comfort, spaciousness and luxury for the passengers.
❖ Develop an aircraft that would be as inherently safe as possible within the existing knowledge of materials, equipment, and the science of aviation.

Construction of the B-314 began at Boeing's plant near Seattle. The aircraft became so big that the hull was mounted on a launching dolly and the stern was moved outside the hangar so that tail surfaces could be attached. It had a wing span of 152 feet, a span larger than any previous practical, operational aircraft.* Length was 106 feet overall. The hull depth was just under 19 feet, and constructed so that the center wing spar would be supported on the upper portion of the fuselage. This was found to reduce wind drag compared to the wing-type mounting on top of the fuselage found on such aircraft as the Martin M-130, the Sikorsky S-40 and S-42, and the Dornier DO-X.

This arrangement also gave the hull more volume for passengers and cargo. The hull bottom was built with a pointed rear step to reduce aerodynamic drag and a main step athwartship. Due to the size of the aircraft, a water rudder was attached to the rear step but was later deleted because test pilots found it was easier to steer on the water with asymmetrical engine power.

The gross takeoff weight of the B-314 came to a whopping 82,500 pounds. The fuel tankage was 4,200 gallons, with a maximum oil tankage of 300 gallons—more than enough to meet the proposed payload, speed, and range requirements.

The aircraft's 14-cylinder, twin-row Wright R-2600-A2 Double Cyclone engines turned out to be the most efficient units of their day. Mounted in a nacelle 69 inches in diameter, it was the first commercial aircraft engine to use 100-octane fuel. The design team also selected Hamilton hydromatic, three-bladed propellers, cutting an arc 14 feet, 9 inches in diameter, that were full-feathering, another first for an airliner.

The B-314 wing was constructed in three pieces. The center sections to a point outboard of the two inner engine nacelles were integrated with the hull; the outer panels were separate and removable pieces, while the outer ends of the wings were actually watertight compartments, intended to float if the aircraft was to dip a wingtip.

Each of the wing's center sections held a fuel tank; four other tanks were built into the hydrostabilizers (sponsons). As in the Martin M-130, the sponsons were used for lateral stability in water instead of floats. First used with the Dornier in 1918, they were also useful work platforms and allowed passengers to step directly from them through the entry door into the hull.

The hull and wing combination was actually so enormous that a

---

*The DO-X's wing span exceeded that of the B-314 by 5 feet 6 inches, but it was not a successful, nor an operational aircraft.

mechanic could use an interior catwalk to work on any of the four engines, including in-flight inspection, a feature that in later years saved more than one B-314 from disastrous consequences.

The hull incorporated a compartmented double bottom, the same process used in ship construction, although there were only two full-depth watertight bulkheads: one ahead of the instrument panel to prevent flooding if the bow was damaged and one between the passenger compartment and the tail.

All control surfaces shared the aluminum-tube-and-channel type of construction. Ailerons were metal-framed, covered with fabric and had one trim tab divided into two separate units to reduce hinge binding that occurred when the wing flexed under a heavy load. The elevators, themselves, were connected to the pilot's controls through springs; the controls moved the tabs, which, in turn, moved the elevator. The metal-frame fabric-covered flaps were the *split* type, that is, they were fitted under the wing's trailing edge, which stayed in place when the flaps were lowered. Normal landing usually required 60° full flaps, while 20° flaps were used for takeoff. The aircraft's rudders used the same tab and spring control system as the elevators.

Controls, however, were heavy by today's standards, and more than once a captain required an assist from his first officer. Crosswind taxiing also continued to be somewhat difficult, and there were times when crewmembers had to scramble out onto a wing to keep the other wing tip from dipping into the water. Occasionally, a stiff crosswind combined with a current or running tide would leave the Boeing skipper no choice but to sail, somewhat awkwardly, backwards to a dock.

The crews' quarters and flight deck were unbelievably large, so spacious, in fact, they will probably never be equaled again in any aircraft. The control deck, designed to reduce crew fatigue and to given them some place to rest, could even put some ocean-going vessels to shame. More than six feet high and more than twenty-one feet long, it was plushly decorated with deeply upholstered chairs and wall-to-wall carpeting. The flight deck, once called the cockpit, had plenty of room for a master (also called the watch officer), first pilot, second pilot, navigator, radio operator and flight engineer. Because of the long, non-stop distances traveled, the B-314 often carried two complete crews, but even the addition of an assistant navigator, another radio operator, and a second engineer did not make it crowded. Two stewards could also be easily accommodated, but they usually remained on the passenger deck below.

The pilot had his engine, propeller, and trim tab controls to the left of his seat, while the copilot had duplicates on the right. The throttles to all four engines could be operated with one hand and were used mainly for maneuvering on the water, while the flight engineer supervised propeller controls, engine cowl flap settings, fuel flow, and cabin air conditioning. The flight engineer also synchronized engine speeds by watching a *synchroscope* that showed a signal light when the engines were in rhythm.

The pilot had a remarkably clean cockpit — certainly nowhere near the clutter found in airliners today — with little more than the ABC's of piloting in front of him: altimeter, airspeed indicator, rate of climb indicator, bank and turn indicator, artificial horizon, and directional gyro. Between these clusters were the gyropilot and above it the only engine instruments on the board: two dual tachometers and two dual manifold pressure gauges. The pilot also had two compasses, an outside air temperature indicator, a flap position indicator, a clock, two pressure gauges for the gyropilot, and an instrument vacuum gauge.

The navigator, on the port side, behind the pilot, had a large table and all the essential navigation instruments, as well as a celestial observation dome and two drift sight stations in the wing roots. On the starboard side of the flight deck a stairway, just behind the copilot's seat, led down to the passenger deck.

Just aft of the stairway was the radio operator's position with three transmitters and three receivers, plus direction finding equipment. Crew members could also communicate with each other through built-in interphone connections.

At the rear of the flight deck, on the port side, was the master's desk, an uninstrumented abode with a table and chair. Like the master of a ship, he kept no watches and seldom did any actual flying.

Directly behind the flight deck was the meteorologist's compartment, sleeping accommodations for the crew, and baggage holds that extended out into the wings. Forward of the flight deck, and accessed by a small door located between the pilot and copilot, on the other side of the main bulkhead, was the marine equipment room, housing mooring gear, extra fold-up bunks for crew sleeping, and sometimes additional cargo and mail. Up in the extreme bow was another ladder that led up to the mooring hatchway. A second hatch, known as the baggage and cargo hatch, opened out on the left side of the fuselage.

Pan Am overdid itself when it came to passenger luxury in the B-314. Everything was first class, no coach or economy air travel in the 314, thank you. Officially, the aircraft could carry up to 74 passengers, but again, at least in the civilian configuration, this seldom happened. Passenger capacity was actually an inverse function of the distance flown: A hop of 1,000 nautical miles, for example, meant a payload of 21,000 pounds. Hike this up to 2,500 nautical miles (the San Francisco-Honolulu run, for example), and payload dropped to 9,000 pounds, or around 30 passengers. For overnight, sleeper flights, passenger capacity was limited to 34, regardless of the distance.

The passenger deck was divided into eleven compartments: five standard compartments that could each hold 10 people; one special compartment seating four; one deluxe bridal suite (no kidding); a 14-seat dining lounge, galley, and two rest rooms. The rest rooms were the first to have in-flight, over-the-ocean disposal. The men's room was equipped with a standing urinal — another first — while the women's powder room had primping stools and large mirrors.

The passenger lounges were furnished with "davenport-type" chairs, upholstered in a beige wool tapestry with leather trim. Carpeting was

Pan American World Airways

Dining room on the Boeing 314 Clipper flying boat. This type of aircraft inaugurated Pan Am's first transatlantic service in 1939, carrying up to 70 passengers.

turquoise green on rust. Kapok and spun glass wool soundproofing was used throughout the ship.

The 10.5-foot by 12-foot dining room offered complete formal place settings, with linen-draped tables, flowers, and silverware. Its blue color scheme was intended to compliment the "rich terra cotta" carpeting. The cuisine, served on real china, came from a galley that was actually a full-service kitchen complete with steam tables. No frozen food was served, except ice cream. Meals came with the best of French wines and champagne; Priester's ban on alcohol on aircraft had finally broken down. On some flights, there was even a "captain's table," where only the best were seated! And across from the galley—a bar that served drinks in-flight.

All this came, of course, very expensively by the standards of the 1930s. The tariff to Europe was a stiff $375 one way, or $675 round-trip, say about $7,000 or $8,000 in today's money, about twice the Concorde fare.

For passenger safety, each standard passenger compartment had two emergency exit doors; counting the regular doors and hatches, there were 15 ways to leave the airplane in a hurry. Each aircraft also carried eight 10-person rafts, four accessible from outside the fuselage. There were also enough life preservers for everyone on board. Other safety equipment— flare pistols, signal lights, buckets, axes—was carried. All upholstery was fire-proofed, another first for an airliner, and a gas-engine generator could be fired up to provide emergency power for the radios. There was even a container of special oil to pour upon troubled waters around the aircraft if abandoning ship became necessary.

Testing on the Duwamish

On June 7, 1938, the first B-314, with Eddie Allen, Boeing's chief test pilot, at the controls, eased its way out onto the Duwamish River near Seattle. It was 6:17 p.m. A brisk wind that had ruffled the surface of the water for most of the day had died down, and a hush had fallen upon the river, broken suddenly now by the roar of the huge aircraft's engines. Allen poured on full power, and the graceful flying boat sped across Lake Washington and rose into the air to the excited cheers and applause of the spectators. The first flight lasted 38 minutes.

Almost immediately Allen noticed a lateral stability problem. The aircraft tended to drift unless the engines were used to maintain direction on the water, nor was the aircraft stable in flight. The problem was the sheer bulk of the airplane; the enormous hull was blocking off airflow to the rudder. A double rudder on a horizontal stabilizer did not seem to solve the problem, so the single rudder was replaced, but this time with another rudder on each side. This seemed to control the situation, although porpoising on landing was such a problem that at one point John Leslie, Pan Am's Pacific Division manger, told Beall that the aircraft was unacceptable.

Altogether, about 450 miles of taxiing and 5,000 miles of in-flight operations were conducted. Amazingly for a 42.5-ton airplane, the pilot could fly the ship with only two fingers on the column. Less force was needed on the rudder pedals than that required to operate a car. Flying with an autogyropilot made it still easier, the remote controls were two little wheels at right angles to each other: one for making turns and one for operating the elevators. When the gyros were operating, the pilot could turn the ship in either direction any number of degrees simply by rotating the right wheel.

The Boeing B-314 weighed 40,105 pounds as a bare airplane, with disposable load of more than 32,000 pounds, a basic ratio of 51:49, equal to the M-130. Later, with upgraded engines, the ratio improved to 40:60. Wing loading was 28.7 pounds. A further comparison between the B-314 and M-130 is shown below:

Boeing B-314 Versus Martin M-130
(weights in pounds except as noted)

	B-314	M-130
Mtow	82,500	52,000
Tare	50,270	28,500
Disposable load	32,230	23,500
Load:tare	51:49	51:49
100% fuel	25,476	20,736
Wing area, sq. ft.	2,867	2,315
Wing loading, lbs/sq. ft.	28.7	22.00
Engines × horsepower	4 × 1,500	4 × 830

Flight tests showed the B-314 to have a cruising speed of 150 mph at 11,000 feet and a range of 4,275 miles. The operational ceiling was 16,000 feet; top ceiling, 21,000 feet. Top cruising speed was 155 knots; Never-exceed redline was 184 knots. At 84,000 pounds of gross weight, with 10° of flap and no wind, the aircraft used 3,200 feet of water to take off in 47 seconds. The optimum climb speed with one engine out was 103 knots. Approaches were flown at 90 knots with 40° of flap, touching down at 80 knots, 70 in rough water.

The 'Yankee Clipper' flies the pond

Following Boeing's tests, the CAB conducted extensive testing of its own, and the B-314 was granted it approved type certificate on January 26, 1939. The first aircraft (NC-18601) was kept in experimental use until after the second and third B-314s were built. NC-18601 was later given the name *Honolulu Clipper*. The second ship out of the factory (NC-18602) was christened the *California Clipper*, delivered to Pan Am on January 29, 1939, and assigned to the Pacific Division.

NC-18603, the third in line, was painted in Pan Am livery and, on March 3 at the Tidal Basin in Washington, dubbed the *Yankee Clipper* by First Lady Eleanor Roosevelt. On March 26, it was flown by Harold Gray on an inspection flight to Europe with a total of 21 people on board, including crew and observers from the federal government and Pan Am's operations department.

Gray — who was one of the first pilots to reach Priester's super rank of Master of Ocean Flying Boats — lifted the Clipper off the waters of the Patapsco River near Baltimore and headed straight for Horta in the Azores. The 2,750 miles was covered in 17 hours at an average speed of almost 160 mph.

After a three-day layover, the *Yankee Clipper* made the 1,060-mile hop to Lisbon, making aerial surveys of the islands of Pico, San Miguel, and Terciera en route. From Lisbon, the next stop was scheduled to be Marseilles, but strong head winds forced a diversion to the French base at Biscarosse, on a coastal lake south of Bordeaux. The French launched their big *Lieutenant de Vaisseau Paris* from Biscarosse on its initial Atlantic flight in

Yankee Clipper before World War II.

1938. By April 3, NC-18603 was in Marseilles, and the next day, it made the jump to the flying boat base at Southhampton, England, or, as the British call it, Southhampton Water.

From England, the Clipper touched down at Foynes in Ireland and then retraced its steps to Lisbon for the cross-Atlantic hop. Again, strong head winds kept speed down to only 104 mph. After touching down once more at Horta, 603 flew on to Bermuda, where Pan Am station operators had a radio-ordered breakfast waiting. The last leg was an easy six-hour flight to Baltimore.

Although Gray had been given discretion to set his own departure times from each stop, the 11,000-mile trip was completed within a few minutes of the predetermined plan. The flight had also given Pan Am crews practice in re-calibrating the direction finding equipment at each stopover, as well as their mooring and servicing techniques.

When the Clipper came in to land at Baltimore, excitement swept through the company, from Trippe down to newest clerk. The flight of the *Yankee Clipper* was the culmination of more than 10 years of effort. Now the way across the Atlantic was clear. Trippe, however, anxious to stay on the good side of Woods-Humpherey, made sure that the head of Imperial Airways was kept informed of all developments. "Washington," said Trippe, rather disingenuously, was pressing Pan Am to start regular service to England and Europe as soon as possible, although he wanted to wait until Imperial was ready.

On May 20, 1939, the *Yankee Clipper* rode at anchor in Manhasset Bay in bright noon sunshine. A crowd was at hand to see off Captain Arthur LaPorte and his crew. Trippe, who was enduring the bitter trial of no longer being in control of Pan American, asked LaPorte if all was in order.

"The *Yankee Clipper* is ready, sir. All stations are manned, standing by for orders, sir," the pilot replied.

Trippe handed LaPorte the cargo manifest and ordered him to cast off. The crew boarded the Clipper, and in a few minutes it had roared over the New York World's Fair and vanished into the eastern sky. Almost 27 hours later, the Boeing 314 landed at Lisbon via the Azores. The payload consisted of some 200,000 letters, about 1,804 pounds, and some cargo. The next day, it continued to Marseilles, completing the first scheduled airmail flight to Europe from North America.

The race to establish the first regular service across the Atlantic was over, and Pan Am had won.

On June 17, 1939, the *Atlantic Clipper* (NC-18604), flown by Captain Culbertson, made the first official crossing of the Atlantic, carrying 16

Atlantic Clipper (NC-18604) being serviced in Bermuda.

passengers, primarily radio and newspaper reporters, and Pan Am officials. Regular passenger service started 11 days later when the *Dixie Clipper* (NC-18605), the fifth B-314 to be completed, with Captain Sullivan at the controls, made the trip with 22 passengers on board, including Mr. and Mrs. Cornelius Whitney and Mrs. Elizabeth Trippe. Faith and patience were rewarded for at least one other passenger; Mr. W.J. Eck had made reservations nine years previously. Boarding the aircraft, he chortled that he had been offered $5,000 for his ticket.

By the end of 1939, Pan Am's Clipper fleet was joined by the sixth B-314, the *American Clipper* (NC-18606).

Following the early transatlantic flights, which made headlines around the world, the giant Pan Am flying boats began three-times-a-week flights to Europe, a gracious mode of travel that has never really been equalled.

A typical trip across the "Pond" would follow the normal flight procedure: at takeoff, the pilot would hold the aircraft just above the water until an airspeed of 120 mph was reached. Then, with all engines performing satisfactorily, they were throttled back from their maximum of

1,550 horsepower each to around 1,200 horsepower. Reaching an altitude of 750 feet, the captain would again throttle back, maintaining a speed of 126 mph at 900 horsepower. The Clipper would then slowly climb to cruising altitude.

Once in the air, everyone settled back and moved around talking to each other. A steward handed out a printed passenger list — just like on board an ocean liner — and people scanning it would often be rewarded with the name of a famous person.

To mention only a few that preferred the convenience of the Clipper that year: Queen Wilhelmina of the Netherlands; Lord and Lady Mountbatten; Madam Chiang Kai-shek; Claire Booth Luce (then married to the publisher of *Time* magazine, she would write: "Fifty years from now, people will look back upon a Clipper flight of today as the most romantic voyage of history."); Lord Halifax, Britain's ambassador to Washington; Sir Winston Churchill; and Noel Coward.

Later, after a dinner that was as good as any served in a restaurant, the captain would come down from the flight deck to smoke a cigarette and chat with the passengers. Ready for bed? The berths were larger and more comfortable than those on the Martin Clippers, although Betty Trippe, on one of the initial flights across the Atlantic, would note the same problem of lack of uniform heating.

At Horta in the Azores, the passengers could get off the aircraft and stretch their legs, maybe buy a straw hat and a bottle of port. Then, refueled, the aircraft was airborne again, knowledgeable passengers clocking the takeoff run, and seven hours later the Tagus River at Lisbon was below them.

In Lisbon, passengers going on would stay overnight at the Aviz, a small hotel that was formerly a palace. It was a charming place, decorated in Louis XV style, with an aura of faded but proud glory. The next morning, passengers were called at 5:30 a.m. They would eat breakfast in the air before the Clipper landed at Marseilles.

It was a brief summer of peace before war engulfed the world.

On October 3, 1939, due to the outbreak of the war in Europe, Pan Am suspended its service to Marseilles and Southhampton. From then on, the only aerial lifeline between the United States and Europe would connect to Lisbon in neutral Portugal.

The government now decided to step in and substantially improve Pan Am's profit picture: the Civil Aeronautics Authority raised the Pacific mail rate from $2 to $3.35 a mile on the Alameda-Manila run and $7.12 a mile from Manila to Hong Kong. What prompted the largess: secret testimony from the U.S. Navy concerning the national interest that Pan Am's Pacific routes served. Said Admiral William Leahy, chief of naval operations, "Pan American activities should be encouraged and expanded."

The outbreak of war in Europe also proved to be a bonanza for the airline. Now, the United States (Pan American Airways) was left as practically the only carrier across the North Atlantic. Mail loads quickly rose to 8,000 pounds per flight on certain Atlantic runs. Pan American was carrying 30 percent of all trans-Atlantic mail by 1942. In Lisbon, hordes of desperate refugees from every country in Europe tried to get their names on the long waiting lists for a seat on a Clipper flight to the United States.

The frequency of flights to Lisbon rose to three times a week in 1940, and then to once a day. From June 1939 to December 1941, Pan Am's Ocean Clippers carried 25,248 passengers, a figure that approached that of the major steamship companies.

By the end of its first year in operation, in fact, the Boeing 314 had flown 393,214 routes miles. Pan American had achieved almost complete control of all air service across the Atlantic from the United States. At no other time in its history, before or since, has it enjoyed such complete hegemony.

The mail rate increase, combined with the sharp rise in passenger traffic across the Atlantic, turned 1939 into the most profitable year in the airline's history, earnings of $2 million on reported revenues of more than $20 million.

Coward on the Clipper

Noel Coward was returning to England in 1940 after an appearance in a Broadway show. "On Sunday, June 9," he wrote in his autobiography, *Future Indefinite*, "I drove out to La Guardia airfield. . . . The Clipper, which according to the schedule should have left the day before, was sitting complacently on the quiet water like a large prehistoric bird. The airport was buzzing with the usual rumors; there would be three hours delay, there would be six hours delay. . . ." He chattered brightly with the small crowd that had come to see him off, including Tallulah Bankhead and Clifton Webb. Playwright Simon Elwes and the beautiful actress Madeleine Carrol, who was trying to get to the South of France where her parents and fiancé lived, were going to be his traveling companions on the Clipper, "and there was a great deal of press photography."

Despite the delay and the sadness of departure, however, the service in the air more than made up for the delay. Coward found the Clipper flight the "acme of comfort." Cocktails and a good dinner mellowed him even further; "Our passage through the upper air was so smooth that there was no sensation of moving at all; we might just as well have been sitting in a well-appointed bus that had become somehow embedded in the sky. . . ."

The *California Clipper* and the *Honolulu Clipper* were assigned to the Pacific. Pan Am established regular fortnightly mail service from Los Angeles to Auckland, New Zealand, on July 12, 1940. Passenger service was inaugurated a month later.

Once again, globe-trotting Noel Coward, entertaining British troops around the world, took the Clipper home. His Boeing Clipper left Auckland at 7:30 a.m. February 3, 1941, and arrived at New Caledonia with enough daylight for the passengers to go ashore, drive around, bathe and dine aboard the Pan American yacht *Southern Seas*, which served as a sort of floating restaurant. "There was no point in going to bed," wrote Coward, "because we had to leave again at three thirty in the morning, and I spent the hours enjoying a light drinking bout with the captain."

In the air again, the Clipper seemed to have met some strong head winds because it was three hours late coming into Canton Island ("a small cluster of winking lights looking like a Cartier bracelet flung onto black velvet"). The Clipper, however, made a perfect landing, the doors were thrown open, and the warm tropical air swept in. Coward found the hotel startling; "I had certainly not bargained for private showers, luxurious beds, shining Fifth Avenue chintzes, and a chromium cocktail bar."

California Clipper (NC-18602), which was the second Boeing 314 manufactured, on San Francisco Bay prior to Pearl Harbor.

Although the Clipper took off at the noon the following day, Coward remained at the hotel for seven more days, swimming, reading, and enjoying himself, apparently an unplanned vacation. While he was on Canton, however, there was the dramatic event of the cyclone.

The New Zealand-bound Clipper was due one evening at 8 p.m., but it was hours overdue because of a huge storm in the Pacific. At Canton, the torrential rain poured down. For hours, Coward and the Pan Am staff sat around waiting. On board the Clipper was the wife and baby of Hal Graves, the Pan Am manager. Several radio messages got through, but they were almost unintelligible. After hours of nail-biting tension, Graves was white faced. The radio operator finally ran in with the news that the Clipper was about to land. Everyone, including Coward, wearing only a swimsuit and a raincoat, rushed outside. They all looked up, straining to see the aircraft through the mist and driving rain. Then, with a roar, it passed over their heads, missing the station roof by inches. Coward remembers "yelling violently with relief." The aircraft landed safely, with Mrs. Graves, baby, and the rest of the passengers unscathed.

Finally ready to leave on the America-bound Clipper a few days later, Coward's departure was again delayed, this time by another storm and then by engine trouble. Returning to the island after two hours of flying, the Clipper was repaired, and then, once again, took off. Coward, now "headed back to the world," craned his neck to look down. "There it lay," he wrote, "that tiny coral circlet in the blue water; the jetty, the lagoon, the coloured fish, the little white terns so tame that they perched on your

Pan American World Airways

The *Honolulu Clipper* (NC-18601) was the first Boeing 314 manufactured, subsequently sunk at sea by U.S. Navy in November 1945. This photograph was probably taken at Treasure Island on San Francisco Bay.

hand, Lordee and Jack, Hal Grave's baby screaming its lungs out, and Frank Fleming, wearing an old pair of khaki shorts, hauling up the flag."

Three weeks' later, Coward was on another Boeing Clipper crossing the Atlantic via Bermuda, the Azores, and Lisbon, until he finally reached England. "The ceiling was low," he said, "but my spirits were high."

On May 10, 1941, the *California Clipper* opened the first scheduled airline service from San Francisco to Singapore, via the stepping-stone bases in the Pacific. Fares were posted as $825 one-way or $1,485 round trip; the bridal suite ran higher. In the Atlantic, meanwhile, still another service began. On September 28, 1941, the *Dixie Clipper* opened the first air express route between the United States and Europe. Among its first shipments was a large afghan for King George's queen.

The next six Boeing 314s off the assemblyline, designated the 314A, were an upgraded model with a new engine, the 1,600-hp, Wright 579C1 4AC1, 14-cylinder, twin-row radial. Takeoff weight was increased to 84,000 pounds, fuel tankage boosted to 5,448 gallons and the props were also modified to give better performance. But Pan Am would only take delivery of three of the new 314As; the rest would go to the British.

Britain was facing dark days in 1940–41. The remnants of the British Army had been pulled back from Dunkirk. France had fallen. Norway, Denmark, Holland had all gone down under the German blitzkrieg. Britain stood alone. Its aircraft industry was totally committed to the war effort, even though it was authorized to conduct services across the Atlantic to the United States on a reciprocal basis with Pan American. Yet Britain badly needed long-range aircraft to keep its lines of communication with its far-flung colonies and allies intact.

With United States government permission, Pan Am sold to the newly formed British Overseas Airways Corporation three of the Boeing 314As at a cost of $1 million each. Between April and June 1941, BOAC took delivery of NC-18607, NC-18608, and NC-18610, respectively named the *Bristol* (G-AGBZ), the *Berwick* (G-AGCA) and the *Bangor* (G-AGCB). All were based at the Pan Am facilities at Baltimore.

Pan American Airways took delivery of the *Pacific Clipper* (NC-18609), the *Anzac Clipper* (NC-18611), and the *Capetown Clipper* (NC-18612).

The first BOAC 314A made its initial flight from New York to Foynes, Ireland, on May 22, 1941, and by the end of the war, British-owned 314s would make approximately 600 Atlantic crossings. They were the only British commercial aircraft not operated under wartime "austerity" conditions and a first-class restaurant was maintained throughout the period.

Although other governments would investigate the possibility of buying 314s from Boeing, no additional foreign sales were made. The B-314 was the only aircraft in existence, and would likely be for some time, that could fly the great distances across the world's oceans with useful quantities of war materials and passengers. The United States decided that the 314 was best kept in the family. In August of 1941, however, the United States government purchased the *Capetown Clipper* for $900,000 from Pan Am to ensure that more supplies would get through to the British, who were fighting desperately to hold Rommel in Africa. Pan Am would continue to operate the aircraft throughout the war, but the government assumed all responsibility for assigning the Clipper routes where there was the possibility of enemy contact.

Saga of the 'Pacific Clipper'

The *Honolulu Clipper* was in San Francisco for overhaul on December 7, 1941. The *California Clipper*, en route from San Francisco to Honolulu, arrived that Sunday morning about a half-hour after the attack on Pearl Harbor began. Pilot Art Peters immediately diverted to Hilo on the big island of Hawaii and landed on a river. Peters and his crew, not knowing if

The *Yankee Clipper* (NC-18603) during routine maintenance; it was probably the most famous Boeing 314.

Japanese aircraft would appear at any moment, concealed the Clipper as best they could and waited.

After a few hours, with no sign of the Japanese, Peters asked the passenger if they wanted to go back to San Francisco with him as going any further westwards into the Pacific was now out of the question. Every passenger opted to stay in Hawaii, and, after unloading everyone with their baggage, Peters took the Clipper back to San Francisco.

Both the *Honolulu Clipper* and the *California Clipper* were immediately taken over by the Army Air Transport Command and operated as the C-98, although they would still be flown and maintained by Pan Am crews. Later, when enough land bases had been established, the army decided it didn't have much use for flying boats and turned its C-98s over the navy. The Pan Am crews simply changed uniforms and continued with business as usual.

The *Pacific Clipper*, meanwhile, was approaching Auckland, New Zealand, at the end of a routine flight. It was summer "Down Under," the talk was of country picnics, outdoor games of bowls and the championship cricket match that was coming up. ANZAC troops were fighting in North Africa and Greece, but that seemed far away. Aboard the Clipper, the talk was of nothing more important than the upcoming shore leave.

Suddenly, they received a flash: "Plan A." With a sharp intake of breath, John Poindexter, the first radio operator, realized that the United States was at war.

National Air and Space Museum, Smithsonian Institution

Flight testing of Boeing 314 NX-18601, which was named *Honolulu Clipper* as NC-18601. It was subsequently sunk at sea by the U.S. Navy on November 4, 1945.

Once the aircraft had landed, Captain Robert Ford, 35 years old, went immediately to the American consul to find out his orders. But he found he was in for a wait. War had caught everyone on the wrong foot. Scores of messages were coming into the consulate, all of them in code, and the clerks were overwhelmed. For seven days, Ford and his 10-man crew marked time, and then his orders arrived. The *Pacific Clipper* could not be risked crossing the Pacific. He was to take it home the long way around.

Pan Am had made advanced arrangements for just such an emergency, but it was still a formidable task. Attached to the Pan Am station in Auckland was Bill Mullahey, the former Columbia University college student who had spent a glorious summer dynamiting out the harbor at Wake Island. Mullahey scurried around, gathering every chart, every map, every school geography book he could find. Not only would the flight be the first round-the-world flight of a commercial aircraft, roughly following the equator, it would also be the longest continuous flight ever of a commercial aircraft.

The Clipper started for home at 10 a.m., December 15, 1941. First stop was Noumea in New Caledonia to pick up all company personnel and fly them to safety. Ford evacuated 22 men, women, and children from the island, giving them one hour to get packed. Six-and-a-half hours later, he dropped them off in Gladstone, Australia. It was another first for the *Pacific Clipper* because no other aircraft had made that crossing.

Unable to find 100-octane fuel in Gladstone, Ford took off the next morning for Darwin, an entire continent away, with his tanks one-third empty. Beneath his aircraft for the entire 11-hour flight was nothing but hot, dusty earth, not even a decent lake to land on. The Clipper arrived at Darwin, Australia's main port on the Timor Sea, and was refueled at the height of a violent electrical storm. There was pandemonium in the town because all women had to be evacuated within 24 hours. Presumably, it was deemed important that the virtue of the women be preserved intact from the marauding Japanese, while the men could fend for themselves.

Next stop was Surabaya in the Dutch East Indies. Under strict radio silence to maintain security, NC-18609 was approaching the Allied port, when suddenly four British fighters rose to meet them. All four moved into position to make a firing pass at the Clipper. The Americans listened wide-eyed as the British discussed among themselves and with their home base whether they should shoot down the big aircraft that refused to identify itself. Ford had had the Boeing painted with camouflage in Auckland, but one of the fighters flew close enough to discern the American flag on the top of one wing. The British didn't shoot, but Ford and his crew were very lucky.

Once again, there was no 100-octane gasoline available, and there was nothing else to do but fill some of the Boeing's tanks with auto gas. The last of the aviation fuel was used up on takeoff, and, engines coughing and spitting, flew NC-18609 over the Indian Ocean toward Ceylon. Anxious not to miss landfall, Ford kept the Boeing low to the water, and at one point flew over a surfaced Japanese submarine. The sub crew was out sunning themselves on deck and it was hard to say who was the more surprised. Then Ceylon appeared on the horizon, and they circled the port of Trincomalee, where no flying boat had landed before. Ford picked out a fairly clear spot among all the harbor craft and dropped the aircraft into the water.

On Christmas Eve, with the engines still knocking, they took off for Karachi, only to have the number three engine blow, oil streaming back over the wing. Back in Ceylon, the two flight engineers on the crew tore down the engine to find that 10 of the 16 studs holding one of the cylinders had broken off. John Parish, second engineer, asked a nearby British warship for the loan of a lathe and some rolled steel, made a needed tool, and repaired the cylinder. December 26 they were on their way to Karachi once more, landing at 4 p.m. for 3,100 gallons of needed aviation fuel. The *Pacific Clipper* skirted the northern coast of the Gulf of Oman, crossed the Persian Gulf to Bahrain, flew over the Arabian peninsula and the Red Sea, and then followed the Nile to Khartoum in the Sudan. Again, engine trouble when part of the exhaust stack blew off number one, and there were no flying boat parts in Khartoum. But the Clipper was not going to be much use to anyone in the middle of Africa, so Ford made his decision. NC-18609 took off and flew across Central Africa to Leopoldville in the Congo. They landed on the river, about 1,700 feet above sea level, and opened the hatch to moist, blanket-like heat.

The next morning, Ford and his crew were ready to take off early. The Boeing had been loaded with 5,100 gallons of fuel that weighed 33,660 pounds. It was a stifling hot day. Ford revved the engines and headed downstream with the current to gain speed for liftoff. The current was about six knots, and just ahead were the cataracts. The 1,500-hp engines strained at full throttle, but the Boeing seemed stuck to the surface of the river. Startled Africans watched from the shore.

Parish shouted that the dials showed they were at redline. And the waterfall was just ahead.

Ford gripped the wheel. Each second was agonizing.

The average takeoff run lasted 30 seconds. This one took 91 very long seconds.

An almost cinematic sense of timing lifted the Clipper from the surface of the water just before the rapids.

Ford held on. The Clipper was up, but just barely. They were down in a narrow gorge. The wings were deforming because of the heavy fuel load, and the ailerons were not working properly. The engines were at the point of burning out, Ford dared not throttle back. Slowly, the Clipper climbed up out of the gorge and winged its way to the west.

The Boeing roared across the South Atlantic for an afternoon and a night, engines hammering. Ford's crew had changed plugs only once in 209 hours. It was nearly noon when they landed at Belem after more than 23 hours in the air. The exhaust stack on number one was wired back into place. It blew off almost immediately on the way to Trinidad, but they landed without incident after a 14-hour flight. The final leg of the odyssey took 16 hours.

January 6, 1942, was a very cold morning. The control officer on duty in the tower at LaGuardia Field, New York, was startled at 5:54 a.m. to hear a voice: "*Pacific Clipper*, inbound from Auckland, New Zealand, Captain Ford reporting. Due arrive Pan American Marine Terminal LaGuardia seven minutes."

The controller had not been warned that something out-of-the-way was expected, and a Pan Am rep was hurriedly called to the tower. Yes, he wasn't hearing things. That really was the *Pacific Clipper* arriving home. The Clipper's journey was not over yet. It was still an hour before sunrise and LaGuardia Field regulations were that no Clipper may land before the sun was up.

Captain Ford and his crew, 22 days out of Auckland, after 34,500 miles, were forced to fly around in circles until after 7 a.m., when the sun was definitely up. When the seaplane landed, the water that splashed up on the wings froze solid. But the *Pacific Clipper* had made it home.

Pan Am later put out a statement, supposedly quoting Captain Ford, that the flight was "a purely routine operation . . . completely without incident" and "simply a further demonstration of the flexibility of long-range aircraft." Wartime gung ho can excuse Pan Am for the exaggerated "let's-get-on-with-the-job" hyperbole, but the odyssey of the *Pacific Clipper* remains a true epic of flight. And one, with all respects to Ford, that had a great deal of incidents.

Special missions

The *Pacific Clipper* was not allowed to bask in the limelight for long, and was soon in urgent war service. On January 30, 1942, it carried 56 delegates home from the Rio de Janeiro Conference, including Undersecretary of State Sumner Welles and his party, and the foreign minister of Mexico. The Clipper reached Miami in 33 hours, covering 4,350 miles, setting a new record for commercial aviation.

That August, out in Africa, NC-18609 made news again. A gust of wind suddenly rammed it against a reef as it was being taxied towards its moorings, ripping the hull from one side to the other. It was a major repair job. A cable brought skilled mechanics from LaGuardia Field on the next eastbound airplane. A makeshift diving helmet was made from a five-gallon flour can with a disc of glass for a window. They pumped water out of the Clipper's flooded compartments, screwed plates over the damage, and poured 1,500 pounds of concrete into the hull. The Clipper was then flown back to New York for permanent repairs.

Other Boeings, meanwhile, criss-crossed the world to help the war effort. Spare airplane parts and tracer ammunition, for example, were flown on the *Capetown Clipper* to India for trans-shipment by CNAC to the Flying Tigers and the Royal Air Force in Burma. Commanded by Captain Gray, the Clipper completed the 29,801-mile New York-Calcutta trip in 207 hours, blazing an aerial trail that later proved invaluable to Air Transport Command supply lines to the Far East. There were also a number of special missions, primarily flying dignitaries and world leaders to conferences around the world, that only the Boeings with their range and power could carry out. Kings and queens, admirals and generals, a book could be written on these flights alone. The *Berwick* carried Winston Churchill back to England in January 1942 after his conference in Washington with President Roosevelt. Churchill, ensconced in the bridal suite, loved every minute of it, and even persuaded the captain to let him take the controls of the flying boat on the way from Bermuda to Britain.

Another important flight occurred in June, when the *Atlantic Clipper* carried Queen Wilhelmina of the Netherlands and her party from Lough Erne, Ulster, to Shediac, New Brunswick. She would return to Europe on another Boeing Clipper. Special Mission Number 22 flew General George C. Marshall and Harry Hopkins, the president's assistant, from Baltimore to Scotland, the return trip marking the first non-stop trans-Atlantic flight from England to New York by a commercial airliner.

A January 1943 special mission carried diving equipment to the French navy to salvage ships damaged and sunk by mines off the African coast. It was also in January that Special Mission Number 71, piloted by Captain

Howard Cone Jr., made ready to depart from Miami to Casablanca, Morocco. The crew did not know who would be on the flight except they would be carrying someone named "Mr. Jones." It all began with great secrecy. John Leslie, now manager of Pan Am's Atlantic Division, suddenly found his Navy reserve commission activated. Back in uniform as a lieutenant-commander, he was told to get two Boeings and their crews ready in Miami for a very important person.

When "Mr. Jones" and his wheelchair were lifted on board, Cone and his crew were startled to recognize President Roosevelt. The President and his entourage, including Harry Hopkins and Admiral Leahy, were flown to Africa to attend the Casablanca Conference with Churchill and Stalin. It was the first out-of-the-country flight, incidentally, flown by a chief executive.

On the way back from Casablanca, Roosevelt celebrated his 61st birthday on the Boeing, complete with an iced cake. He was also initiated into the "Short Snorters Club." According to Harry Hopkins, the president enjoyed the flights tremendously as it was the first time he was able to fly since taking office.

There is a footnote to Special Mission 71. Captain Bill Masland, flying a Boeing with the designation Special Mission 72, arrived in Bahrain on the Persian Gulf under orders to wait until the Casablanca Conference was over and then to fly Roosevelt, Churchill, and Stalin to Australia for a meeting with Chiang Kai-shek. Apparently, the Japanese got wind of the fight, and it was abruptly canceled for security reasons. But Masland would make the trip anyway, carrying General Wedemeyer and his staff.

Admiral Chester Nimitz, Eddie Rickenbacker, Darryl Zanuck (now a major in the Signal Corps), Prince Bernard of the Netherlands, Captain James Roosevelt: Scanning the Boeing's passenger lists during those years is like reading a who's who of the famous and near-famous. The great 314s became indispensable workhorses, making a tremendous contribution to the war effort.

The *Atlantic Clipper* (NC-18606), alone, accomplished 20 transocean crossings in one month, flying 55,000 miles, including two round-trips to Brazil from the United States, and hauling 213,000 pounds of cargo. Its utilization rate was 12.58 hours per day. Together, the American and British Boeing 314s made more than 4,100 transocean crossings by September 1945 providing transportation for 61,000 passengers and carried seven million pounds of mail.

"London calling: When does the next Clipper leave Lisbon?"
"Washington calling: Who was on yesterday's Clipper?"
"Havana calling: Reserve four seats on the first Clipper from Miami."

"New York calling: Rush shipment!"

And so it went, long-distance operators far and wide contacting Pan American Airways for the famous Boeing Clipper. Whether it was surveying the Indian Ocean for bases (the *Capetown Clipper*) or making a tremendous 36,728-mile flight around the world (the *Anzac Clipper* piloted by Masland), the B-314 became a vital part of the free world's battle against the totalitarian foe.

And the crews that flew those missions were the same as always: well-trained, professional, a little older now. Perhaps the wild streak of individualism that marked their early years of flying had been wrestled into submission under the blue uniform of Pan Am. But they still stared off at the horizon, still felt that surge of excitement when their huge aircraft left the water.

Bill Masland remembers those war years as filled with tension and back-aching hard work, but he also remembers an anchor watch on a clear cold night in the Persian Gulf, a mass of stars above him in the velvety darkness, hanging as low "as the lamps in a mosque," and then there was the flight to the remote port of Angra dos Reis (Anchorage of the Kings) on the Brazilian coast, where the sea was so calm and beautiful.

Performance Data
Boeing B-314

	B-314	B-314A
Type	Boat	———
Length	106 feet	———
Span	152 feet	———
Height	28 feet	———
Gross Weight	82,000 pounds	84,000 pounds
Engines	Wright Cyclone × 4	———
Horsepower	1,500	1,600
Range	3,500 statute miles	4,275 statute miles
Fuel Capacity	4,200 gallons	5,448 gallons
Useful load	23,500 pounds	31,360 pounds
Cruising Speed	150 mph	———
Service Ceiling	21,000 feet	———
Passengers	74 (34 at night)	———
Crew	10 - 16	———

Pan American's Boeing B-314s
(in order of construction)

Model	Reg. No.	Name	Remarks
B-314	NC-18601	*Honolulu Clipper*	Assigned to Pacific. Sunk at sea by U.S. Navy, 11/8/45.
B-314	NC-18602	*California Clipper*	Assigned to Pacific; inaugurated trans-Pacific passenger service San Francisco-Singapore, 3/29/39. Scrapped 1950.
B-314	NC-18603	*Yankee Clipper*	Inaugurated first trans-Atlantic mail service. 5/20/39. Sank in Tagus River, Lisbon, 2/22/43.
B-314	NC-18604	*Atlantic Clipper*	Assigned to Atlantic. Scrapped for parts 1946.
B-314	NC-18605	*Dixie Clipper*	Inaugurated first trans-Atlantic passenger service, 6/28/39. Scrapped 1950.
B-314	NC-18606	*American Clipper*	Assigned to Atlantic. Scrapped 1950.
B-314A	NC-18607	*Bristol*	Operated by BOAC (G-AGBZ). Sold to World Airways and scrapped, 1951.
B-314A	NC-18608	*Berwick*	Operated by BOAC (G-AGCA). Sold to World Airways and scrapped, approx. 1950.
B-314A	NC-18609	*Pacific Clipper*	Assigned to Pacific. Damaged by storm and salvaged for parts, approx. 1948.
B-314A	NC-18610	*Bangor*	Operated by BOAC (G-AGCB). Sold to World Airways and scrapped, approx. 1950.
B-314A	NC-18611	*Anzac Clipper*	Assigned to Pacific/Atlantic. Destroyed Baltimore, 1951.
B-314A	NC-18612	*Capetown Clipper*	Assigned to Atlantic. Sunk at sea by U.S. Coast Guard, 10/14/47.

12

The end
of an era

Pan American Airways was a sizable industry by the end of 1942. Gross revenues for the year were $109 million, more than half of which were government payments for new airport construction and flight operations carried out under army and navy contract. More than 88,000 men and women were now employed by the company, and its operations spread out over three quarters of the globe.

Nor was Pan Am neglecting its civilian business, which had more than doubled since the beginning of the war. Wartime travel meant more people, more money, and less time. The only shortage was aircraft. But Trippe could not have it all because the wartime emergency also brought competition, and slowly Pan Am's competitive edge began to crumble. American Export Airlines, a creation of the shipping company United States Lines, was now carrying passenger traffic across the Atlantic.

Even in Pan Am's dominion of Latin America, aircraft wearing the colors of American Airlines, Braniff, and Eastern could be seen parked at airports. What the government giveth, the government can take away was an omen of Pan Am's future. Trippe even had to take time off from the war to battle, and finally destroy, TACA (Transportes Aereos Centro-Americanos), a Honduran-based airline begun by a New Zealand-born entrepreneur named Lowell Yerex that had begun to branch out all over Central America.

The Tagus disaster

There is a saying among those who fly that there are old pilots and there are bold pilots, but there are no old, bold pilots. Captain Rod Sullivan leaned a little toward the bold side. A former navy enlisted man who had earned aviator's wings, he was known for his tendency to fly aircraft with a heavy hand on the controls.

Flying a load of newspaper publishers in 1939 on a publicity flight to Europe, he had landed his Boeing 314 at Horta, and a "maverick swell" had stoved in the bow. Sullivan believed in landing an aircraft flat and fast, instead of the more normal steeper and slower method used by most other pilots. Trouble was, in flight the 314 was exceptional, but on water the aircraft also was something of a "maverick."

Wing tips had a habit of suddenly digging into a swell, and at approximately 20 mph, pilots would suddenly realize that there was nothing under the boat but air. The problem was traced to the 314's huge bow wave, which had a tendency to carve the water out from under the sponsons. A wooden block extending the hull step 20 inches aft improved matters considerably, but the very size of the 314 dictated that it be handled with more than the usual amount of care.

Sullivan lifted the *Yankee Clipper* off Bowery Bay, LaGuardia Field, on the morning of February 21, 1943, for Foynes, Ireland, via Bermuda, Horta, and Lisbon. A month earlier Sullivan had made his 100th trip across the Pond, a mark no other airman at that time had equalled. For its part, the *Yankee Clipper*, with 240 ocean crossings and over one million miles in the air, had become one of the most famous ocean flying boats in the world.

The Clipper carried 39 passengers and crew, among them seven U.S.O. entertainers — all well-known Broadway stars, including singing star Jane Froman and singer Tamara Drasin, who had introduced Jeremy Kern's "Smoke Gets in Your Eyes" — and Ben Robertson Jr., novelist and top correspondent for the New York *Herald Tribune*.

The *Yankee Clipper* approached the Tagus River on February 22 at 6:35 p.m., almost dusk, for its landing at Lisbon. A thunderstorm had just passed to the south of the city and a light rain was falling. The flying boat landing area was 11.5 miles up the river from the coast. Watchers on the Pan Am launch thought the approach seemed normal, a little shallow perhaps, but, well, that was Sullivan's way. Passengers thought nothing seemed out of the ordinary.

There is another old rule in flying: making a turn when you are flying low is asking for trouble. As Langewiesche puts it: ". . .you ask a pilot how most people get killed in airplanes and he will tell you anything except the fact that most of them lose control of their airplanes in turning flight close to the ground." *

---

*Wolfgang Langewiesche, *Stick and Rudder: An Explanation of the Art of Flying*. McGraw-Hill Book Company, New York, 1972.

The 314 banked to port for its final approach at 6:47 p.m., almost dark. The left wing was skimming the river, then catastrophe. Watchers stared in horror as the big flying boat's left wing tip dug into the water, and then sheared off just outboard of the Number One engine. The aircraft seemed to stagger in the air, and then smashed into the river.

The final moments of the *Yankee Clipper* were like a replay of the *Titanic*. Silhouetted against the gloomy sky, the huge ship floundered in agony. The Boeing had careened for some yards along the surface of the Tagus, ripping open the bottom of the hull and destroying the watertight bulkheads. For approximately 10 minutes, what was left on the flying boat remained on the surface before sinking into the dark, cold waters of the Tagus.

Twenty-four people died, including Ben Robertson and the lovely singer Tamara Drasin. Jane Froman, badly injured, was kept afloat by John C. Burns, fourth officer, who she would later marry. There were 13 other survivors, including Captain Sullivan. Taken to a Lisbon hospital, he was unable to explain the cause of the accident. Referring to his own condition, he said, "Nothing is broken, but my heart."

Jane Froman gradually recovered from her injuries and later testified on the disaster. "The crash itself I remember as a sudden shocking confusion of noise and violence," she said. "I was conscious of being flung across the compartment, of the sound of ripping, crumbling metal and breaking glass and then I was in the icy water of the Tagus River, fighting to keep myself alive."

The remains of NC-18603 were pulled to the surface, but a CAB investigation failed to find any malfunction of the aircraft or its controls. The initial thought was that a sudden low air current must have made the 314 veer sharply to the left. Even enemy sabotage was investigated. But finally, the accident was attributed to pilot error. Captain Sullivan had simply misjudged his height above the water when he was making a turn. He was forced to resign from the airline.

The *Yankee Clipper* was the only Boeing 314 lost in a flying accident.

Winding down

Pan Am did not repurchase the Boeing 314s from the U.S. Navy after the war because better long-range, land-type aircraft were on the way: the Douglas DC-4 and the Lockheed Constellation. Nearly all the Clippers were placed in dry dock in 1946 at San Diego, California, and put up for sale by the War Assets Administration. Pan Am flew its last Boeing 314 on April 8, 1946, when the *American Clipper* arrived in San Francisco. It, too, joined the rest of the retirees at San Diego.

The American-operated 314s had flown a total of 8.3 million miles on 3,650 flights, with an average of 2,270 miles per flight. They had averaged 18,000 hours of flight time during their service with Pan Am.

BOAC took its three B-314s off the transatlantic route in 1946, but continued to fly them on the Baltimore-Bermuda run until January 1948 when they were finally withdrawn from service. They had flown six and one-half years of operation without an accident or mishap of any kind. Between them, they had flown a total of 4,258,876 miles and carried 40,042 passengers.

One of the last dramas of the Boeing 314s occurred just after the war ended. The *Honolulu Clipper*, the first 314 built by Boeing, was on a night flight from Honolulu to San Francisco on November 4, 1945, when sparks and flames shot from Number Three engine, and it began backfiring and running rough. The loss of one engine was not a critical problem, and for awhile there did not seem much to worry about. Then the crew saw smoke around the engineer's station on the flight deck and within the catwalk in the starboard wing. That was something to worry about.

Number Three was feathered. But in a few minutes, Number Four engine began to run rough, and it, too, was feathered.

Only two engines were keeping the giant flying boat in the air. S.E. Robbins, the pilot, applied maximum power, and a radio call went out to Station Ship Number 4. They had an emergency, radioed the Clipper, and they were heading for the station ship's position. Emergency landing operations were in progress. Robbins ordered all excess gasoline and the cargo jettisoned. In the meantime, the ship's engineers were struggling with the balky engines. They managed to restart Number Four, but the huge aircraft was still unable to maintain altitude. Station Ship Number 4 came into view. The *Honolulu Clipper* circled and Robbins brought it down to a smooth landing on the ocean.

While the Boeing floated, with the station ship standing off nearby, the crew inspected the two engines. They found an oil leak around the three lower cylinders of Number Three as well as inside the inboard exhaust stack. Number Four had also lost a cylinder head.

The Clipper could not be repaired at sea, and the passengers and crew were taken off by the *Manila Bay*, a baby carrier that took NC-18601 under tow. For seven hours, the flattop plowed through steadily worsening seas toward Honolulu towing the huge flying boat. Then the tow parted.

Next on the scene was the seaplane tender *San Pablo* to attempt a salvage. The sea was now very rough. As the tender attempted to get a line across to the violently pitching seaplane, the 314 suddenly slammed against the ship's side. There was not much the navy could do for the flying boat now because its starboard wing was sheared off and water was pouring in through its stoved-in bow. The Clipper was being operated by Pan Am for the Naval Air Transport Service (NATS), and naval authorities declared the airplane a derelict. It was a hazard to navigation and had to be sunk. But the *Honolulu Clipper* died hard. It took 1,300 rounds of 20 mm ammo for NC-18601 to finally slide beneath the waves. The *Honolulu Clipper* had 18,000 hours of flying time on its logbooks when it sank, representing enough miles to circle the globe 80 times.

The 'Bermuda Sky Queen'

The three Boeings operated by BOAC were put up for sale and purchased by General Phoenix Corporation of Baltimore, an aircraft broker. General Phoenix sold the aircraft in 1948 to World Airways, which was operating as a nonscheduled airline, largely with government contracts. World Airways went on to acquire three more 314s from the War Assets Administration: the *American Clipper*, the *California Clipper* and the *Dixie Clipper*. The six Boeings were flown by World Airways until 1949, when the company was in financial trouble and the aircraft apparently were sold for scrap. Their registrations were cancelled by the FAA in May 1954 for non-compliance.

The *Atlantic Clipper* was salvaged for parts by the War Assets Administration in 1946.

Universal Airlines, Incorporated, acquired the *Pacific Clipper* and the *Anzac Clipper* in 1946. The *Pacific Clipper* was damaged by a storm, and Universal salvaged it for parts to keep the other 314 in the air. The *Anzac Clipper* was then sold to American International Airways, another "nonsked," in 1947, which, in turn, sold it to World Airways in 1948.

NC-18611 ended up in private hands in 1951 and was berthed at Baltimore. It sank in a sudden storm and, for a time, someone calling himself Master X was reported to have plans to raise the flying boat, repair it, and fly it to Russia to talk peace with Stalin. But nothing came of the idea, and the aircraft was eventually sold for scrap.

The *Capetown Clipper* had a more interesting end. Sold to American International in 1947, it was given the name *Bermuda Sky Queen* and operated on nonscheduled flights across the Atlantic from Poole, England, to Baltimore via Foynes and Gander. On October 14, 1947, carrying 62 passengers and a crew of seven, it was forced down into the ocean after bucking such strong head winds that it ran short of fuel. For 24 hours, it drifted almost 100 miles before help arrived in the shape of the U.S. Coast Guard cutter *Bibb*.

In a dramatic rescue that made headlines around the world, all the passengers and crew were safely transferred to the cutter. But there was no rescue for the flying boat. In a replay of the *Honolulu Clipper* ordeal, the *Sky Queen* smashed against the ship's side and was badly damaged. Water was pouring into the aircraft, and it could not be flown nor towed. Sadly, the aircraft's captain, Charles Martin, turned away. The cutter riddled the Boeing with bullets, and it sank beneath the waves in a shroud of fire and smoke.

American International was later called on the carpet by the Civil Aeronautics Board. An investigation had determined that the aircraft was carrying more than 5,000 pounds over its certificated 84,000 pounds, it did not receive a full load of fuel in Foynes, and the crew had failed to use cruise control or utilize available weather data. In all, it was a sad end to a once proud fleet.

Last flight of a legend

There was once a legend that flew the blue skies of the Pacific, flying to a far-off continent where there were mystical temples, tigers, sailing junks, and opportunity, perhaps riches, beyond men's dreams. The legend of the *China Clipper* was created partly by Hollywood, partly by the publicity drums of Pan American Airways and partly by the public fascination with the name. In a way, the *China Clipper* was a symbol of America's manifest destiny to control the Pacific long after it had departed for another ocean. What became of the legend?

Marshall Zhukov's armies were sweeping around Warsaw and pounding the city of Cracow in January 1945. General Mark Clark's 15th Army Group was attacking a crumbling German front trying to hold a line from Genoa on the Mediterranean towards Bologna. In western Europe, Patton's tanks were preparing to break through the German defenses in the Ardennes to reach the Rhine. In a few weeks, the Americans would capture the bridge at Remagen. Out in the Pacific, B-29s were bombing Tokyo, and Halsey's Third Fleet was sending daily air strikes against Iwo Jima in preparation for a landing.

Since October 1943 the *China Clipper*, which had been returned to Pan Am by the U.S. Navy, was flying from Miami to Allied-controlled Leopoldville in the Congo. From there, war supplies and passengers were flown across Africa to the Middle East and even to India and China.

The *China Clipper* approached Port of Spain, Trinidad, on the night of January 8, 1945. There were 30 souls aboard Flight 161 that night: 18 passengers and 12 crew members, with Captain Cyril Gayette at the controls. The weather was fine, in fact, beautiful, with a bright moon and few clouds. Approaching Port of Spain, Gayette decided to change seats with Captain Leonard Cramer, who was acting as first officer — a common occurrence on long-distance flights — to give Cramer some practice in night landings. Cramer would make the landing from the left seat.

Flight 161 received instructions from Pan American-Miami at 7:30 p.m. to contact Port of Spain for the weather. The Martin flying boat was number one to land in the Corcorite area at 9 p.m., an anchorage about ten miles off the Trinidad coast. Crossing the north coast of the island, the *China Clipper's* altitude was 4,000 feet, still too high to land on a final approach, so Cramer started a 360-degree turn to the left to come around again. But there were hills in that direction. Gayette told Cramer to make his turn to the right instead.

Final approach placed the aircraft three miles from the number one light at the anchorage at approximately 1,000 feet. The rate of descent was 600 feet per minute at 105 knots. The aircraft was right on course. Eight hundred feet above the water, rate of descent was 300 feet per minute and speed was 100 to 105 knots. There was a light haze at around 400 feet, but this was of little consequence. The Clipper was approximately one-half mile from the first anchorage light. The huge ship cast a giant shadow on the water, silvery in the moonlight, 250 feet, 100 knots.

Suddenly, there was a terrific crash. Captain Leonard Cramer would later describe it as "a shearing noise followed by a sudden lurch."

The Martin Clipper came to a sudden stop, the hull broken in two; water poured into the cabin, and a major part of the aircraft sank immediately. Sixteen passengers and nine crewmembers died.

The official investigation gave the probable cause of the crash as the pilot's "failure to realize his proximity to the water and to correct his altitude for a normal landing and lack of adequate supervision by the captain during the landing, resulting in . . . excess landing speed in a nose-down attitude." No mention was made of the M-130 hitting an unidentified object on the water, although unofficial versions of the accident frequently say that the *China Clipper* hit something, such as a small boat.

Flight Engineer John Morse, who survived the accident, probably gave the most damaging testimony, which, in part, ran like this:

> (Said Morse when questioned about the approach to the anchorage at Port of Spain) The string of landing lights were [sic] distinctly visible, strung out in approximately an east-west direction, and I noticed one launch in its proper position . . . I could see ripples on the surface (of the water), and it seemed odd to me that the surface of the water and the top surface of the sea wing seemed parallel, so I concluded we were in a gliding

Naval recovery effort salvages debris following the crash of the Martin M-130 *China Clipper* (NC-14716) near Port of Spain, Trinidad.

position. [Normally, at that height above the water the upper surface of the hydrostabilizer would have been pointing at an up-angle of approximately 15 degrees with the surface of the water — AUTHOR]

Question: Could you see the neon landing markers?

Answer: I could see no light whatsoever except that given by the left landing light. When I realized the imminence of our landing, I tightened my safety belt and at that instant, as far as I can remember, we touched the water. . . .

And so the *China Clipper* met the same fate as the other two Martin 130s — the aircraft that had probably done more to stimulate aircraft development and public acceptance than any others of their age. Strangely, the death of the *China Clipper*, with so much else happening in the world at that time, went almost unnoticed by the public. Perhaps it was just as well, better to remember the giant Clipper as she was in her heyday, the romantic lead in one of the best shows on earth.

Today, Pan American World Airways is still a major international airline, flying its Airbus A300s, Lockheed L-1011s, and Boeing 747s bearing names that begin with Clipper. The years have been both good and bad to the airline, with periods of prosperity and times of financial stress. Buffeted by the competition of deregulation, Pan Am sold its Pacific Division routes, built at so much human cost and treasure, to United in April 1985.

Juan Trippe did not live to see it. The man who had been at the controls of the airline since almost its inception, retired in 1975 at the age of 76. He continued to regularly attend meetings of the board past the age of 80, sitting at the right hand of William Seawell, company chairman, and not saying a word no matter how long the meeting lasted.

Trippe died in April 1981.

Midway has become a supply base for missile submarines, and civilian aircraft rarely call there. In 1970, Canton Island became a down-range tracking station for the U.S. Air Force. Guam is as busy as ever, a refueling point for transpacific jets. But the jet age has by-passed Wake. The buildings there stand empty, desolate, each storm that passes gradually destroying them year by year. Perhaps one day, when all this is no more than a mere blip in some electronic history book, the coral will be seen again in the lagoon.

And so Pan Am continues to ply the skies, always reminding us that it is "the world's most experienced airline." Many of those who know its story, however, will always feel that the company's most glorious moment was on that distant day in November 1935 when the *China Clipper*,

Captain Ed Musick at the controls, shook off the water of San Francisco Bay and flew out over the Golden Gate toward the Orient, so distant, but suddenly so near.

Color schemes

Earliest color schemes of Pan American amphibians and flying boats would leave the fuselage and wings the natural silvery aluminum color, with block lettering in a shade called "Mumsell Blue" on the twin booms or near fuselage. When the Clipper name was introduced with S-40, *American Clipper*, it appeared in block letters and painted on the nose, just below the cockpit.

The S-42 carried its name, *Brazilian Clipper* , in slanted, windswept lettering. Also below the cockpit was Pan Am's logo, the winged globe, which had both silver and white lettering and continents on Mumsell Blue at various times, and the words "PAA" in windswept lettering beside it.

Surprisingly, despite the transoceanic routes of the airline, the Pan Am globe continued to show only the Western Hemisphere and was not changed until the airline introduced its DC-4s after World War II. The registration of the aircraft, NV-80V, for example, was in block letters on the tail surface, lower side left wing, and upper side right wing in black.

All marine aircraft from the S-38 to the Boeing 314 carried the company name as the "Pan American Airways System" in Mumsell Blue on the side of the fuselage. The Martin M-130 and the Boeing 314 also had the letters in the more modern windswept slant instead of straight. To complicate matters, however, there are photographs of an S-42 in Pan Am service that show the words, "Pan American Clipper" in windswept lettering below the cockpit, but no name on the nose. This could be the unnamed NC-824M, or, more likely, this was a color scheme that was later discarded.

The S-38, S-40 and S-42 had a "Winged S" and the name Sikorsky on their tails, but the manufacturer's name did not seem to appear in a visible spot on the Martins and Boeings.

As an example of the Pan Am color scheme, the specifications for the S-42 are shown below:

Black	Hull.
	Lower side pontoons.
	Bow in front of cockpit.
	Lettering (e.g., NC-16736)
	under side left wing;
	upper side right wing.
	Number registration on outside
	of each tail surface.
Mumsell Blue	PAN AMERICAN AIRWAYS SYSTEM
International Orange	Strip across top of wing.
Aluminum	Fuselage.
	Tail surface, all except registration.
	Wings, except for International Orange.
	Pontoons, upper side.
	Struts.

In 1938, due to war conditions in the Far East and China, the Martin Clippers were given a wavy American flag on the bow and wings. The Pan Am logo was moved from the bow to a pylon at the rear of the pilot's compartment.

When the Martins entered navy service at the entry of the United States into World War II, they were painted "blue and gray" and given a straight flag on the nose and wings. All three Clippers also received a Navy BuAer number, but this does not appear to have been painted on. In all cases, the Pan American name remained on the side. The *Philippine Clipper*, after its dramatic escape from Wake Island, also carried a "wound stripe" on its nose.

The policy with the Boeing 314s, before the U.S. entered the war, seems to have been more varied. There is a photograph showing the *California Clipper* anchored in Auckland, New Zealand, on its inaugural flight in 1939, and it is wearing a wavy flag. A picture of the *Yankee Clipper* in Bermuda in 1940, however, reveals no flag.

There is also a photo of the *Honolulu Clipper*, taken "just before World War II," that shows it without a flag. On the other hand, we know from the story of the *Pacific Clipper's* flight around the world, that it left Auckland with at least a partial American flag on the wings; the aircraft had been hastily "camouflaged," which presumably meant the United States flag on the nose had been obliterated.

Apparently, then, Pan Am's policy on painting its aircraft was not related to its theater of operations. After Pearl Harbor, however, there is no doubt that all Boeing 314s, except those flown by BOAC, wore the straight American flag.

Once the war was over, the flags seemed to have been immediately removed from those aircraft that remained in service. No flag, for example, is in evidence on a photograph of the *Honolulu Clipper* sinking in November 1945.

Specifications glossary

maximum takeoff weight (Mtow)   Often called "gross weight," Mtow includes the weight of the aircraft and everything in it. This is a legal definition, however, based on the certificate of airworthiness, and does not necessarily indicate the airplane's ultimate capabilities.

manufacturer's empty weight   The aircraft, complete with engines, ready to fly, although with nothing on board. This is usually the aircraft described in the initial contract between the manufacturer and the airline, entirely without furnishings, which is a variable resting with the buyer.

operating tare   The weight of the aircraft ready for flight with a fully equipped cabin but without crew, payload, fuel, oil, or other miscellaneous consumables.

payload   Passengers, mail, and cargo, either individually or any combination thereof. Payload is one aspect of *disposable load*.

disposable load   The difference between Mtow and tare, including crew, payload, fuel, oil and a variety of other consumables. The disposable load of an aircraft fresh from the factory includes all cabin furnishings, such as seats, galley, lavatories, ventilation, soundproofing, and the like.

C Route Maps

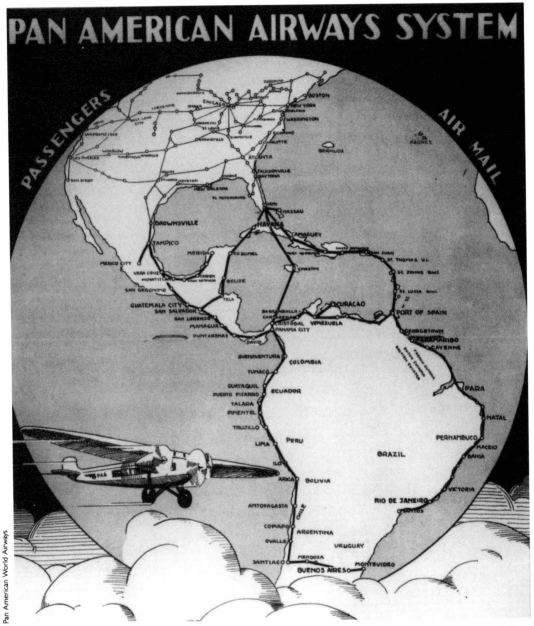

Pan American World Airways

Route map from the 1930 Pan American Airways annual report. The company reported that aircraft had flown 9,080,134 passenger miles on 20,000 miles of routes.

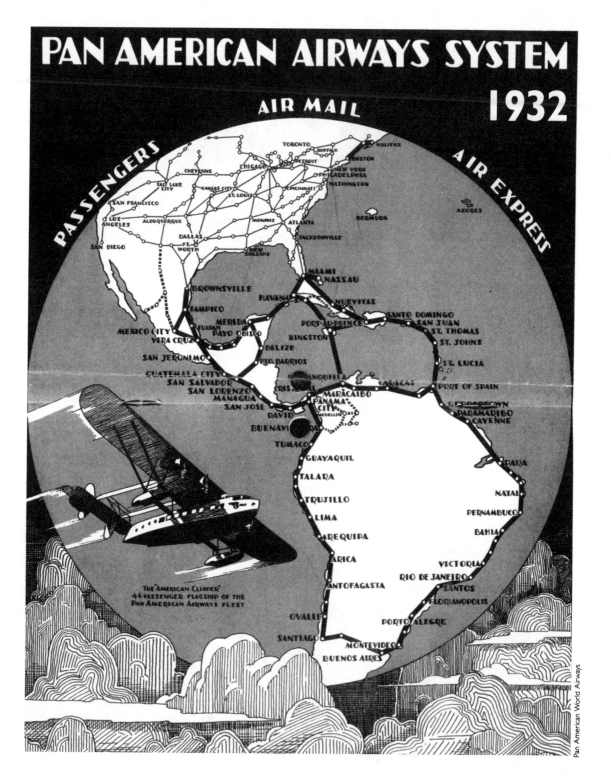

Pan American World Airways

PAN AMERICAN AIRWAYS SYSTEM

PASSENGERS · AIR MAIL · AIR EXPRESS

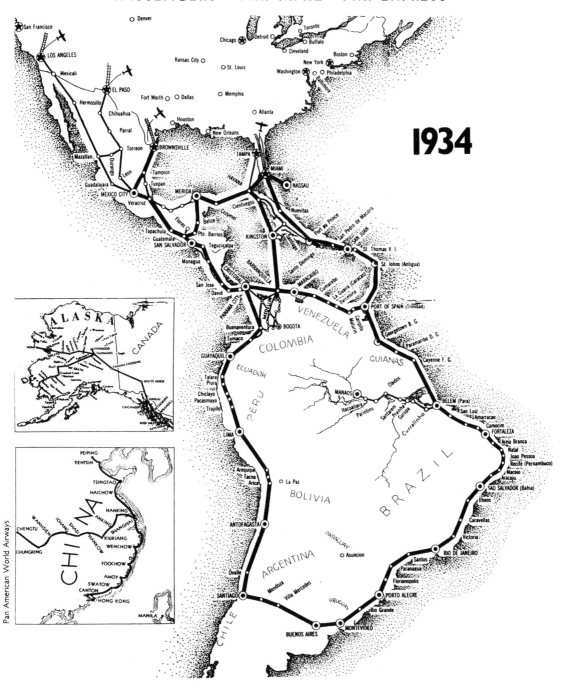

1934

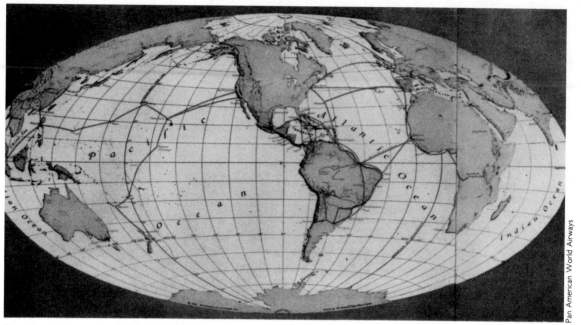

Pan American Airways' routes on December 7, 1941, according to the company's 1941 annual report. Routileage in 1941 was 98,582 with 227 million passenger miles flown that year.

Bibliography

Arnold, Henry H. *Global Mission*, New York: Harper & Bros., 1949.

Beaty, David. *The Water Jump: The Story of Transatlantic Flight*, New York: Harper & Row, 1976.

Bender, Marylin and Altschul, Selig. *The Chosen Instrument*, New York: Simon and Schuster, 1982.

Burden, William A.M. *The Struggle for Airways in Latin America*, New York: Council on Foreign Relations, 1943.

Corn, Joseph J. *The Winged Gospel: America's Romance with Aviation, 1900–1950*, New York: Oxford University Press, 1983.

Coward, Noel. *Future Indefinite*, New York: Doubleday & Company, 1954.

Daley, Robert. *An American Saga: Juan Trippe and his Pan Am Empire*, New York: Random House, 1980.

Davies, R.E.G. *Pan Am: An Airline and its Aircraft*, New York: Orion Books, 1987.

_____. *Airlines of the United States Since 1914*, London: Putnam, 1972.

_____. *A History of the World's Airlines*, London: Oxford University Press, 1964.

Grooch, William Stephen. *From Crate to Clipper*, New York: Longmans, Green and Co., 1939.

_____. *Skyway to Asia*, New York: Longmans, Green and Co., 1936.

Jablonski, Edward. *Seawings: The Romance of the Flying Boats*, New York: Doubleday & Company, 1972.

Jackson, Ronald W. *China Clipper*, New York: Everest House, 1980.

Josephson, Matthew. *Empire of the Air*, New York: Harcourt, Brace & Company, 1944.

Kaucher, Dorothy. *Wings Over Wake*, San Francisco: John Howell, Publisher, 1947.

Langewiesche, Wolfgang. *Stick and Rudder: An Explanation of the Art of Flying.* New York: McGraw-Hill Book Company, 1972.

Lindbergh, Anne Morrow. *North to the Orient*, New York: Harcourt, Brace and Company, 1935.

———. *Listen, the Wind*, New York: Harcourt, Brace and Company, 1938.

Munson, Kenneth. *Flying Boats and Seaplanes Since 1910*, New York: The Macmillan Company, 1971.

Rowe, Basil L. *Under My Wings*, New York: The Bobbs-Merrill Company, Inc., 1956.

Sikorsky, Igor. *The Story of the Winged-S*, New York: Dodd, Mead & Co., 1958.

The following articles were also useful sources of information.

Anderson, Charles E. "Philippine Clipper." *Journal* of the American Aviation Historical Society, Fall, 1965.

Hyer, Charles. "A Clipper Captain Remembers the Early Days." *Journal* of the American Aviation Historical Society, Fall, 1988.

Klass, M.D. "Last of the Flying Clipper Ships." *Journal* of the American Aviation Historical Society," Vol. 13, No. 2, Summer, 1968.

Mayborn, Mitch. "Sikorsky S-40 Amphibian." *Airline Quarterly*, Vol. 2, No. 1, Spring, 1978.

———. "The Ugly Duckling — Sikorsky's S-38." *Journal* of the American Aviation Historical Society, Vol. 4, No. 3, Fall, 1959.

Reingold, Lester. "Lindbergh's Second Crossing." *Air Line Pilot*, June, 1985.

Rowe, Basil L. "Flying the Caribbean with Lindbergh." *S.P.A. Journal*, September, 1968.

Schepper, Robert H. and Charles E. Anderson, "The Martin Clippers." *Journal* of the American Aviation Historical Society, Vol. 10, No. 3, Fall 1965.

Smith, Richard K. "The Intercontinental Airliner and the Essence of Airplane Performance, 1929 – 1939." *Technology and Culture*, Vol. 24, No. 1, July, 1983.

"First Lady Names American Clipper." *Pan American Air Ways*, Vol. 2, No. 7, November, 1931.

"A.A. Radio Stands By in Belize Hurricane." *Pan American Air Ways*, Vol. 2, No. 7, November, 1931.

"North Haven Sails for Canton Isle to Set Up Base." *Pan American Air Ways*, Vol. 10, No. 2, April, 1939.

"Pacific Clipper Circles the World to Avoid Clash." *Travel Trade*, January, 1942.

"The Great Clippers." *Air Power*, Vol. 7, No. 6, November, 1977.

"Wake Escape." *New Horizons*, January, 1942.

"Yankee Clipper Completes Final Inspection Trip." *Pan American Air Ways*, Vol. 10, No. 2, April, 1939.

Also   *New York Times*
       San Francisco Chronicle
       Life
       Time

Index

North Haven, 81, 86, 122, 128, 129, 131
North to the Orient Lindbergh's Pacific flight, 52
North Wind steamer, 129
Northland Lindbergh supply ship, 53

O
Ostfriesland battleship, 109
O'Neill, Ralph, 21

P
Pacific Clipper, 174-180, 183, 189, 196
Paley, William S., 147
Pan Am Clipper II, 98
Pan American Airports Corporation, 148
Pan American Clipper, 74, 84-89, 120, 128, 195
Pan American Clipper III, 93, 94, 95, 96, 98
Pan American-Grace Airways, 8
PANAGRA, 8, 27, 80, 101
Panair do Brazil, 101
Parker, Ivan, 145
Parker, Kenneth, 136
Pearl Harbor, 46, 150-154
Peruvian Airlines, 8
Peters, Art, 42, 44, 100, 150, 175-179
Philadelphia Rapid Transit Airline, 36
Philippine Clipper, 112, 120-121, 123, 125-133, 135, 136, 150, 151, 152, 155-157, 196
piloting for Pan Am, 141-143
pitch-controlled propellers, 72
Poindexter, John, 176
point of no return, 86
Post, Wiley, 89, 128
President Lincoln liner, 117
Priester, Andre, 8, 35, 70, 72, 76, 77, 112, 141

Q
QANTAS, 127
Quezon, Manuel, 107, 126
Quick, Raymond, 74

R
R100 airship, 91

radio communications, WKDL, 18, 89
radio navigation, 86
Ralph, Fred, 152, 153
Rebozo, Charles B., 40
Relyea, Charles, 152
Rickenbacker, Eddie, 6, 181
Robbins, David, 3
Robertson, Ben, 186, 187
Rockefeller, Percy, 6
Rockefeller, Williams, 3
Rodenbaugh, E.S., 19
Rogers, Ginger, 42
Roosevelt, Eleanor, 167
Roosevelt, Franklin D., 7, 79, 80, 107, 124, 131, 154, 180, 181
Roosevelt, James, 181
Roseville motorship, 117
Rossi, Angelo, 104
route maps, 201-204
Rowe, Basil, 7, 9, 10, 15, 16, 17, 19, 38, 40, 44, 142, 143
Royal Air Force, 180

S
SACO, 27
salvage operation, 192
Samoan Clipper, 130, 146
San Pablo tender, 188
Santa Maria, 7
Savale, Victor, 135
Savoia-Marchetti, 91
SCADTA, 5, 8, 27
Schafer, Charles, 154
Scripps-Howard newspapers, 125
Seawell, William, 193
Selznick, David O., 147
Sergievsky, Boris, 74-75
Shangai, bombing of, 139-140
Short Class C flying boats, 93, 130
Short Snorters Club, 181
Short-Mayo Composite, 96
Short-Snorters Club, 89-90, 95
Sikorsky Aero Engineering Corporation, 8
Sikorsky Aircraft, 159
Sikorsky, Igor, 8-11, 35, 41, 69-102
Smith, Richard K., 71
Southern Clipper, 41, 42, 46, 47
Spaatz, Caroll, 5, 6
specifications glossary, 199
Spirit of St. Louis, 68

sponsoons, 113
Stalin, 181
Stinson SM6B, 57
Sullivan, Rod, 79, 88, 107, 120, 122, 169, 185-187
Sun Yat-Sen, 154
Sweet Sixteen China Clipper, 105, 112, 116, 123, 149, 150, 157-158, 190-194
S-38 amphibians, 9-12, 14, 16-22, 24, 35, 57, 59-60, 82
  areas of use, Pan Am, 29-30
  color scheme, 195
  performance data for, 28
  prototypes, 16, 18
S-40 Clippers, 33-46, 69, 73
  bizarre events aboard, 42-44
  cockpit crew of, 45
  color scheme, 195
  development of, 35-40
  first flight of, 40-41
  interior appointments of, 42
  nautical theme of, 39
  order of construction, individual, 47
  performance data, 47
  redesign of, 46
  removal of landing gear in, 45
  retirement of, 46
  specifications for, 36-39
  testing, 39
  'Flying Down To Rio' movie use of,, 41
S-42, 69-99, 101, 111, 121, 128, 130, 140, 152
  Atlantic competition for, 90
  color schemes, 195-196
  design and development of, 70
  Ed Musick, test pilot for, 75
  first commercial flight of, 77
  fuel capacity, 73
  icing problems over Atlantic, 94
  initial ideas for, 69
  interior appointments, 73, 73
  modifications to, 90
  navigation, 78, 79
  order of construction, 97, 97
  Pacific bases established, 81
  performance data, 97
  price of, 74
  propeller design, pitch-controlled, 72

range and payload capacity, 71, 73
Short S.23 performance vs., 95
South American routes for, 89
takeoff, 72
test flight, 75-79
testing, 74-75
trans-Pacific flight, 84
wing design, 72
world records set by, 77
S-43 Baby Clipper, 99-102
design and development of, 100
order of construction, 102
performance data, 101
wing-landing gear design, 100
S-44 flying boat, 160

T
TACA, 185
Tagus disaster, 185-187
Terletzky, Leo, 20-21, 143-146
Tilton, John, 88, 121
Tingmissartoq Lindbergh trans-Atlantic plane, 64, 68
trans-atlantic mail service, 50
trans-Atlantic air service, 67-68
Treasure Island, 148-150
Tripartite Agreement of 1930, 50
Trippe, Elizabeth Stettinius, 12-13, 125, 169
Trippe, Henry, 2
Trippe, John, 2
Trippe, Juan T., 33, 49, 70, 77, 91, 92, 96, 104, 107, 110, 111,
116, 121, 123, 145, 159, 185, 193
around the world flight, 1936, 125
loss of Pan Am control by, 146
Pan American Airways development, 2
personal history of, 1-31
TWA, 155

U
Under My Wings, Rowe autobiography, 17
United Airlines, 159
United States Lines, 185
Universal Airlines, 189

V
Vanderbilt, Cornelius, 4
Vanderbilt, William H., 3
Vianna, John A., 121
Vidal, Eugene, 77

W
Wah Sun CHoy, 146
Wake, 81-84, 88, 104, 117, 118, 119, 125, 138, 151, 152, 177, 193, 196
Walker, M.A., 143-146
Webb, Clifton, 171
Wedemeyer, General, 181
Welles, Sumner, 180
Wells, Hugh, 2
West Indian Aerial Express, 6-7, 10

West Indies Clipper, 84, 97
Whitbeck, Jack, 1
Whitney, Cornelius V., 3, 123, 125, 147, 148, 169
Whitney, John Hay, 4
Wilcockson, Captain, 94
Wilhelmina, Queen of Netherlands, 170, 180
windmilling, 73
Winged Gospel, The, 63
Winged S, The Sikorsky autobiography, 70
WKDL Pan Am radio communications, 18, 89
Woods-Humpherey, George, 91, 92, 96, 168
Woolworth, Frank, 4
World Airways, 189
Wright, USS warship, 117
Wright, C.D., 107
Wright, Vic, 79, 107
W.R. Grace Corporation, 8

X
XB-15 experimental aircraft, 160

Y
Yankee Clipper, 167-171, 175, 183, 186-187, 196
Yerex, Lowell, 185
Young, Clarence, 104
Younkins, John, 66

Z
Zanuck, Darryl, 181